D0152927

Bloom's Modern Critical Views

Bloom's Modern Critical Views

Bloom's Modern Critical Views

ALDOUS HUXLEY

Edited and with an introduction by
Harold Bloom
Sterling Professor of the Humanities
Yale University

Mishawaka-Penn-Harris
Public Library
Mishawaka, Indiana

CHELSEA HOUSE
PUBLISHERS
A Haights Cross Communications Company
Philadelphia

©2003 by Chelsea House Publishers, a subsidiary of
Haights Cross Communications.

A Haights Cross Communications ✦ Company

Introduction © 2003 by Harold Bloom.

Printed and bound in the United States of America
10 9 8 7 6 5 4 3 2 1

Library of Congress Cataloging-in-Publication Data

Bloom's modern critical views: Aldous Huxley / edited with an
introduction by Harold Bloom.
        p. cm. -- (Bloom's modern critical views)
Includes bibliographical references and index.
   ISBN 0-7910-7040-9
   1. Huxley, Aldous, 1894–1963--Criticism and interpretation. I.
Bloom, Harold. II. Series.
   PR6015.U9 Z564 2002
   823'.912--dc21
                                            2002009631

Chelsea House Publishers
1974 Sproul Road, Suite 400
Broomall, PA 19008-0914

http://www.chelseahouse.com

Contributing Editor: Gabriel Welsch

Cover designed by Terry Mallon

Cover: Associated Press

Layout by EJB Publishing Services

Contents

Editor's Note

My Introduction is an attempt to come to terms with Aldous Huxley's version of the mystical tradition, which he termed the "perennial philosophy."

In an overview of Huxley's career as a person-of-letters, Milton Birnbaum praises the novelist-essayist for stoicism, intellectual vibrancy, acuteness of language, and prophetic insight. *Brave New World* is the focus of John Attarian, who sees the dystopia as an evasion of transcendence.

Huxley's quest for the spirit, from agnosticism to gnosticism, is traced by Salley A. Paulsell, after which Jerome Meckier gives us two essays on Huxley's verse, the first analyzing "Leda," and the second turning to the sonnet, "The Decameron," and later experiments at converting the sonnet form to satiric purposes.

Huxley's influences upon Russian writers and readers is considered by Nina Diakonova, while James R. Baker contrasts William Golding's *Lord of the Flies* with Huxley's *Ape and Essence*.

Ape and Essence is placed in the context of the Age of the atom bomb by Sanford E. Marovitz, after which Kerwin Lee Klein compares Huxley's California dystopias with Robert V. Hine's much sunnier *California's Utopian Colonies* (1953).

The influences of the scientific journalist J. W. N. Sullivan upon Huxley is expounded by David Bradshaw, while Ronald Hope centers upon Huxley's anthology *The Perennial Philosophy*.

Finally, Huxley's synopsis for turning *Alice in Wonderland* into a film script is investigated by David Leon Higdon and Phill Lehrman.

Introduction

Aldous Huxley cannot be judged to have achieved lasting eminence either as a novelist or as a spiritual guide. The best of his novels were *Antic Hay* and *Point Counter Point*, which I enjoyed in my youth, but now regard as very literate Period Pieces. His most famous fiction, *Brave New World*, scarcely sustains rereading: its basic metaphor, in which Henry Ford replaces Jesus Christ, now seems strained and even silly. Huxley's one great book is his *Collected Essays*, which includes such superb performances as "Wordsworth in the Tropics," "Tragedy and the Whole Truth," and "Music at Night." In this Introduction, I turn mostly aside from Huxley-as-essayist in order to center upon his anthology-with-comments, *The Perennial Philosophy*, and two curious little books, *The Doors of Perception* and *Heaven and Hell*, both concerned with his visionary experiences induced by taking drugs.

Huxley defines the Perennial Philosophy as: "the metaphysic that recognizes a divine Reality substantial to the world of things and lives and minds; the psychology that finds in the soul something similar to, or even identical with, divine Reality; the ethic that places man's final end in the knowledge of the immanent and transcendent Ground of all being." The figures and texts testifying to this metaphysic, psychology, and ethic are very various: St. Augustine, St. Bernard, the Bhaghvad-Gita, the Buddha, St. Catherine of Siena, Chuang Tzu, *The Cloud of Unknowing*, Meister Eckhart, Fénelon, St. Francis de Sales, St. John of the Cross, Lao Tzu, Jalal-uddin Rumi, *Theologica Germanica*, Thomas Traherne. It will be noted that my list of these fifteen spiritual authorities is alphabetical, they being so diverse that no other ordering seems possible. But, to Aldous Huxley, they are all One Big Thing: The Perennial Philosophy. This Californian eclecticism helped to make Huxley one of the gurus of the New Age, but it renders me uneasy,

1

despite my own spiritual convictions, which are not wholly antithetical to Huxley's.

Huxley's second wife, Laura, wrote a poignant memoir of her husband, *This Timeless Moment*, in which she reveals that she aided him in his dying moments with a substantial shot of LSD, as he desired. One hesitates to call the death of any distinguished author a Period Piece, but 1963 (the year of Huxley's death) cultivated very different fashions than 2003, when the dying are likelier to prefer morphine to mescalin or lysergic acid. I recall reading *The Doors of Perception*, and its sequel, *Heaven and Hell*, when they were published in the mid-Fifties, with a certain skepticism, as to whether aesthetic or spiritual experiences ought to be so palpably ascribed or reduced to a chemical base. Almost half a century later, rereading these treaties, my skepticism increases. Is there a difference, *in kind*, between the strawberry ice-cream *soma* of *Brave New World* and swallowing mescalin dissolved in water, as Huxley does at the onset of *The Doors of Perception*.

Huxley would have pointed out, with exquisite courtesy, that his mescalin-induced visions increased his awareness of Art and of God, while the Brave New Worlders, stuffed with *soma*, merely danced a sort of conga, spanking one another to the beat of:

> Orgy-porgy, Ford and fun
> Kiss the girls and make them One.
> Boys at one with girls at peace;
> Orgy-porgy gives release.

It is rather a distance from that to the Perennial Philosophy, but in each instance a chemical substance gives release. New Ages are always destined to become Old Ages, and Huxleyan spirituality alas now seems antique. Aldous Huxley was a superb essayist, but not quite either a novelist or a sage.

MILTON BIRNBAUM

Marking and Remembering: Aldous Huxley (1894–1963)

$\mathbf{M}$ention Aldous Huxley to the average reader and if he remembers him at all, he will probably say, "Oh yes, didn't he write *Brave New World*?" Occasionally, his name will appear in news stories in connection with his predictions made in that dystopian novel or his experiments with psychedelic drugs. It is unlikely that he will be recalled for much else. And yet perhaps much more than any other significant literary figure in the twentieth century, he embodies the ten traits of the man of letters as ideal human being.

1. STOIC ACCEPTANCE OF FATE

First there is the ability to overcome personal adversity with a kind of stoic resignation. Although a brilliant student at Eton, Huxley became temporarily blind at sixteen, and so was prevented from preparing for a medical career. He took this affliction in stride and years later wrote with his typical grace, "Providence is sometimes kind even when it seems to be harsh. My temporary blindness also preserved me from becoming a doctor, for which I am also grateful. For seeing that I nearly died of overwork as a journalist, I should infallibly have killed myself in the much more strenuous profession of medicine." When a fire destroyed nearly all his valuable books

From *Modern Age* 37, 1 (Fall 1994) © 1994 by the Intercollegiate Studies Institute, Inc.

and letters and manuscripts a few years before his death, he remarked, "It was quite an experience, but it did make one feel extraordinarily clean." And his second wife, Laura Archera Huxley, writes that when, in a moment of compulsive restlessness, she asked for a divorce, "Aldous looked at me, with such deep love, with such dissolving tenderness. He took my hand and kissed it; 'I caught a nymph,' he said, 'I must let her go,' and released my hand."

2. Intellectual Diversity

The second trait of the man of letters is a profound intellectual curiosity and diversity of interests. Huxley's favorite reading was *The Encyclopaedia Britannica*. Although noted chiefly for his brilliantly satiric novels, by no means was he limited to fiction. He was equally at home with his first love, science (he once said that if he would be given a choice of being either Michael Faraday or William Shakespeare, he would prefer to be Michael Faraday), semantics, music, painting, philosophy, religion, psychology, sociology, politics, history—and dabbled in other fields as well. His writings allude not only to the usual literary figures—Chaucer, Dante, Shakespeare, etc.—but also to Mozart, Michelangelo, Kropotkin, Cardinal Newman, Buddha, William Sheldon, Freud, Vico, etc. Besides his eleven novels, his works include collections of short stories, biographies, poetry, an encyclopedia of pacifism, philosophical tracts, an interpretive anthology of religious excerpts, screen scripts, commentaries on painting and music, lectures to college audiences. He even used his own blindness as a basis for a book on blindness. This wealth of interests left little room for brooding or for boredom.

3. Rootedness in the Past

A third trait of the man of letters is a strong rootedness in the past. Not that Huxley was a blind conformist to tradition. He realized—as any thinking person must realize—that to improve the future one must know the past. Thus, he was knowledgeable not only in Homer, Chaucer, Shakespeare, but he knew, with Santayana, that unless we learn from the errors of history we are likely to repeat those errors. He recognized that a study of the past could improve the quality of life in the present. Sometimes the past could teach us to avoid tragic mistakes—the futility of wars, the need for decentralized governments, the importance of putting into political power people who are certified to be sane. Would Hitler, Stalin, Mussolini—not to mention some infamous leaders in power today—ever pass a sanity test? It seems strange that to get an electrician's license or a plumber's license, the applicant must fulfill certain requirements. To get control of a government, one needs no license but a manipulative skill in the licentiousness of power.

4. AWARENESS OF PRESENT

The fourth requirement facing the man of letters is a realistic awareness of the present. It is sometimes tempting for a scholar to isolate himself from the turbulence of the present by withdrawal to comforts of the past alone. Not Huxley! Long before it became fashionable to do so, Huxley vividly portrayed the dangers of overpopulation, exploitation of natural resources, and jingoistic nationalism. Time after time he warned us that unless we learn to curb our lust for material aggrandizement, we would be headed for perdition. With uncanny prophecy, his *Brave New World* (1932) portrayed the dehumanized world of the present—where, besides being overwhelmed with technological overkill, we are also being exposed to a psychological tyranny of the most subtle kind.

5. AWARENESS OF FUTURE

His awareness of the past, his attention to the present, and his scathing analysis of the soulless world he presented in his *Brave New World* did not blind Huxley to the possibility of a better world, and so in his last published novel, *Island* (1962), he projected a utopian nation. The encyclopedic knowledge that he had amassed during his lifetime he now tried to synthesize in his attempt to mold a perfect society: "Pharmacology, sociology, physiology, not to mention a pure and applied ontology, neurotheology, metachemistry, myco-mysticism, and the ultimate science ... the science that sooner or later we shall all have to be examined in—thanatology." Mind, body, and spirit have been harmoniously united. The synthesis, however, turns out to be synthetic—and although Huxley had intended to create a utopia, the tale reveals his basic belief that utopia will continue to be unattainable. "Utopia" retains its etymological meaning, "Nowhere."

6. Sense of Humor

And yet despite the seriousness with which Huxley viewed the many problems of the world, he never took himself too seriously and certainly never pompously. He could puncture the solemnity of foolish romance by writing,

> And here we sit in blissful calm Quietly sweating palm to palm.

He also recalled a Russian historian's comment that the ideal life would consist of picking one's nose while watching the sunset. Thus, aesthetic longings could be satisfied without neglecting physical needs. Of course, some people may say, "We cannot afford the sense of humor in these days of grave crisis." Perhaps if we had more of a sense of humor, there would not be so many grave crises.

7. Civility and Personal Decency

Added to all of these qualities must be a sense of personal decency and morality. Recent years have witnessed the growth of courses in assertiveness training. I recall seeing a cartoon in which a sign outside the door of an Assertiveness Training office said: "Out to lunch. Will be back whenever I damn please." Well, barbarism is not always funny. Life is barbaric enough without our adding to it by being discourteous and excessively aggressive. Despite the Swiftian irony in his novels and essays, Huxley was essentially a very decent person. All the people who reminisced about him when he died (and there is an excellent collection of these reminiscences edited by Sir Julian Huxley, Aldous' distinguished brother) testify to his essentially decent nature. Shortly before his death, as his widow noted about him in her book, he told an audience, "It is a little embarrassing that, after forty-five years of research and study, the best advice I can give to people is to be a little kinder to each other." One could listen to worse advice.

8. Commitment to Society

Huxley was more than a nice person who affected only the lives of his friends. He had a sense of commitment to society. He was opposed to both World Wars and was actively involved in fighting for his pacifism. He wrote pamphlets, gave talks, joined organizations—just as he continued doing for a variety of other causes all his life. Despite his innate shyness, he recognized that words by themselves mean little unless translated into action. He did not, however, allow his pacifist stance to blind him to the realities of existence. In a letter to John Atkins in 1955, he wrote: "I don't think that the pacifist position will ever be generally accepted on religious or ethical grounds—but it may be forced on the world by the logic of technological advance. Meanwhile the best way to further peace is [for a writer] to call attention to the psychological and demographic factors making for war."

9. Precision in Language

Although Huxley knew that words, unless followed by action, are powerless, he recognized the need for precision in language. It is his remarkable knowledge and use of language which marks the ninth trait of the man of letters. Like George Orwell, he knew that language can be used to obfuscate, to agitate, to inspire. Obviously, the language one employs in imaginative literature is not the same language one should employ in the quotidian world of politics, government, interpersonal involvement. Concrete language should replace euphemistic abstractions. Using clear language may be difficult but as he tells us in his *Perennial Philosophy* (1945), this "guard of the tongue ... the most difficult and searching of all mortifications ... is also the most fruitful."

10. Sense of Transcendence

Lastly, and above all, the man of letters as ideal human being must be aware of the transience of life and the spirituality which underlies all material existence. Like Spinoza, whom Huxley admired very much, Huxley eventually became a God-intoxicated man. Not god or religion in a narrow ritualistic or creedal sense. Even though he tended to lean to Eastern religion, particularly, to Buddhism, Huxley tried to combine the best inherent in all religions. He wanted to achieve a union with the Godhead because he recognized that the goodness of life is really the godliness of life. He realized that without a sense of transcendence, life becomes pointless.

Although he knew for a long time before his death that he was suffering from terminal cancer, he did not allow this knowledge to curtail either the congeniality he showered upon his family and friends, or his intellectual creativity. A day before his death, he finished an essay on "Shakespeare and Religion." Death held no dark fears for him; for his life was filled with beatific enlightenment.

We could use more of his kind today.

JOHN ATTARIAN

Brave New World *and the Flight from God*

Aldous Huxley's *Brave New World* (1932) is commonly seen as an indictment of both tyranny and technology. Huxley himself described its theme as "the advancement of science as it affects human individuals."[1] *Brave New World Revisited* (1958) deplored its vision of the over-orderly dystopia "where perfect efficiency left no room for freedom or personal initiative."[2] Yet *Brave New World* has a deeper meaning: a warning, by way of a grim portrait, of life in a world which has fled from God and lost all awareness of the transcendent. Reading the signs of his times, Huxley saw awaiting us a soulless utilitarian existence, incompatible with our nature and purpose. Subsequent history has vindicated his pessimism.

Brave New World's significations flow from Huxley's vision of reality and human nature and its implications for proper living. As Milton Birnbaum points out, by the early thirties, Huxley was in transition from cynicism to a mystical religion,[3] which held that a transcendent God exists, and that one's proper final end, as the foreword to the 1946 edition of *Brave New World* notes, is "attaining unitive knowledge of the immanent Tao or Logos, the transcendent Godhead or Brahman."[4] (Indeed, with its religious theme, *Brave New World* emerges as a milestone in Huxley's odyssey.)

Man, Huxley maintained, is an "embodied spirit."[5] As such, he is governed by belief:

From *Modern Age* 38, 1 (Fall 1995) © 1995 by the Intercollegiate Studies Institute, Inc.

It is in the light of our beliefs about the ultimate nature of reality that we formulate our conceptions of right and wrong; and it is in the light of our conceptions of right and wrong that we frame our conduct, not only in the relations of private life, but also in the sphere of politics and economics. So far from being irrelevant, our metaphysical beliefs are the finally determining factor in all our actions.[6]

Moreover, people possess not only a will to self-assertion but also a will to self-transcendence. "In a word, they long to get out of themselves, to pass beyond the limits of that tiny island universe, within which every individual finds himself confined."[7] This longing arises because, "in some obscure way and in spite of our conscious ignorance, we know who we are. We know ... that the ground of our individual knowing is identical with the Ground of all knowing and being."[8] Our mission in life, then, is "upward self-transcendence," metaphysically upward affiliation culminating in union with the Divinity. Unfortunately, much self-transcendence is horizontal (toward "some cause wider than their own immediate interests," but not metaphysically higher, from hobbies and family to science or politics) or even downward (toward drugs, loveless sex, etc.).[9]

Huxley saw self-restraint as essential to human dignity and proper living. His 1931 essay "Obstacle Race," published while *Brave New World* was in progress, depicted nineteenth-century life as "a kind of obstacle race," with conventions and taboos restricting behavior being the obstacles. While psychologically painful, it was worth the cost, because "the dignity of man consists precisely in his ability to restrain himself from dashing away along the flat, in his capacity to raise obstacles in his own path." Turning back from those obstacles is often "the most nobly and dignifiedly human thing a man can do."[10] This resembles Irving Babbitt's view that "what is specifically human in man and ultimately divine is a certain quality of will, a will that is felt in its relation to his ordinary self as a will to refrain."[11] For both men, this self-mortification was an act of loyalty to standards, and indispensable for upward self-transcendence.

The struggle against adversity which this entails is essential for fulfilling emotional life. The "pleasurable excitements" from surmounting (even sometimes not surmounting) psychological obstacles surpass those of life without such restraints.[12] Huxley did not explain why, but we may speculate: Striving toward God entails surmounting obstacles, overcoming adversity. Hence we exult in meeting challenges; it is a microcosm of the victorious metaphysically-upward striving which our fulfillment requires.

II

Even before *Brave New World*, Huxley realized that the main tendency in the West was away from upward self-transcendence.

The fundamental beliefs shaping thought and conduct were shifting. *Music at Night* (1931) observed that Christian beliefs "are now only lukewarmly believed in or even rejected outright." Likewise the once inspiring tenets of classical liberalism. Instead, "The modern emphasis is on personality. We justify our feelings and moods by an appeal to the 'right to happiness,' the 'right to self-expression.'"[13] Western man was also, Huxley pointed out in 1927, embracing substitute religions, from democracy and egalitarianism to the cult of business efficiency.[14] All these, of course, embody horizontal self-transcendence.

Moreover, science, technology, and mass production had seemingly removed many external constraints and disciplines, *e.g.*, economic scarcity and the consequences of sexual license. Religion's decline and applied science's advance were, Huxley believed, working synergistically to undermine self-restraint by making moral taboos seem absurd (*e.g.*, contraception)[15] and self-indulgence seem good (overconsumption to absorb overproduction).[16]

On causality Huxley was undecided. In 1927 he averred that "material circumstances are driving all nations" to emulate America's machine civilization. "Fate acts within and without; there is no resisting."[17] But "Ideals and the Machine Tool" (1931) rejected economic determinism. Huxley acknowledged "certain definite correlations" between men's world views and the economic situation. Hence "a correlation exists between the present popularity of the ideal of happiness [identified with comfort] and the rise of mass production." Unlike goodness, truth, and beauty, pursuit of happiness sustains production. Yet ideals—truth, beauty, goodness, happiness—arise apart from economics. Economics only determine which ideals shall be prevalent.[18] *Brave New World* reverted to determinism. Huxley's wavering is unimportant. What matters is his realization that Western awareness of transcendent Reality was withering.

Huxley divined too that machine civilization, and "liberation" from religion and religious morality, were exacting terrible forfeits. It was axiomatic to Huxley that getting something for nothing is impossible.[19] Even before *Brave New World* he warned that success demands "nothing short of spiritual self-mutilation."[20] Machinery was inflicting similar mutilations. As Richard M. Weaver put it, "What had been created in response to the human spirit and had referential justification began to be autotelic and to make its own demands."[21] Thus, as Huxley concluded,

> Fordism, or the philosophy of industrialism, demands that we should sacrifice the animal man (and ... large portions of the thinking, spiritual man) ... to the Machine. There is no place in the factory, or in that larger factory which is the modern industrialized world, for animals on the one hand, or for artists, mystics, or even, finally, individuals on the other. Of all the ascetic religions Fordism is that which demands the cruelest mutilations of the human psyche ... and offers the smallest spiritual returns. Rigorously practiced for a few generations, this dreadful religion will end by destroying the human race.[22]

One mutilation he observed was a spreading mediocrity of aspiration. Demanding goals—pleasing God, living morally, partaking of high culture—were being replaced by lesser ones: "fun," comfort, conformity.[23] Unfortunately, multitudes are not interested in having their souls stretched by either a demanding religion and morality or an inspiring high culture—hence the great danger that the majority would cheerfully make a Faustian bargain, selling their souls for bread, baubles, comfort and amusement.[24]

In particular, American modernity was pressuring higher and more intelligent independent souls to conform to mediocrity.[25] Beyond the evils of value inversion and intelligence emulating stupidity, those most likely to heed calls from the divine Ground were being drawn away from the upward path.

With technology, secularization, and affluence flattening the "obstacle course," people, having neither inclination nor need for self-restraint, were forfeiting their dignity too.[26] And, Huxley warned, life bereft of "exaltations and agonies" would be boring.[27] The worst forfeit, and the true and ultimate peril, of modern history's main tendency is not political, abhorrent though tyranny and regimentation were to Huxley, but religious. Loss of awareness of the transcendent is cumulative and ultimately total. Living in a secularized world, immersed in the powerful distractions of horizontal and downward self-transcendence presented by a consumption-and-fun economy, with the path of upward self-transcendence increasingly forgotten, people have nowhere to go except into ways of life unworthy of beings with souls, utterly incapable of fulfilling a higher purpose: attaining knowledge of God.

In *Grey Eminence* (1941), his biography of Father Joseph, Cardinal Richelieu's adviser, Huxley observed that the West had been increasingly forsaking such knowledge for centuries:

The acquisition of one-pointedness and the cultivation of genuine mysticism were tasks no easier in the fourteenth century, or the seventeenth, than under Queen Victoria; they merely seemed more reasonable, more worthy of consideration by men of culture and intelligence.[28]

[W]here there is no vision, the people perish; and ... if those who are the salt of the earth lose their savour, there is nothing to keep that earth disinfected, nothing to prevent it from falling into complete decay. The mystics are channels through which a little knowledge of reality filters down into our human universe of ignorance and illusion. A totally unmystical world would be a world totally blind and insane. From the beginnings of the eighteenth century onwards, the sources of mystical knowledge have been steadily diminishing in number, all over the planet. We are dangerously far advanced into the darkness.[29]

In *Those Barren Leaves* (1925), Francis Chelifer's brooding, culminating in a cynical catechism, shows that, long before *Brave New World*, Huxley had spotted this danger:

Why am I doing this? What is it all for? Did I come into the world, *supplied with a soul which may very likely be immortal*, for the sole purpose of sitting every day at this desk? ... .

Q. On what condition can I live a life of contentment?
A. *On the condition that you do not think.*

Q. What is the function of newspapers, cinemas, radios, motor-bikes, jazz bands, etc.?
A. The function of these things is *the prevention of thought* and the killing of time. They are the most powerful instruments of human happiness.

Q. What did Buddha consider *the most deadly of the deadly sins*?
A. *Unawareness, stupidity.* (italics added)[30]

III

Seen in this light, *Brave New World* is a warning that modern life threatens to inflict "the most deadly of the deadly sins": to annihilate awareness of the transcendent God and divert us from our true purpose.

Dystopia's people live in a continuous state of "unawareness, stupidity." Incomprehension, indeed, is one of the novel's themes. People are kept unaware of old age, strong feeling, death; they flee anything unpleasant into the drug *soma*. Underlying all this unawareness is deliberately-fostered unawareness of God. Abundant evidence in the novel proves that this, not runaway science or totalitarianism, was Huxley's actual chief concern.

In Chapter 3, World Controller Mustapha Mond's enumeration of the former world's discarded features focuses on elements of transcendent religion: God, heaven, soul, immortality. The Henry Ford cult replaced religion, with crosses decapitated into T's, and Ford's Day celebrations, Community Sings, and orgiastic "Solidarity Services" as "religious" rites.

Just a few pages later, a moronic elevator operator is overwhelmed by reaching his building's roof and encountering "the warm glory of afternoon sunlight": "'Oh, roof!' he repeated in a voice of rapture. He was as though suddenly and joyfully awakened from a dark annihilating stupor. 'Roof!'" To Peter Firchow, this shows that people can achieve fleeting awareness of a different reality despite conditioning.[31] True; but, more profoundly, it is a metaphor for attaining the Beatific Vision. And the elevator operator's prompt return, duty-called, to darkness and "habitual stupor" warns that our enslavement to machine civilization keeps awareness of God fleeting at best.

Religious books are "smut," accessible only to World Controllers. The only self-transcendence permitted is horizontal: social solidarity and service. And it is God's existence and its implications for conduct, not science, economics, or politics, which dominates the dialogue between Mond and the Savage, where the novel's central argument appears.

Preventing awareness of God motivates Mond's suppression of "A New Theory of Biology," which addresses "the conception of purpose," as "heretical and ... dangerous and potentially disruptive." Why? Because, Mond muses.

> ... once you began admitting explanations in terms of purpose—
> well, you didn't know what the result might be. It ... might make
> [intelligent people] lose their faith in happiness as the Sovereign
> Good and take to believing, instead, that the goal was somewhere
> beyond, somewhere outside the present human sphere; that the

purpose of life was not the maintenance of well-being, but some intensification and refining of consciousness, some enlargement of knowledge.

This dread alternative purpose is none other than attaining unitive knowledge of God. That this is life's purpose Mond deems "quite possibly true. But not, in the present circumstance, admissible."

Blocking awareness of God arguably underlies more mundane awareness-blocks. As Lenina Crowne and Henry Foster embark on a date, advertising-bearing electric sky-signs keep them "*fortunately* unaware" of the "*depressing* fact" of a starry night. Afterward, though the sky-signs' "*separating screen*" had largely dissolved, *soma*, which had "raised a quite impenetrable wall between the actual universe and their minds," enables them to retain "happy ignorance" of the "*depressing* stars" (italics added). Why "depressing"? Because a starry night is one of Creation's classic witnesses for its Creator, before which mundane concerns pale into insignificance bordering on ridiculousness.

As Huxley knew, unitive knowledge of God requires silence; distractions are its mortal enemy;[32] and by the twenties life was already distraction-ridden.[33] In his dystopia distraction via synthetic music and television is continuous, a favorite escape from anything disquieting for people sharing Lenina's determination "to preserve her incomprehension intact." The careful insulation of civilization's inmates from awareness of frustration, intense feeling, and death is partly to ensure the individual stability on which social stability and civilization depend: "When the individual feels, the community reels." But beyond that, beauty, love, heroism, pain, suffering and death are windows and channels to a transcendent reality, to God. Ecstasy and suffering are the whetstones of the soul, sharpening it to a keen edge of awareness. Beauty is a directly perceptible experience of, and witness for, God's perfection and goodness, and the natural response to it is joyful appreciation; and, beyond this, awe, reverence, and thanksgiving for its Creator. Romantic love inspires, and finds expression in, tenderness, devotion, and reverence for the beloved—self-transcendent sentiments all.

Unlike fun and comfort, which make no spiritual demands on us, suffering—one's own or others'—compels a response; it seldom leaves us where we were. It provokes an anguished "Why?" demanding an answer. It prompts reflection on life's purpose and meaning, its fairness or unfairness—in short, upon the ultimate nature of reality. This leads ineluctably to the religious question. All this is especially true of death, the most poignant pain of all, irreversible and irrevocable, the unanswerable proof that reality is not malleable, that earthly existence is in at least some measure tragic, that its fleeting pleasures are not adequate recompense for its hurts.

That Huxley knew this is revealed by Mond's reading to the Savage from Cardinal Newman and Maine de Biran on how only the young and prosperous can be independent of God, and how aging, afflicted, death-conscious people turn to God for compensation. Mond assures the Savage that the moderns have preserved youth and prosperity, hence allowing this independence, and abolished loss, rendering religion superfluous. The Savage knows better, having felt the reality of loss at his mother's death in Park Lane Hospital: "'Oh, God, God, God ...' the Savage kept repeating to himself. In the chaos of grief and remorse that filled his mind it was *the one articulate word*. 'God!' he whispered it aloud. 'God ...'" (italics added). To which a visiting child, unawareness personified, responds: "Whatever is he saying?"

Suffering and death, rightly considered, give the lie to the cult of comfort. As Aleksandr Solzhenitsyn divined:

> If, as claimed by humanism, man were born only to be happy, he would not be born to die. Since his body is doomed to death, his task on earth evidently must be more spiritual: not a total engrossment in everyday life, not the search for the best ways to obtain material goods and then their carefree consumption. It has to be the fulfillment of a permanent, earnest duty so that one's life journey may become above all an experience of moral growth: to leave life a better human being than one started it.[34]

Once aware of God and one's proper "task on earth," this implies, one will forsake "carefree consumption." But a poor consumer is a threat to prosperity. Hence not only religion but also awareness of anything that could prompt dangerous sentiments of ecstasy and suffering, which could draw one Godward, must be stifled. Hence the war against awareness.

Solzhenitsyn's words neatly express the Savage's view. His intense religiosity, and Huxley's handling of it, proves further that religion is *Brave New World's* true concern. At the Reservation the flashbacks about his upbringing culminate in his breakthrough to discovering "Time and Death and God," his mystical, ascetic quest for God in the mountains, and his emulation of Jesus on the Cross. This religiosity is in counterpoint to civilization's relentless secularism. To "unawareness, stupidity," he opposes an almost visionarily keen awareness of the Deity; to engrossment in material existence, his focus, as Bernard Marx complains, "on what he calls 'the soul,' which he persists in regarding as an entity independent of the physical environment"; to self-indulgence and *acedie*, a ferocious penitential asceticism of purification and flagellation, and a rigorous sense of sin. His last words are a remorseful "Oh, my God, my God!"—his last act an atonement-by-suicide, on which, fittingly, the novel ends.

"If you had a God, you'd have a reason for self-denial," he observes. "But industrial civilization is only possible when there's no self-denial," Mond retorts. "Self-indulgence up to the very limits imposed by hygiene and economics. Otherwise the wheels stop turning." Machinery, Huxley contends, had forced a choice: stability or death. It had permitted vast population growth, but should the wheels stop turning, famine would ensue. And wheels require attendants,

> ... men as steady as the wheels upon their axles, sane men, obedient men, men stable in contentment.

> Crying: My baby, my mother, my only, only love; groaning: My sin, my terrible God; screaming with pain, muttering with fever, bemoaning old age and poverty— how can they tend the wheels? And if they cannot tend the wheels ...

Riding a tiger, daring not dismount, humanity warped itself to fit the machine, forsaking truth and beauty for comfort and happiness. "Mass production demanded the shift. Universal happiness keeps the wheels steadily turning; truth and beauty can't." But this entailed sacrificing the divine source of truth and beauty. "God isn't compatible with machinery and scientific medicine and universal happiness. You must make your choice. Our civilization has chosen machinery and medicine and happiness."

Indeed. You pays your money and you takes your choice, as the 1946 edition's gloomy foreword noted. But "One can't have something for nothing. Happiness has got to be paid for." Forsaking God and enslaving itself to its own creation to avoid physical ruin, humanity inflicts on itself spiritual ruin.

For, as the Savage knows, awareness of God precludes allowing oneself "to be degraded by pleasant vices. You'd have a reason for bearing things patiently and with courage.... God's the reason for everything noble and fine and heroic." All virtue, all righteous conduct, is loyalty to standards of excellence. Excellence, in turn, presupposes a conception of perfection. And perfection requires a transcendent metaphysic; a secular, materialist metaphysic will not support it; the imperfection of earthly existence, with its impermanence, its frequently realized potentials of ugliness, evil, suffering and death, is clear to any awareness above the sensual.

The great choice in life—as *Brave New World* makes clear—is between self-transcendence and self-indulgence. Virtue flows from the former, sin from the latter. And without a transcendent God to stretch our souls upward, to demand that we become more than we were, no truly compelling motive to self-transcending virtue exists. As history abundantly demonstrates, the entities inspiring horizontal self-transcendence can inspire sin at least as readily as virtue. And in a reductive, materialist world unaware of God, the prevailing ethic will be pragmatic, utilitarian, self-indulgent, pleasure-seeking, pain-shunning—because that is the only ethic supportable by such a metaphysic. Virtue atrophies for want of compelling or even plausible reason.

All that makes for truly human existence atrophies too. Human dignity disappears. If we are not "embodied spirits," then we are mere matter, and there is nothing awe-inspiring or reverential about us. Corpses reduce to utilitarian objects. The Brave New World cremates its dead and recovers their constituent chemicals. Flying with Lenina past a crematorium, Henry Foster sums up materialist reductionism and its radical egalitarianism in one phrase: "All men are physico-chemically equal." Live people fare no better. Being mere matter, Lenina, Bernard notes, "thinks of herself that way. She doesn't mind being meat." She worries at his seeming indifference, is relieved when he emotionlessly fondles her breasts, and frets constantly about her appearance.

A religious outlook—with its emotions of faith, trust, devotion, reverence for the other, and self-transcendence—orients one toward love as unbelief does not. As the Hound of Heaven warned, "Thou dravest love from thee, who dravest Me." Only soulless fun and sex remain. In the meeting between the Savage and Lenina, the taut, upwardly stretched, self-transcending, vividly aware soul collides with the slack, horizontal, self-indulgent, unaware one in perfect counterpoint. He kneels reverently before Lenina and kisses her hand; she leans forward lustfully. He proclaims his desire to perform some service to prove his love and worthiness of her; she listens in incomprehension and rising annoyance:

> "At Malpais," the Savage was incoherently mumbling, "you had to bring her the skin of a mountain lion—I mean, when you wanted to marry some one. Or else a wolf."

"There aren't any lions in England," Lenina almost snapped.

"And even if there were," the Savage added, with sudden contemptuous resentment, "people would kill them out of helicopters, I suppose.... I'll do anything," he went on, more and more incoherently. "Anything you tell me.... I mean I'd sweep the floor if you wanted."

"But we've got vacuum cleaners here," said Lenina in bewilderment. "It isn't necessary."

"No, of course it isn't *necessary*. But some kinds of baseness are nobly undergone. I'd like to undergo something nobly. Don't you see?"

She doesn't see. She recoils in horror at his mention of marriage and greets his profession of love with a sexual advance.

Without struggle, without a demanding moral call to self-transcendence, without pain and ecstasy, all vivid interior life disappears. Indeed a corollary theme of *Brave New World* is that suffering and mortification are the price of transcendence, of fulfillment, of anything worthwhile, and that when life is purged of all occasion for paying this price, attaining these things becomes impossible. Note that Dystopia's rebels, seeking more intense, meaningful life, choose mortification. Helmholtz Watson adopts asceticism and experiences "a kind of mental excess"; Bernard wants "to try the effect of arresting my impulses"—*i.e.*, resurrect Babbitt's "inner check." The Savage's discovery of "Time and Death and God" comes after being driven from the manhood initiation rite, "despised and rejected of men"; his initiation into divine mysteries follows a five-day fast. "The tears are necessary," he tells Mond, and recounts the tale of the Girl of Mataski, whose troth could be won only by a morning's hoeing in her garden, enduring magic flies and mosquitoes. "What you need," he concludes, "is something *with* tears for a change. Nothing costs enough here." Slackness pervades the Brave New World; the "obstacle course" is gone. Every peaceful self-indulgence is encouraged; no demands are made on anyone. Without passion or purpose, time exists only to be frittered away.

With souls slack, high art disappears. Helmholtz Watson, Emotional Engineer, accomplished minstrel of infantile "happiness," grasps the idiocy of trying to "say something about nothing." He could, he senses, write something "more important. Yes, and more intense, more violent." But nothing in his safe, easy existence evokes such writing. Capable of appreciating *Romeo and Juliet* only as regards literary technique, he laughs when the Savage reads from it, then admits that

"… one needs ridiculous, mad situations like that; one can't write really well about anything else. Why was that old fellow such a marvellous propaganda technician? Because he had so many insane, excruciating things to get excited about. You've got to be hurt and upset; otherwise you can't think of the really good, penetrating, X rayish phrases…. We need some other kind of madness and violence. But what? What? Where can one find it?" He was silent; then, shaking his head, "I don't know," he said at last, "I don't know."

Huxley's dystopia, then, merely extrapolated the flight from God which he had observed for years. But whereas the Brave New World had deliberately chosen spiritually suicidal comfortable stupor, the West of the twenties was so exteriorized, so engrossed in affluence and seeming freedom from God, and so unaware of their costs, that it was drifting insensibly toward an oblivion of slack-souled "unawareness, stupidity." An increasingly mystical, religious man in an increasingly unmystical, irreligious world, Huxley was warning mankind to turn back before it was too late.

IV

Largely misread, the warning went unheeded. (This was partly Huxley's fault, as *Brave New World Revisited* stresses freedom, not religion.) The flight from God into a transcendence-purged world has intensified, while countervailing forces have withered. Just as the urban America of the Roaring Twenties was for Huxley the prefiguration of humanity's future, so is America today an index of heedless progress toward "a world totally blind and insane." America's secularization is already familiar. More ominously, our government is increasingly persecuting religion—an aping of the Brave New World far more sinister than the State's tightening stranglehold on our economic life.

Pursuit of secular Utopia is stronger than ever. Not even in the dictionary[35] when Weaver flayed the "spoiled-child mentality," "lifestyle" is now on every lip. Our staggering consumer debt, Americans' increasing gluttony and obesity, and the proliferation of superfluous costly articles (*e.g.,* walking shoes, running tights, skating blades), all confirm Huxley's warning of overconsumption deliberately fostered to sustain the economy—and of the warping of human nature to fit machinery.

Modern Americans typically see matter, in Simone Weil's phrase, as "a machine for manufacturing the good."[36] Technology is the idolized tool for this process, and the advent of computers has only intensified our idolatry. Liberalism's cherished welfare state and the consumer capitalism trumpeted by "Conservatives" share the Brave New World's secularist-materialist premise: the good consists of pleasant sensations, attainable by optimally arranging matter and services and the purchasing power needed to acquire them. They share too its corollary goal of purging life of unpleasantness. They differ only in their methods and in who is assigned to serve these goals.

As in Huxley's dystopia, awareness of the mysterious, transcendent significations of life and death is fading. Concerning the first, witness the utilitarian Moloch's hecatomb of abortion; and concerning the second, note Henry Foster's chirp while passing the crematorium: "Fine to think we can go on being socially useful even after we're dead. Making plants grow," informs the chilling vogue for organ harvesting, which has gone beyond willingness to give an organ posthumously to a family member and is becoming almost a social obligation. Death is demystified accordingly, and not even the integrity of a corpse is beyond Moloch's reach. Which presupposes a broad, deep repudiation of that hallmark of spiritual decency, respect for the dead—and the dogmas of bodily resurrection and of body as temple of the Holy Spirit.

Though death is regarded "like any other physiological process," suffering increasingly terrifies Americans, as witness the rising popularity of Dr. Kevorkian. This is merely the most lurid and ghastly symptom of the comfort cult's corollary: our national tendency to flinch from anything unpleasant, from petty inconveniences to suffering for principles. But virtue, spiritual growth, upward self-transcendence, and unitive knowledge of God cannot be attained by people craving an easy life.

Nor are these attainments open to the unaware, and America is increasingly rendering itself stuporous and grace-proof. Our *somas* include drugs, drink, TV, and athletics. Almost throughout their waking hours, Americans are immersed in distractions: TV, radio, tapes, CDs, computers, movies. And if "a crevice of time should yawn in the solid substance of their distractions," the Walkman tape player will fill it. With increasing frequency, one encounters on our sidewalks dead-eyed, blank-faced or Walkman-engrossed specimens, staring mindlessly like zombies. "Virtual reality" technology, uncannily like Huxley's "feelies," will only worsen our stupor.

Blocking awareness further is Americans' accelerating decerebration. The lack of widespread outrage over our disastrous system of education, and of any serious attempt to undo it, indicates that our educators are giving our slack-souled population what it wants. The popularity of "no-brainer" activities and the cretin-celebrating movie *Forrest Gump* confirm this.

Self-transcending conduct and emotions are increasingly viewed as disruptive. "Civilization," Mond tells the Savage, "has absolutely no need of nobility or heroism. These things are symptoms of political inefficiency. In a properly organized society like ours, nobody has any opportunities for being noble or heroic." David Brooks, writing in *The Wall Street Journal*, disparaged the courage, heroism, even manhood of diehard Communist Russians and Zulus opposing Mandela's African National Congress. "Today we place a higher emphasis on compromise and reconciliation, and are not so concerned that people should have fight in them."[37] Better to be "technocratic and prosaic" epicene sheep docilely turning the wheels and guzzling products, too immersed in commercialized distractions ever to grasp that they have sold their souls for comfort.

Love is withering in an atmosphere of fear, childish self-centeredness, and carnality.[38] The fervent love lauded for centuries in Western high culture is deprecated in self-help literature, and too often in real life, as "dysfunctional" or "obsessive," in favor of safe, casual companionability seeking only meaningless fun. Love is frequently replaced by dystopia's obsessive, casual sex. In this—and in popular obsessions with physical appearance, diet, and exercise (which consumes far more of a typical American's time than religion)—today's Americans see themselves as "so much meat."

Modern America, then, is primarily oriented toward soulless self-indulgence, away from upward self-transcendence. And the two possible obstacles to this Juggernaut of unawareness, culture and religion, are today, as in Huxley's dystopia, smoothing its path.

For centuries Western high art was inspired and informed by a transcendent metaphysic. Today's high art bleakly confirms Huxley's prophecies. Fashionable minimalist art, music, and literature are merely Helmholtz's "saying something about nothing." Minimalism may, as Mond says, "require the most enormous ingenuity," making art "out of the absolute minimum ... practically nothing but pure sensation," but it is also, as Helmholtz, the Savage, and our better critics grasp, "idiotic." Like Huxley's dystopian art, it imprisons its consumers in the unremitting banality and barbarism of modernity, instead of opening a window to a higher reality.

Religion has largely betrayed its mission as the conservator of awareness of the metaphysically transcendent. Roman Catholicism is pervaded by the insidious, seemingly innocuous but devastating heresy that worship is not "vertical" but "horizontal." Vertical worship seeks after upward self-transcendence, straining toward a God who is metaphysically other. Horizontal worship, "seeing the Christ in one's brothers and sisters," with the Mass as a "meal," is disturbingly near the "Solidarity Service" (*sans* orgy). It speaks volumes about the Church's loss of metaphysical acumen and vigilance that this heresy spreads unchecked.

Much popular religion is infantile and undemanding. Witness the angels fad, which reduces the metaphysically other to relentlessly cute figures on calendars. Mainstream religious morality is attenuated; demanding sanctions, especially in matters carnal, are increasingly jettisoned for fear of being "judgmental." Religion often merely exhorts us to niceness and "compassion"—a horizontalist heresy insofar as it substitutes for and thus forestalls love of God and upward self-transcendence.

Religion's recent rehabilitation among neoconservatives is not disproof, for it seeks not after upward self-transcendence. Rather, it has the same pragmatic motive as the suppression of religion in Huxley's dystopia: to improve social control and stability, the better to keep the wheels turning.

In its essentials, *Brave New World* is dangerously near fulfilled prophecy. America's mental and spiritual life increasingly resembles a skyscraper whose inhabitants, having closed the blinds on the "depressing" starry Heaven, with its silent calls to transcendence, are turning out the lights floor by floor, as their aspirations descend to the mediocrity of the Brave New World's dark basement of unawareness and fun. A politically and culturally marginalized reactionary remnant resists, Savage-like; but barring a massive revaluation of values, it seems likely, as Huxley grimly forecast in 1946, that "the horror may be upon us within a single century."

NOTES

1. *Brave New World* (New York, 1946 ed.; 1953 paperback ed.), ix.

2. *Brave New World Revisited* (New York, 1958; 1965 paperback ed.), 1–2.

3. *Aldous Huxley's Quest for Values* (Knoxville, Tenn., 1971), 166–167.

4. *Brave New World*, viii–ix.

5. *Tomorrow and Tomorrow and Tomorrow* (New York, 1956), 1.

6. *Ends and Means* (New York, 1937), 11.

7. *The Devils of Loudun* (New York, 1953), 67.

8. Ibid., 69.

9. Ibid., 313–327.

10. "Obstacle Race," *The Adelphi*, April 1931, 40, 41.

11. *Democracy and Leadership* (Indianapolis, 1979), 28.

12. "Obstacle Race," 40.

13. *Music at Night* (Garden City, N.Y., 1931), 101–102, 105.

14. "The Substitutes for Religion," in Huxley, *Proper Studies* (London, 1927), 207–229.

15. "Obstacle Race," 37.

16. *Jesting Pilate* (London, 1926), 266–270; "Foreheads Villainous Low," in *Music at Night*, 184–185.

17. "The Outlook for American Culture," *Harper's Magazine*, August 1927, 265.

18. "Ideals and the Machine Tool" (1931), in *Aldous Huxley's Hearst Essays* (New York, 1994), 14.

19. *Proper Studies* (London, 1927), 297; "Something for Nothing" (1933) in *Aldous Huxley's Hearst Essays*, 239; *The Perennial Philosophy* (New York, 1945), 79, 171.

20. *Proper Studies*, 270.

21. *Visions of Order* (Bryn Mawr, 1995), 80.

22. *Music at Night*, 159–160.

23. See, e.g., Huxley, *Jesting Pilate* (London, 1926), 266–270, 280.

24. Huxley, "Outlook for American Culture," 267.

25. *Jesting Pilate*, 279–280; "Foreheads Villainous Low," *passim*.

26. "Obstacle Race," 40.

27. Ibid., 36, 39.

28. *Grey Eminence* (New York, 1941), 77.

29. Ibid., 103–104.

30. *Those Barren Leaves* (London, 1925), 106–107.

31. *The End of Utopia: A Study of Aldous Huxley's* Brave New World, (London, 1984), 24.

32. *The Perennial Philosophy*, 216–219; *Grey Eminence*, 70–74.

33. See the quote from *Those Barren Leaves*.

34. "A World Split Apart," in *Solzhenitsyn at Harvard* (Washington, DC, 1980), 19.

35. See the 1951 *Webster's New Collegiate Dictionary*.

36. Quoted in George A. Panichas, *The Courage of Judgment: Essays in Criticism, Culture, and Society* (Knoxville, 1982), 32.

37. "Last Stand of the Old Believers," *The Wall Street Journal*, October 5, 1993; "The Zulus: Victorian Warriors in the Modern Age," *The Wall Street Journal*, April 12, 1994.

38. See Kay Hymowitz, "The L Word: Love as Taboo," *City Journal*, Spring 1995.

SALLY A. PAULSELL

Color and Light: Huxley's Pathway to Spiritual Reality

Unlike modern British writers such as T. S. Eliot and Evelyn Waugh, Aldous Huxley did not convert to a specific religious community indigenous to Western culture; however, his entire life embraced a consciousness-expanding search for ultimate reality revealed to him through the mystical qualities of color and light. Like Eliot and Waugh, Huxley found himself regarded by many critics as unfaithful to his earlier writing after his conversion to a spiritual faith. Huxley's friend Christopher Isherwood states that Huxley's developing beliefs were "widely represented as the selling-out of a once-brilliant intellect" (Clark 303), and Donald Watt concurs that "in the minds of a majority of critics Huxley was fixed as an entertaining recorder of the frenetic 1920s who later recoiled into an aesthetically suicidal mysticism" (*AH* 31).[1] More recent critics still tend to divide Huxley's canon into two halves in which *Eyeless in Gaza* (1936) is sometimes referred to as his "conversion" novel (Bowering 114, Watt *AH* 19). Although the assumption has been weakening, what many critics mistakenly took to be an abrupt change of direction and attitude in Huxley's writing actually represents a continuation of his search for theological idealism. The writer's steps on the pathway to spiritual reality can be charted—from his first book of poetry in 1916 to his last novel in 1962—through his distinctive use of the imagery of color and light. By 1936 Huxley had already started his troubled spiritual

From *Twentieth Century Literature* 41, 1 (Spring 1995) © 1995 by Hofstra University.

journey from despair toward mystical union with the "pure light of the void." Despite elements of wishful thinking and open doubt in Huxley's life and work, his conscious commitment to the struggle to believe in the Divine Light can be traced as early as 1922 in his first novel, *Crome Yellow*.

Confirmation of Huxley's intentional use of color is summarized in his "Natural History of Visions," a 1959 lecture posing the question, "Why are precious stones precious?" (*Human* 216). These brightly colored pebbles, says Huxley, are not beautifully harmonized like a work of art or a piece of music; they are single objects which the human mind responds to in an unaccountable way. He states that one reason for our interest can be found in the *Phaedo* where Socrates speaks about the ideal world of which our world is in a sense a rather bad copy. Socrates says: "In this other earth the colors are much purer and more brilliant than they are down here. The mountains and stones have a richer gloss, a livelier transparency and intensity of hue" (217). Plato writes not merely about a metaphysical idea but also about another inner world which has landscape and beautiful regions of memory, fantasy, imagination, dreams, and—most remote—"the world of visions" (218). Huxley explains the importance of light and color in this world of visions:

> This experience of the pure light of the void is a visionary experience of what may be called the highest, the most mystical, kind. On a rather lower level the lights seem to be broken up and become, so to speak, incorporated in different objects and persons and figures. It is as though this tremendous white light were somehow refracted through a prism and broken up into different coloured lights. In this lower form of vision we have the intensification of light in some way associated with the story-telling faculty, so that there are visions of great complexity and elaboration in which light plays a tremendous part, but it is not the pure white light of the great theophanies. (228–29)

Huxley deduces, therefore, that precious stones are precious because they are objects in the external world—along with fire, stained glass, fireworks, pageantry, theatrical spectacle, Christmas-tree lights, rainbows, and sunlight—which most nearly resemble the things that people see in the visionary world (232–35). Poets and storytellers, by giving us a mystic vision of these objects with gemlike qualities, bring us into contact with the visionary world and potentially stimulate our own visions within us.

Mysticism, difficult to define, becomes more difficult with Huxley's encompassing of Eastern and Western mystical thought evident in *The Perennial Philosophy* (1944). The *Abingdon Dictionary of Living Religions* summarizes a variety of inclusive definitions: "an apprehension of an ultimate nonsensuous unity in all things, a direct apperception of deity, the art of union with reality, an immediate contact or union of the self with a larger-than-self." Several schemas for the stages in a mystic's experience are also listed, such as the "fivefold classification of awakening, purgation, surrender, illumination, and union" (508). Saint John of the Cross includes the "dark night of the soul" between the last two steps reflecting an experience of isolation from deity or reality just before union.[2] Many persons in search of the Divine Presence (including Huxley) commonly report experiencing the dark night of the soul more than once and at different stages of their mystic quest. The question for many observers and presumably for Huxley himself is whether they ever achieved this last stage of union with Absolute Reality.

Like most true mystics, Huxley never claims for himself mystical status; in fact, in his essay "One and Many" (1929) he states that he is "officially" an agnostic. He goes on to say that some days he believes that "God's in his heaven and all's right with the world" while on other days he believes he is living in an "uncaring universe" (*Do* 1–2). As late as 1962 he wrote to Reid Gardner, "I remain an agnostic who aspires to be a gnostic" (*Letters* 935). In another letter to Gardner a few months later, Huxley confided that he had a "sense of the world's fundamental All Rightness" (938). Huxley's inquiring mind typically juxtaposes skepticism with affirmation; the stages of his mystical experience do not fall into a doubt-free steady continuum. Eliot, the friend and poet whose themes Huxley often emulates, writes that "doubt and uncertainty are merely a variety of belief."

Julian Huxley recognized the mystical quality in his brother's personality when they were children:

> From early boyhood, I knew in some intuitive way that Aldous possessed some innate superiority and moved on a different level of being from us other children. This recognition dawned when Aldous was five and I a prep school boy of twelve: and it remained for the rest of his life. (21)

Others also writing in Julian's memorial volume remember his perception of the mystery of the universe; for example, David Cecil reminisces that "he had a profound sense of some spiritual reality, not to be apprehended by the senses, existing beyond the confines of time and space, serene, inviolate, ineffable" (14). Whatever our conclusion to the question of whether Huxley ever achieved union with a larger-than-self, clearly this searcher for truth signals his progress toward visionary experience through color imagery in his poetry and fiction. We can best follow Huxley's spiritual journey in this way because he connects his natural affinity to color and light imagery with his progression toward inner visionary union. Thus he uses the imagery of luminous color and richly hued colored objects in a positive way to mark movement approaching unity with the Divine. Whereas a clear white light represents ideal mystical union, the bright colors that precede this ideal depict positive steps toward acceptance—toward unity with the "one and many."

Huxley's interest in color may have intensified during an illness when he was sixteen. In 1911 while at Eton, Huxley had trouble with his eyes. The school matron, thinking the boy had pinkeye, advised him to stay in the dark—an experience Huxley did not like (Bedford 32). Years later he wrote about his illness:

> At sixteen I had a violent attack of keratitis punctato, which left
> me (after eighteen months of near-blindness, during which I had
> to depend on Braille for my reading and a guide for my walking)
> with one eye just capable of light perception.   (*Art* vii)

"Light perception" remained an important ingredient in Huxley's creative life as a poet and novelist as well as in his pursuit of the mystical experience. The murky, blurred colors seen through near blindness would represent for Huxley stagnation (the symbolic dark night of the soul, if you will) as opposed to luminous colors which forecast mystical visionary experience. Even though Huxley does not use an abundance of metaphoric imagery in his writing,[3] when he does, color imagery usually constitutes an integral part of the figurative language.

Looking at his spiritual journey chronologically, we see that in 1915 when Huxley published his first book of poetry, *The Burning Wheel*— reminiscent of the Buddhist "wheel of becoming"—he was already exploring the importance of light and color as it relates to mysticism in his need to find order in his grievous, chaotic world. Doubtful of every solution, however, the poems in the volume are either contrapuntal arguments between Huxley's different voices or parodies of Wordsworth's reassurance that unity with God is possible. Looking back from a perspective of many years, Huxley calls this earlier self a "Pyrrhonic aesthete" (one who doubts everything) (*Brave* viii). This early poetry, deliberately written in many voices, moves toward parody and satire. In "Darkness" Huxley presents the dichotomy between desired union with God and despair in terms of a brilliant, blinding vision and a wounded, twisted spirit. The darkness in the first stanza (which the speaker has never known) is an experience of dazzling beauty:

> My close-walled soul has never known That innermost darkness, dazzling sight, Like the blind point, whence the visions spring In the core of the gazer's chrysolite.... The mystic darkness that laps God's throne In a splendour beyond imagining,
>   So passing bright.

The "mystic darkness" (in the language of Christian mysticism) "blinds" the human mind due to the brilliance of God's light. The second stanza, however, counterpoints with mean-spirited darkness "of lust and avarice, / Of the crippled body and the crooked heart" (*Collected* 17)—darkness with which the speaker is all too well acquainted.

Even though the poet gives no hint that the speaker's spiritual quest can be fulfilled, images of light, darkness, and color describe the glorious sight in the first stanza. "Chrysolite," a mineral in the form of a gemlike, gold-colored stone, resides in the center ("core") of the stanza surrounded by images of darkness which are actually images of the blinding brilliance of God. The darkness in the second stanza remains "static" and "rather undeveloped," according to Donald Watt, but he also agrees that it expresses Huxley's enduring theme of "the need for some guiding light in the dark night of the soul" (Meditative" 116–17).

The seeds of Huxley's developing ideas about the levels of vision in the external world also emerge in a compatible poem in *The Burning Wheel*. In "Two Realities" "I," possibly the poet, sees life in its brilliant colors—"A waggon passed with scarlet wheels / And a yellow body, shining new" and feels a sense of the beauty of life. The speaker becomes disillusioned, however, when he realizes that his companion's vision differs—the companion sees "a child that was kicking an obscene / Brown ordure with his feet" (*Collected* 20). The poet feels the futility of life because our limitations of perception imprison us.[4] The bright, shining colors of scarlet and yellow give hope because, unaccountably, the mind responds to them while the "obscene / Brown ordure," which has no brightness, represents life in a confused, muddled world of despair. Huxley (the Pyrrhonic aesthete) in modernist counterpoint juxtaposes both views but cannot choose.

In *Defeat of Youth* (1918) several poems introduce specific connections between soothing thoughts and the generic term "color." In "Stanzas," for example, the speaker would like to live in a beautiful world free from pain "like a pure angel, thinking colour and form / ... Spilling my love like sunlight, golden and warm / On noonday flowers" (73). "Poem" begins: "Books and a coloured skein of thoughts were mine; / And magic words lay ripening in my soul" (73). Frequently used images such as "Coloured skein" and "Coloured strands" symbolize for Huxley the band or spectrum of colors (like those in the rainbow) which develop from a white light after passing through a prism. These skeins and strands have the potential to recombine into white light—the pure white light of the void.

"Scenes of the Mind" introduces ideas developed further in later novels, such as the potential for making bright colors out of dull lead (symbolically the potential for visions of ecstatic experience as opposed to deathlike paralysis in the disordered waste land of modern society) and the calm pastoral hush of "crystal silence" where in contented evenings:

> I held a wealth of coloured strands,
> Shimmering plaits of silk and skeins
> Of soft bright wool. Each colour drains
> New life at the lamp's round pool of Gold.   (74)

The optical illusion of the "pool of Gold" from the lamp's light enlivens the color in the spectrum of strands, plaits, and skeins. Miraculous transformation takes place within the mind when

> Beauty or sudden love has shined
> And wakened colour in what was dead
> And turned to gold the sullen lead.   (75)

The poet equates non-specific color citations with purity and enchanting supernatural effects of inner quiet; moreover, the "dead" "sullen lead" which "turned to gold" describes the process of developing the paint pigment, chrome yellow. This compound of chromic acid and lead becomes golden yellow in its purest hue. In idyllic moments in "Scenes of the Mind," a Wordsworthian God is seen in the waterfall or in the flame of a fire. However, in swift counterpoint the scene freezes into stone, causing "the death of gems" (75). Although Huxley cannot ultimately accept these color-filled scenes of the mind as reality, they demonstrate the importance of color to the poet's emerging mystical vision.

Leda (1920) continues with poetry of disillusionment, and Huxley uses the myth of Leda and Jove as a framework for shaping the world's chaos and perversion. In "Leda" Huxley describes the young queen in terms of ironical perfection. She undresses to become "dazzlingly naked" (85) while bathing with her maidens. "The sun's golden heat" clothes her "in softest flame" (94). This scene of carefree innocence, however, fills Jove with lust; and with help from another god he schemes to rape her. Jove, disguised as a "dazzling white" swan, feigns attack by "an eagle, tawny and black" (95). This "colorless" pair's destructive plot results in a pointless, sensuous seduction of Leda. Now instead of playing in the light of joyful innocence, she must veil her body "from the shame / Of naked light and the sun's noonday flame" (98). Offering no hope for deliverance from the negation of this spiritually barren world, the poet emphasizes colorlessness in *Leda*.

Huxley turned to short stories, novels, and essays during the twenties. His first novel, *Crome Yellow*, takes its name from the country house named Crome where the novel's house party gathers but more importantly from "chrome yellow," the compound of substances used as pigment in paints ranging in hue from light greenish yellow to reddish medium yellow. Chrome yellow, one of the chrome colors noted for its clearness and brilliance, reflects golden yellow in its purest hue; thus, the luminescence of both chrome yellow and the house party at Crome has the potential to captivate with its dazzling brilliance. The creative guests (including a writer, a poet, an artist, and a philosopher) arrive bringing bright promise of sparkling conversation; they fall short of their promise, however, because they cling only to their own pet topics.

Crome Yellow centers around the young poet Denis Stone, who, as his name implies, has the opportunity of being a "sparkling stone" with a bright and colorful poetic future of depth and intensity and a warm future full of love. Just as the fire in "Scenes of the Mind" freezes into the dullness of visually impenetrable stone and in "Stanzas" hardens into "chiselled stone" (*Collected* 73), Denis Stone remains colorless and opaque—not a precious gem. Through color imagery early in the novel we get a hint of the young poet's potential for a meaningful life and of his ultimate failure to develop that potential. Huxley describes Denis (reminiscent of Eliot's Prufrock trying to decide whether to wear his white flannel trousers rolled) on his first morning at the Wimbush estate where he has joined a house party:

> Denis woke up next morning to find the sun shining, the sky serene. He decided to wear white flannel trousers—white flannel trousers and a black jacket, with a silk shirt and his new peach-colored tie. And what shoes? White was the obvious choice, but there was something rather pleasing about the notion of black

patent leather.... His hair might have been more golden, he
reflected. As it was, its yellowness had the hint of a greenish tinge
in it. (14)

Although he selects rather color-free attire, Denis's white flannel trousers,
silk shirt, peach-colored tie, and black patent-leather shoes have a certain
sparkle and gloss. His hair (yellow with green tinges—a hue of chrome
yellow), however, suggests dullness and loss of purity in color. This streaked
mixture of yellow and green, which "might have been more golden"—the
purest hue of chrome yellow—symbolically foreshadows Denis's lack of
courage to declare his love and to stimulate his own inner poetic vision.

The poet evades reality and writes insipid Georgian verse rather than
examining his life and thereby creating ironic, satirical poetry. In addition to
this professional failure, Denis also fails to pursue his love for Anne
Wimbush. For one brief mystical moment, however, he comes in contact
with his feelings and takes positive action. The scene occurs at night in the
garden where Denis assists Anne after she falls and hurts herself:

He felt in his pockets for the match-box. The light spurted and
then grew steady. Magically, a little universe had been created, a
world of colours and forms—Anne's face, the shimmering orange
of her dress, her white, bare arms, a patch of green turf—and
round about a darkness that had become solid and utterly blind.
(82)

This vision of "colours and forms" gives Denis self-confidence, and
instinctively he begins to comfort and to kiss the woman he loves. For once
the young poet discards his Prufrockian inertia and acts on honest emotions.
The flaming match goes out, however, and the vision (Huxley's frequent
sight-enhancing image of an optical illusion provided by a temporary circle
of light) disappears. The inept lover's boastful offer to carry Anne back to the
house ends in humiliation as he staggers out of control; again he becomes the
object of laughter. Discouraged at the way others perceive him, Denis
decides to end his holiday at Crome on the subterfuge of urgent family
business; he feels as if he is planning his funeral. Denis mistakenly believes
he has acted decisively (albeit unwisely), but his inability to face his feelings
with integrity has only served to deepen his paralysis.

The artist, Gombauld, rivals Denis for Anne's attention and for artistic
veracity. Huxley's imagery of color and light in Gombauld's painting holds
the most promise for mystical vision at Crome; in fact, Denis tells Anne, "I

have to say that art is the process by which one reconstructs the divine reality out of chaos" (18). Denis prostitutes his art while Gombauld strives to complete his creative vision. Gombauld's half-finished picture inspired by Caravaggio involves a man fallen from a horse:

> A white, relentless light poured down from a point in the right foreground. The beast, the fallen man, were sharply illuminated; round them, beyond and behind them, was the night. They were alone in the darkness, a universe in themselves.... A central gulf of darkness surrounded by luminous forms. (53)

According to Sir Kenneth Clark, the picture being imitated is Caravaggio's "Conversion of St. Paul" (Julian Huxley, *Aldous Huxley* 15–18)—a painting which coincides with Huxley's spiritual quest. Art critic John Canaday notes:

> Caravaggio dramatized otherwise realistic scenes by means of brilliant artificial light, sometimes from a miraculous source. His most spectacular use of this device [is] *The Conversion of Saint Paul....* The light itself is a symbol of spiritual transfiguration— and is visible only to Saul. (70–71)

This pure, luminous form of chrome yellow (amber light seen as crystal white in its piercing brilliance) signifies the pure light of heaven—a vision which only Saul has seen. Sanford Marovitz misses the significance of Huxley's use of Caravaggio's painting in *Crome Yellow* when he writes that the painting "has little if any relation to the rest of the novel" (174). In fact, Huxley desperately desires this "spiritual transfiguration," but, like Gombauld, he wonders about his ability to free himself from the despair of the world. How would he know if he had seen the mystical vision of God? Gombauld looks at his canvas and thinks: "But that something he was after, that something that would be so terrific if only he could catch it—had he caught it? Would he ever catch it?" (*Crome* 53)

Not only was Huxley struggling with the mysticism of spiritual reality, he was also struggling with the question of Western versus Eastern mysticism. One important scene from the novel reveals, through form, light, and color, his attraction to both religious disciplines. As Denis and Anne take a morning tour of the grounds at Crome, Denis sees:

> That part of the garden that sloped down from the foot of the terrace to the pool had a beauty which did not depend on colour

so much as on forms. It was as beautiful by moonlight as in the
sun. The silver of water, the dark shapes of yew and ilex trees
remained, at all hours and seasons, the dominant features of the
scene. It was a landscape in black and white. For colour there was
the flowergarden; it lay to one side of the pool, separated from it
by a huge Babylonian wall of yews. You passed through a tunnel
in the hedge, you opened a wicket in a wall, and you found
yourself, startingly and suddenly, in the world of colour. The July
borders blazed and flared under the sun. Within its high brick
walls the garden was like a great tank of warmth and perfume and
colour. Denis held open the little iron gate for his companion.
"It's like passing from a cloister into an oriental palace," he said.
(16)

The black and white landscape, equally beautiful by moonlight as by
sunlight, depends on forms for its beauty. Huxley compares this staid garden
to a cloister—a place devoted to religious seclusion such as a monastery.
Western monastic life depends on forms for its beauty: mass, liturgical
offices, chanting the Psalms. The holy "hours and seasons" provide the
dominant forms for observance. The "huge Babylonian wall of yews"
separating the formal garden from the flower garden has to be negotiated
through tunnels and a wicket in the wall. Babylon, the place of exile and
captivity for the people of Israel and Judah, also symbolizes the modern,
corrupt, warring world represented as the realm of resistance to God. The
tunnel in the hedge, akin to the black tunnels where the mole creeps in
Huxley's poem "Mole" and the dim tunnels in "The Reef" where the
sightless fish swim, represent restraint, chaos, and uncertainty. Once through
the mazey tunnels formed by poisonous yew trees one emerges in a flower
garden of warmth, perfume, and color. This bright "oriental palace" of
Eastern mysticism stirred the poorly sighted Huxley who, nevertheless,
remained unconvinced that he could find his way through the tunnel to
mystical union.

Huxley continues his search for spiritual belief in *Antic Hay* (1923),
where Theodore Gumbril, Jr., just like Denis Stone, loses his opportunity for
love and happiness through indecision. Gumbril takes Emily to see the
flowers at Kew Gardens, where he had been happy as a child with his mother.
He had drawn maps of the gardens "and coloured them elaborately with
different coloured inks to show where the different flowers grew" (161).
Now the green grass "glowed in the sunlight, as if it were lighted from

inside" (163), and the trees make a dark shadow against the sky or sometimes a filtered pattern with moving light shining through. Gumbril meditatively compares this outward quiet of grass and trees with an inward quiet which dispels the frenetic noise of factories, jazz bands, and newspaper vendors. Once touched by this equally beautiful and terrifying "crystal quiet" (163), he finds all the noise of daily activity in this world unimportant. "One would have to begin living arduously in the quiet, arduously in some strange unheard-of manner" (164). This quiet crystal world of mystical contemplation seems native to Emily, who tells Gumbril: "Being happy is rather melancholy—like the most beautiful landscape, like those trees and the grass and the clouds and the sunshine to-day" (170). They attend a symphony concert; then, filled with happiness, they go to Gumbril's rooms, where they spend a tender night in the enchanting atmosphere of the lights of two candles burning—"two shining eyes of flame" (171). This image is used similarly in Huxley's poem "By the Fire" in *The Defeat of Youth*. "And candles watch with tireless eyes" (*Collected* 63) two lovers who sit contentedly by the fire until one of them begins to think of the world outside and its problems. The candles only temporarily push back the gloom.

The "eyes" of the candles and the "crystal silence," like that in Huxley's poem "Scenes of the Mind," do not last. The enchantment shatters because Gumbril is frightened by this contemplative inner world of quiet; therefore he sabotages his relationship with Emily by allowing his drunken friends to draw him back into their fellowship. He even entertains his friends by revealing intimate details of Emily's life. Gumbril delays his departure for his appointment in the country with her. When he finally makes his journey, he finds the cottage empty. Gumbril's indecision smashes any possibility of entering the (contrapuntally both feared and desired) symbolic "crystal silence" of visionary experience.

Using Eliot's images, Huxley writes, "Aridly, the desiccated waste extended" (212). Gumbril's friends, involved in sordid affairs, live lives of desperation while he continues to carouse with Myra Viveash. They spend one night endlessly circling the West End in a taxi looking for an end to boredom. Each time they crisscross London, they pass through Piccadilly Circus with its garish neon lights creating a St. Vitus's dance of animated pictures. This satirical perversion of the sanctity of colors in the world of visionary experience reinforces other symbols of meaningless activity: the blinking neon lights create the illusion of motion in their circular patterns; the antic-hay ring dance moves circularly to the music of Pan; Myra and Gumbril circle London aimlessly; Shearwater pedals his stationary bicycle mile after mile. In a parody of the Buddhist wheel of life, death, and rebirth, this pointless activity precludes any inner growth in—what Eliot would later call "the still point of the turning world"—the crystal quiet of the soul.

In *Those Barren Leaves* (1925) mystical solitude finally emerges as a feasible alternative to the frantic circular emptiness of modern life. Calamy, a house-party guest (similar to those in *Crome Yellow*), contemplates the mystery of the universe. He wishes to fix his spirit on the secret of the other world until "its symbols cease to be opaque and the light filters through from beyond" (267). During a sensual night with Mary Thriplow, Calamy performs a basic exercise of mystical contemplation. In the dark bedroom he holds his opened hand against a window with the starlit night shining through and ponders "all the different ways in which these five fingers ... have reality and exist" (340). He believes that if he had the freedom to concentrate on his fingers for a period of time (even months) he might cut "right through the mystery and really get at something—some kind of truth, some explanation" (340). In *The Perennial Philosophy* Huxley writes that many Eastern and Western spiritual teachers recommend intense concentration on an image or idea. Such an exercise is helpful when it results in "mental stillness, such a silence of intellect, will and feeling, that the divine Word can be uttered within the soul" (32).

In the final scene of the book a melancholy yet determined Calamy withdraws from the world to begin his silent, contemplative quest for union with absolute reality. Huxley directly links Calamy's vision of clear color and sparkle with the inner world of mystical experience:

> The cottage was in the shadow now. Looking up the slope he could see a clump of trees still glittering as though prepared for a festival above the rising flood of darkness. And at the head of the valley, like an immense precious stone, glowing with its cold inward fire, the limestone crags reached up through the clouds into the pale sky. Perhaps he had been a fool, thought Calamy. But looking at that shining peak, he was somehow reassured. (379–80)

The trees "glittering as though prepared for a festival" and the limestone crags "like an immense precious stone, glowing with its cold inward fire" represent those brilliantly colored objects in the external world which Huxley believes lead people to mystical experiences in the visionary world. Huxley's "cold inward fire" does not burn with heat; instead, it gives forth a glow, a light from within, a nimbus illuminating the hope that life can be ordered through the discipline of mind and body in meditation. Calamy has seen the "shining peak" and although it may not be the "pure light of the void" (*Perennial* 32) he feels "reassured." From his first book of poetry, Huxley has used imagery of color and light to suggest a quest for union with the infinite, but until now he has been unable to surrender himself to the possibilities of mystical illumination.

By 1928 Huxley (excessively influenced by the "life force" philosophy of D. H. Lawrence represented by Rampion in *Point Counter Point*) temporarily neglects the literary expression of his mystical vision, seen through images of color and light, in order to satirize perverted sexual relationships and perverted scientific reason. Jerome Meckier states that "It is possible to assume that under the impact of renewed acquaintanceship with Lawrence, Huxley, in 1926, makes an about face from the semi-mystical conclusions Calamy comes to at the end of *Those Barren Leaves*" (*Aldous Huxley* 80–81). This assumption is borne out by the absence of familiar imagery of color and light.

Huxley returned to poetry at the end of the decade in two short volumes: *Arabia Infelix* (1929) and *The Cicadas* (1931). For Huxley spiritual crises scar these years, and poem after poem reflects the torment of his soul. As Meckier emphasizes, no longer can Huxley's persona of the sceptical "Pyrrhonic aesthete" contentedly expose the "apparent meaninglessness of modern, that is, post-war life" (*Aldous Huxley* 210). Huxley strives in these poems to overcome his own despair, i.e., his own dark night of the soul, and reach out to the visionary world signified by pure, wondrous color. In "The Yellow Mustard," the final poem in Huxley's 1931 collection, Huxley describes the shadowy mustard fields which are concealed by low clouds and entombed by "Grey mountain-heaps of slag and stone" (*Collected* 165). These emblems of the poet's mind "dark with repinings" turn to "glory," however, when the clouds open and a "conquering ray" reveals the pure chrome yellow of the glittering mustard field:

> And touched, transfiguringly bright
>   In that dull plain, one luminous field;
> And there the miracle of light
>   Lay goldenly revealed.

Although the external world offers no consolation—"despair / Hung dark, without one rift of blue"—there "sleeps" within each one of us "some grain of mustard seed" (166). By alluding to these synoptic Gospel references to the power of faith and the Kingdom of God within each human being,

Huxley emphasizes that we must waken this hallowed core of our existence (the ground of our being) which is revealed through the mystical power of color and light.

Brave New World (1932) explores colorlessness, the polar opposite of positive mystical color imagery. This dystopian novel, continuing to reflect Huxley's spiritual crisis, portrays a strictly controlled society which has scientifically eliminated individuality. "Happiness" is programmed through sexual freedom and a drug (soma) which creates feelings of euphoria. Scent and color organs provide music and momentary pictures on the ceiling such as an artificial tropical sunset followed by a bogus sunrise (51). In this synthetic world Huxley eschews bright primary color imagery in favor of dull, dark hues which border on colorlessness. To identify the stereotyped levels of society, for example, Deltas wear khaki, Epsilons (genetically manipulated to be stupid) wear black, hard working Alphas wear grey, upper-caste Gammas wear green, and so on. These drab colors, far from translucent or glossy, serve utilitarian purposes; they in no way lead to creativity outside of this genetically controlled community. Religious thought becomes virtually impossible in a society that forbids being alone and seeking silence. A note of affirmation resides in the novel, however, because Helmholtz Watson defies the laws and his genetic conditioning and writes a poem which celebrates silence and acclaims a spiritual "presence."

Huxley named Helmholtz Watson, at least in part, for Hermann Ludwig Ferdinand Von Helmholtz (1821–1894) the noted German physiologist, psychologist, mathematician, and physicist (Meckier "Our Ford" 47).[5] This modern Renaissance man wrote what is probably the most important work on the physics and physiology of vision. His three-volume *Physiological Optics* (1856–1866) includes his conception of the structure and action of color perception and how light illumination changes the vision. Von Helmholtz also invented the ophthalmoscope, an optical instrument for examining and focusing light on the interior of the eye. This brilliant scientist and color theorist perfectly symbolizes his namesake Helmholtz Watson, who has a mental excess which makes him aware of his individuality and sets him apart from other people. A lecturer at the college of emotional engineering, Watson ably invents phrases, but he wants to write penetrating ones which look beneath surface reality. Just as the scientist Von Helmholtz invented an instrument for looking into the interior of the eye in an effort to understand the effects of color and light on one's vision, Huxley's Helmholtz Watson wants to invent brilliantly colored phrases which look into one's soul to a world of mystical vision. The authorities exile this poet and a fellow maverick to the Falkland Islands, where they can think or write poetry amid the silence of wind and storm. Watson will survive and continue his creative development because the spiritual "presence" in his poetry triggers theocentric stirrings within him. His retreat from the brave new world's soma-controlled society will free him to pursue mystical oneness—the same goal Huxley desires for his own life.

Eyeless in Gaza (1936), rather than a "conversion" novel, acts as a summation of Huxley's spiritual journey up to this point. It functions as a Bildungsroman not only of Huxley's development from adolescence to maturity but also of the evolution of his mystical vision seen in the color and light imagery in his work. The title refers to the Israelite, Samson (solar or sun's man), who became blinded by vanity and thereupon revealed the secret of his strength. Having failed to rely upon the Lord, Samson lost his legendary power, allowing his Philistine captors to put out his eyes. Samson remains eyeless in Gaza until he again calls upon the Lord for strength. Feeling his strength and his divine purpose returning, he receives second sight and pulls down the Philistine temple upon himself and his captors. Huxley's play on sight, loss of sight, insight, and second-sight embraces not only the biblical story of Samson but also Milton's interpretation of this story in *Samson Agonistes*, Milton's own blindness, and Huxley's near-blindness. By the end of the novel, the synthesis of the spiritual journeys of author and protagonist culminates in the guise of Dr. Miller (modeled after Huxley's friend Gerald Heard, among others), who instructs Anthony Beavis in mystical meditation.

In adolescence young Anthony travels on a train with his father and uncle to Lollingdon for his mother's funeral service. Anthony has a mystical reverie; the wheels of the train begin to chant "dead-a-dead-a-dead," and he cannot keep the refrain from shouting in his head, "for ever." Anthony begins to cry and has to wipe his eyes. Then, "luminous under the sun, the world before him was like one vast and intricate jewel. The elms had withered to a pale gold. Huge above the fields, and motionless, they seemed to be meditating in the crystal light of the morning" (18). As in his first book of poetry, Huxley parodies Wordsworth's philosophy found in "Tintern Abbey" and *The Prelude*. Whereas Wordsworth describes his childhood as a time of unconscious mystical oneness with the universe, Huxley satirically counterpoints Anthony's paradisiacal reveries with intrusive images of death. The mixture of nightmare imagery with the glowing hopefulness of light continues as the three mourners make their way to the burial plot. "The old horse drew them; slowly along lanes, into the heart of the great autumnal jewel of gold and crystal, and stopped at last at the very core of it. In the sunshine, the church tower was like grey amber" (21). But as they move to the church, Anthony becomes trapped like a dwarf in the middle of a black well of adults. It was as though "Their blackness hemmed him in, obscured the sky, eclipsed the amber tower and the trees.... This black well was dark with the concentrated horror of death. There was no escape. His sobs broke out uncontrollably" (23–24). Although Anthony, like the child in "Tintern Abbey" and *The Prelude*, has an affinity for supernatural beauty in his mystical reverie, fragmentation and grief emerge instead of oneness and peace.

Anthony (now at Oxford) and his friend Brian Foxe have a theological debate about mystical books such as *The Way of Perfection*. Anthony admits that he believes "in the fundamental metaphysical theory of mysticism" (81), but this is known truth and not experienced truth. At a party that evening, drunk on champagne, Anthony suddenly sees the world in a new light:

> The apples and oranges in the silver bowl were like enormous gems. Each glass under the candles, contained, not wine, but a great yellow beryl, solid and translucent. The roses had the glossy texture of satin and the shining hardness and distinctness of form belonging to metal or glass. Even sound was frozen and crystalline. (90)

This vision resonates with Huxley's earlier writing. The gemlike colors of the apples and oranges trigger recollections of the shimmering orange of Anne's face in Denis's match light in *Crome Yellow*. The wine transformed into "yellow beryl" in the light of the candles recalls the shining eyes of candle flame in Gumbril's room in *Antic Hay*. Although Anthony is opening his mind to new ideas through his reading at Oxford, it is only while in a drunken reverie that he feels free enough to experience these ideas. Sober again, Anthony mirrors societal mores, and participates in the "alien element" by repeatedly betraying his friend Brian; his betrayal of the confidences of Brian's fiancée (similar to Gumbril's betrayal of Emily in *Antic Hay*) results in Brian's suicide.

A most unusual incident in 1933 catapults Anthony into a search for meaning in his life. He and his lover, Helen Amberley (her last name a variant of the color amber—a translucent yellow, one of the chrome-yellow hues used in stage lighting to simulate sunlight), sunbathing on the flat roof of Anthony's house, are spattered by the bright red blood of a dog dropped from an airplane. The dried blood quickly turns dull brown, and this distributing baptism leads first Helen and finally Anthony to the realization that their purely physical relationship has no future. They must search for detachment from ego, not detachment from duty. Anthony finds a way to serve others, and in so doing internalizes what he already knows mentally—the "Unity of mankind, unity of all life, all being even" (417). A mystical vision follows, and Huxley uses imagery of light and dark to describe it. Anthony's mind passes from "stormy light" to "dark peace"—from "widening darkness into another light" (422). The intensity and profundity of peace grow until

> the final consummation, the ultimate light that is the source and substance of all things; source of the darkness, the void, the submarine night of living calm; source finally of the waves and the frenzy of the spray—forgotten now. For now there is only the darkness expanding and deepening, into light; there is only this final peace, this consciousness of being no more separate, this illumination. (423)

In this way *Eyeless in Gaza* emerges as a pivotal novel in which Huxley sums up the movement in his life and in his writing toward mystical vision and union with God using both satire and the illumination of the pure light of the void to mark his progress.

In *After Many a Summer Dies the Swan* (1939), Huxley satirizes Californian excess. Like Miller in *Eyeless in Gaza*, Mr. Propter embodies the Eastern mystical philosophy of Gerald Heard. Although Huxley primarily assigns to Propter the rather static role of lecturer and conscience to the sinful surrounding community, Huxley does write one scene of Propter deep in mystical contemplation which simulates Huxley's own periods of meditation. Propter, an advocate for migrant workers, lives in a white bungalow where he often meditates on a bench under a eucalyptus tree (noted for its healing oil, strength, and shelter) on questions such as "What is man?" and "What is God?" In a scene reminiscent of Gautama Buddha meditating under the Bo tree—tree of enlightenment or wisdom—in the Buddhist tradition, Propter "had come to this bench under the eucalyptus tree in order to recollect himself, in order to realize for a moment the existence of that other consciousness… that free, pure power greater than his own" (76–77).

> He looked again at the mountains, at the pale sky between the leaves, at the soft russet pinks and purples and greys of the eucalyptus trunks; then shut his eyes once more.
> "A nothingness surrounded by God, indigent of God, capable

of God and filled with God if man so desires." And what is
God?... For little by little these thoughts and wishes and feelings
had settled like a muddy sediment in a jar of water, and as they
settled, his vigilance was free to transform itself into a kind of
effortless unattached awareness, at once intense and still, alert
and passive.... The busy nothingness of his being experienced
itself as transcended in the felt capacity for peace and purity, for
the withdrawal from revulsions and desires, for the blissful
freedom from personality. (77–78)

Even though Huxley introduces Propter's mystical state using colors of the
"pale sky" and the "pinks and purples and greys of the eucalyptus trunks," the
ecstatic experience itself is described in the language used ecumenically by
mystics. In his enthusiasm for the universal language of mystical
experience—especially the Vedantist philosophy promoted by Heard—
Huxley uses less color imagery related to mystical union. However, imagery
of color and light reemerges prominently in *Time Must Have a Stop* (1944).

Softer, yet still luminous and transparent colors in *Time Must Have a
Stop* signal progress on the journey to the crystal, pure white light of spiritual
union with the Divine. The color blue emerges as a passive/aggressive
"hound of heaven" spiritual entity. The color is associated not only with the
spiritual mystic Bruno Rontini, but also with the mystical presence that will
not let Eustace Barnack rest after his death. As Huxley draws his readers
deeper into a mystical experience of the clear pure light, the bright gemlike
colors recede in favor of a more tranquil yet piercing blue.

In his quest for spiritual synthesis, Huxley offers several spiritual
models in various stages of their religious journeys in *Time Must Have a Stop*:
Bruno Rontini, the mystic; Eustace Barnack, the spiritual resister; and
Sebastian Barnack, the poet in the process of achieving mystical union. Two
of these models appear in earlier novels, for example, the mystic depicted by
Miller (*Eyeless*) and Propter (*After*) and the searching poet depicted by
Calamy (*Those*) and Beavis (*Eyeless*). The spiritual resister, however, who is
aware of and troubled by the mystical dimension and yet struggles to
maintain his ego and his identity, adds a new dimension to Huxley's
characters.

Bruno Rontini, a second-hand bookshop owner who basks in a
"crystal silence" even in the midst of city noises, has a great compassion for
Eustace. Huxley describes Bruno's remarks to Eustace about the freedom of
the will to resist spirituality:

> People had been able to say no even to Filippo Neri and Francois
> de Sales, even to the Christ and the Buddha. As he named them
> to himself, the little flame in his heart seemed to expand, as it
> were, and aspire, until it touched that other light beyond it and
> within, and for a moment it was still in the timeless intensity of a
> yearning that was also consummation.   (96)

This sparkling "little flame" within Bruno, which expands at the thought of
Christ and the Buddha, brings him into contact with the visionary world and
stimulates visions of "that other light." He urges Eustace to drop his
resistance and experience this same paradoxical yearning/consummation.
Because of the energy expended in Bruno's concern for the salvation of
others, he always looks physically tired and emaciated; however, there is a
peace and gaiety about him, and his eyes are always "blue and bright" (91).
When Sebastian meets Bruno he notices "the eyes were blue and very bright.
Blue fires in bone-cups" (211). Subsequently, when Sebastian sees Bruno
after his ten years of imprisonment, Bruno is very ill, but "the blue bright
eyes were full of joy, alive with an intense and yet somehow disinterested
tenderness" (253). The blue here is probably related to Christian symbolism,
which somewhat arbitrarily has been taken "to represent eternity, faith,
fidelity, loyalty, truth and spotless reputation" (Hulme 29).

As Eustace Barnack lies dying on a dark bathroom floor, he has a faint
awareness of God or what he always derisively refers to as the Gaseous
Vertebrate. This awareness turns into a bright light bringing with it an
eternity of joy (125–26). Later, in the Bardo state (that intermediate stage
between this world and rebirth into another incarnation), he feels himself in
contact with Bruno, and the overpowering light becomes "tenderly blue"
(154). Eustace resists the seductive power of the blue light:

> Out there, in here, the silence shone with a blue imploring
> tenderness. But none of that, none of that! The light was always
> his enemy. Always, whether it was blue or white, pink or pea
> green. He was shaken by another long, harrowing convulsion of
> derision.   (207)

Eustace will not let himself be fooled by the special color of the light because
all light threatens to engulf him. The light's liveliness and transparency lead
to the pure white light of the void. Later, "He knew what the light was up to.
He knew what that blue tenderness of silence was beseeching him to do"
(209). In Eustace's last thoughts from his purgatorial/Bardo Thodol

existence, he still resists salvation/reincarnation: "But there was the light again, the shining of the silence. None of that, none of that. Firmly and with decision, he averted his attention" (237).

Huxley introduces Eustace's nephew, Sebastian Barnack, into the novel as a self-centered, baby-faced adolescent who writes poetry. Bruno initiates Sebastian's spiritual journey because the young poet senses the depth of the bookseller's mystical spirituality. When Sebastian goes to see Bruno for the first time after his uncle's death, he notices "a square of sunlight, glowing like a huge ruby on the tiled floor" (211). This combination of color and light provides Bruno with the only luxury he desires. At the end of that visit Bruno advises Sebastian to "Try to be more honest, to think less of himself. To live with people and real events and not so exclusively with words" (227). On the way home, Sebastian composes the last verse recorded in the novel:

> Walking on Grape Nuts and imagination
> Among recollected crucifixion and these jewels
> Of horizontal sunlight. (227)

Through the incandescent brilliance of the "jewels" and the "sunlight," Sebastian, the young poet, begins his long spiritual journey toward salvation and the "world of visions." Eventually he stops writing poetry altogether to devote himself to the completion of Bruno Rontini's philosophical and spiritual writings—the Minimum Working Hypothesis—a prototype for Huxley's *Perennial Philosophy*, published the following year.

Huxley's efforts to maintain his vision were tested in *Ape and Essence* (1948) which reflects Huxley's anguish over World War II and its aftermath. In the frame story a producer looks for the author of a discarded Hollywood movie script. The narrator for this frame story observes the spectacular view as he and the producer drive through the desert:

> Out there, on the floor of the desert, there had been a noiseless, but almost explosive transformation. The clouds had shifted and the sun was now shining on the nearest of those abrupt and jagged buttes, which rose so inexplicably, like islands, out of the enormous plain. A moment before they had been black and dead. Now suddenly they came to life between a shadowed foreground and a background of cloudy darkness. They shone as if with their own incandescence. (17–18)

Reflecting Huxley's own mystical experience in his beloved California desert, a scene (or person) which had seemed "black and dead" could suddenly be transformed by the sun bursting through the clouds (or an illumination within the soul). In the midst of war and devastation, Huxley perceived that the land (or human spirit) could suddenly shine with the intensity and brilliance found in the love of God—a luminous island surrounded by darkness.

Ape and Essence, the fantasy of nightmare existence following a thermonuclear holocaust, describes scavenging barbarians digging up California's famous cemetery plots in the ruins of suburban Los Angeles to plunder the expensively appointed caskets. The narrator describes the way the world used to look: "The sea, the bright planet, the boundless crystal of the sky—surely you remember them!" (38). War has produced "the black serrated shape of a rocky island" (38), "stagnant plague-fog," and "a wreath of pus-colored vapor" (53).

The hero of the movie script, botanist Dr. Alfred Poole, is called "Stagnant Poole" (55) by his students and colleagues because he has not lived up to his potential. "It is as though he lived behind plate glass, could see and be seen, but never establish contact" (55). When he does make contact with another captive he finds love, and dares to plan an escape from the baboons who control them. Images of color and light relating to mystical vision persist in this satire through the mystical poetry of Shelley, a volume of whose poems Poole rescued from the furnace in much the same way that this script has been rescued. Shelley's poetry reveals to the two lovers (who have set themselves free) the meaning of the soul:

> An image of some bright Eternity,
> A shadow of some golden dream; a Splendor
> Leaving the third sphere pilotless; a tender
> Reflection of the eternal Moon of Love.   (164)

After escaping from their captors, Poole quotes Shelley again:

> That Light whose smile kindles the Universe ...
> Burns bright or dim, as each are mirrors of
> The fire for which all thirst, now beams on me
> Consuming the last clouds of cold mortality.   (204)

Sitting beside the grave of their dramatist creator, these two people—an island in the midst of chaos—dare to believe in the "Light."

Huxley wrote his next novelette, *The Genius and the Goddess* (1955), during the months of his wife's failing health; she died only four months after the book was finished. Although Huxley confided that he modeled the goddess, Katy, after Frieda Lawrence and her symbiotic relationship with her genius husband, D. H. Lawrence (*Letters* 831), Huxley's fatalistic attitude in the novel about the senselessness of suffering mirrors his personal sorrow. Spiritual grace found in the mystical imagery of light and color in this work combines with animal grace and human grace to form "The Unknown Quantity" needed to know oneself. The narrator, John Rivers, explains:

> "At one end of the spectrum it's pure spirit, it's the Clear Light of the Void; and at the other end it's instinct, it's health, it's the perfect functioning of an organism that's infallible so long as we don't interfere with it; and somewhere between the two extremes is what St. Paul called 'Christ' the divine made human."   (99)

Although Rivers gains spiritual insight from his experiences, ultimately the novel gives little hope for most of us to be open to all three aspects of the same underlying mystery.

Emerging from this latest dark night of the soul at a deeper level of mystical experience, Huxley wrote a Utopian novel in which he explored principles expressed in *The Perennial Philosophy*, such as the potential for all human beings to be identified with the Godhead and the beneficence of humility rather than ego. Here, instead of an island made up of two people escaping the chaos of life in the fable *Ape and Essence*, a whole society joins together on the pathway to inner mystical vision. Huxley's philosophical teaching, paramount in *Island* (1962), harmonizes with the writer's colorful descriptive passages which suggest the world of visions. All of nature on the island of Pala has an intensity of hue, an iridescent, glowing quality which leads to the visionary world in each of us. For instance, a flock of pigeons fly "green-winged and coral-billed, their breasts changing color in the light like mother-of-pearl" (23). Even the children have gemlike qualities: a little Palanese girl "wore a full crimson skirt ... in the sunlight her skin glowed like pale copper flush with rose" (8). This idyllic place and its people, although subject to the sins and diseases of the world, have progressed a long way toward unity with the Divine.

Huxley's lifelong interest in art and its ability to bring divine order to one's life reaches its apex in *Island*. A guest in Pala, Will Farnaby, visits a meditation room where he beholds a landscape painting by a Palanese artist. Like Caravaggio's painting, the light transports:

"What clouds!" said Will. "And the light!"

"The light," Vijaya elaborated, "of the last hour before dusk. It's just stopped raining and the sun has come out again, brighter than ever. Bright with the preternatural brightness of slanting light under a ceiling of cloud, the last, doomed, afternoon brightness that stipples every surface it touches and deepens every shadow."... And between dark and dark was the blaze of young rice, or the red heat of plowed earth, the incandescence of naked limestone, the sumptuous darks and diamond glitter of evergreen foliage. (186)

Will's host sees the painting as "a manifestation of Mind with a large M" (185) and as "a genuinely religious image" (186). Landscapes are religious because they remind us who we are, they compel us "to perform an act of self-knowing," and they reflect distance which "reminds us that there are mental spaces inside our skulls as enormous as the spaces out there":

"Mysteries of darkness; but the darkness teems with life. Apocalypses of light; and the light shines out as brightly from the flimsy little houses as from the trees, the grass, the blue spaces between the clouds. We do our best to disprove the fact, but a fact it remains; man is as divine as nature, as infinite as the void." (187)

Thus, in *Island* Huxley creates a society in which the highest visionary experience is possible; one can move beyond brilliant colors to the transcending Clear Light. For instance, as Lakshmi, a deeply religious woman, moves closer to death, her daughter-in-law, Susila, reminds her of the occasion when she was a little girl of eight and first saw the Clear Light:

"An orange butterfly on a leaf, opening and shutting its wings in the sunshine—and suddenly there was the Clear Light of pure Suchness blazing through it, like another sun."

"Much brighter than the sun," Lakshmi whispered. "But much gentler. You can look into the Clear Light and not be blinded. And now remember it. A butterfly on a green leaf, opening and shutting its wings—and it's the Buddha Nature totally present, it's the Clear Light outshining the sun."   (265)

This mystical vision is not limited to selected people on Pala. Only those persons on the island who are deeply involved in evil fail "to discover their Buddha Nature" (244). As Donald Watt reminds us in his discussion of Huxley's symbolic use of the word "island," people are isolated, like islands, only on the surface of their routine lives; "they are nevertheless united, like islands, beneath the uneasy, oceanic flux.... They are joined in a unitive psychic land which, for Huxley, is the mystical 'Divine Ground'" ("Vision" 177). Only those who know nothing experientially of a divine vision—like the Fordians (the citizens in *Brave New Worlds* whose hygienic lives are controlled by advanced scientific and behaviorist methods), John Barnack, Jo Stoyte, Murugan, or Colonel Dipa—are truly isolated from themselves, from other people, and from the inner world. Sebastian Barnack, for instance, gains the capacity to love other people while on his quest for mystical union with the "pure light of the void."

Just as Sebastian no longer needs to write poetry, the Palanese in *Island* who are nearing the end of their spiritual journeys no longer need color for an awareness of the visionary world. Huxley defines the "prayer of quiet" as "the prayer of waiting upon the Lord in a state of alert passivity and permitting the deepest elements within the mind to come to the surface" (*Human* 203). Complementing this definition, Huxley writes in "Natural History of Visions":

> In these highest forms of vision ["prayer of quiet"], the light is undifferentiated; it is what in Buddhist literature is called the "pure light of the void." It is an immense white light of extraordinary power.   (*Human* 227)

The "pure light," analogous to silence or the "prayer of quiet," represents direct experience of the divine. For Huxley, the beauty of the lively transparency of brilliantly lighted color leads us closer and closer to the internal visionary world and unity with the Ground of All Being.

Huxley parallels Lakshmi's death scene in *Island* with his own experience of his wife Maria's death. Again the light and the divine become one:

> "In the desert and, later under hypnosis, all Maria's visionary and mystical experiences had been associated with light.... Light had been the element in which her spirit had lived, and it was therefore to light that all my words referred. I would begin by reminding her of the desert she had loved so much, of the vast

crystalline silence ... of the snow-covered mountains at whose feet we had lived.... And I would ask her to look at these lights of her beloved desert and to realize that they were not merely symbols, but actual expression of the divine nature; an expression of Pure Being, an expression of the peace that passeth all understanding ... an expression of the love which is at the heart of things, at the core, along with peace and joy and being, of every human mind.... I would urge her to advance into those lights." (Bedford II 185–86)

Using hypnosis or psychedelic drugs (what the Palanese call moksha-medicine), Huxley believed he enhanced the enlightenment of the mystical experience by diminishing the human ego.[6]

Huxley makes clear, however, that the mystical experience often begins before a person is consciously aware of the phenomenon. Just as the dying Lakshmi remembers first seeing the Clear Light when she was eight years old, she also remembers a view from the old Shiva temple above the High Altitude station which looks out over the sea. Susila gently guides the dying woman's thoughts:

"Blue, green, purple—and the shadows of the clouds were like ink. And the clouds themselves—snow, lead, charcoal, satin. And while we were looking, you asked a question. Do you remember, Lakshmi?"

"You mean, about the Clear Light?"

"About the Clear Light," Susila confirmed. "Why do people speak of Mind in terms of Light? Is it because they've seen the sunshine and found it so beautiful that it seems only natural to identify the Buddha Nature with the clearest of all possible Clear Lights? Or do they find the sunshine beautiful because, consciously or unconsciously, they've been having revelations of Mind in the form of Light ever since they were born?"   (*Island* 264)

Huxley may have been thinking of his own life and his own "revelations of Mind in the form of Light ever since [he was] born." Remember that Aldous's brother Julian recognized at age twelve that five-year-old Aldous lived on a different level of being and continued to do so all of his life. Huxley's mystical attachment to color and light—ranging from bright jewel colors to the clear light of mystical union—encompassed his forty-seven years as a writer. As early as 1922, his use of color and light in *Crome Yellow* connects with his explorations into mysticism. His spiritual quest materializes not only through the light which blinds and transforms Saul on the road to Damascus, but also through his symbolic use of color, light, and form in examining the relative merits of Western and Eastern religions. By 1925 Calamy's hope for mystical illumination emerges as a dominant theme in *Those Barren Leaves*. Poetry such as "The Yellow Mustard" conjoins color and light with inner faith in 1931. One year later in *Brave New World* Helmholtz Watson seeks mystical union in the silence of the island on which he is exiled, foreshadowing Huxley's utopian *Island* with its bright colors and transcendent Clear Light—the unity of all things. Aptly, that color of light can be produced by blending all the tints in the spectrum; thus, light is a symbol of the union of every virtue (Hulme 20). Huxley's intense focus in his writing on the high mystical quality of color and light as a link with the pure light of the void permeated his life. For Huxley, everyone who sees beauty in the light is on the path to mystical experience—just at different stages of the journey.

NOTES

1. Elizabeth Bowen in 1936 stated that Huxley was "preaching a new asceticism: if he presses the point further he will not be popular" (148). Orville Prescott in 1944 wrote, "In recent years Mr. Huxley has seen visions and become a convert to a private mystic faith. His last three or four books have been contrite attempts to live down his earlier ones. Unfortunately, though spiritually elevated, they have been dull and mediocre." C. E. M. Joad in 1946 stated, "If a choice must be made, the unregenerate Huxley of sixteen years ago seems to be infinitely preferable to the sour-faced moralist of today."

2. Evelyn Underhill has a chapter (380–412) explaining "the dark night of the soul" in its many manifestations. She concludes that "all these types of 'darkness' with their accompanying and overwhelming sensations of impotence and distress, are common in the lives of the mystics" (393; cited in *Abingdon* 512).

3. "I am and, for as long as I can remember, I always have been a poor visualizer. Words, even the pregnant words of poets, do not evoke pictures in my mind" (*Doors* 15). Huxley makes similar statements in letters and other personal writing.

4. The "obscene / Brown ordure" (possibly elephant excrement) parallels Huxley's frequent mentions of "mud" representing a limitation of vision. In his last novel, *Island*, however, a succulent plant, symbolic of enlightenment, grows out of the mud (108).

5. Von Helmholtz was first cited as one of several possible sources for Helmholtz Watson's name by Meckier. He writes, "Watson's name is a meaningful amalgam that links the thoughts of Freud, Brucker, and Herman Von Helmholtz with Pavlov and the practices of the American behaviorist John Broadus Watson." No mention is made, however, of *Helmholtz's Treatise on Physiological Optics*, ed. James P. C. Southall, 3 vols. Trans. 1909. New York: Dover, 1962.

6. Zaehner argues that Huxley recants the position that the psychedelic experience is identical to mystical experience. He claims that Huxley in the last days of his life came to see the psychedelic experience as a form of self-worship (108–09).

Works Cited

Abingdon Dictionary of Living Religion. Keith Crim, ed. Nashville: Abingdon, 1981.

Bedford, Sybille. *Aldous Huxley: A Biography.* 2 vols. New York: Knopf, 1974.

Bowen, Elizabeth. *Collected Impressions.* London: Longmans, 1950.

Bowering, Peter. *Aldous Huxley: A Study of the Major Novels.* New York: Oxford UP, 1969.

Canaday, John. *What Is Art?* New York: Knopf, 1980.

Clark, Ronald W. *The Huxleys.* New York: McGraw, 1968.

Eliot, T. S. "A Note on Poetry and Belief." *The Enemy* 1 (Jan. 1927) 15–17.

Hulme, Edward. *Symbolism in Christian Art.* Poole, England: Blandford P, 1976.

Huxley, Aldous. *After Many a Summer Dies the Swan.* 1939. New York: Harper, 1983.

———. *Antic Hay.* 1923. New York: Harper, 1969.

———. *Ape and Essence.* New York: Harper, 1948.

———. *The Art of Seeing.* 1924. Seattle: Montana Books, 1975.

———. *Brave New World.* 1932. New York: Harper, 1969.

———. *The Collected Poetry of Aldous Huxley.* Ed. Donald J. Watt. London: Chatto, 1971.

———. *Crome Yellow.* 1922. New York: Harper, 1939.

———. *Do What You Will.* London: Chatto, 1929.

————. *The Doors of Perception* and *Heaven and Hell*. 1954, 1956. New York: Harper, 1963.

————. *Eyeless in Gaza*. 1936. New York: Harper, 1968.

————. *The Genius and the Goddess*. London: Chatto, 1955.

————. *Island*. 1962. Harper: 1972.

————. *The Human Situation: Lectures at Santa Barbara*. Ed. Pierro Ferrucci. New York: Harper, 1977.

————. *Letters of Aldous Huxley*. Ed. Grover Smith. New York: Harper, 1969.

————. *The Perennial Philosophy*. 1944. New York: Harper, 1970.

————. *Point Counter Point*. 1928. New York: Harper, 1956.

————. *Those Barren Leaves*. London: Chatto, 1925.

————. *Time Must Have a Stop*. 1944. New York: Harper, 1965.

Huxley, Julian Sorell, ed. *Aldous Huxley 1894–1963: A Memorial Volume*. London: Chatto: 1965.

Joad, C. E. M. "Huxley Gone Sour." Rev. of *The Perennial Philosophy*. *New Statesman and Nation* 32 (5 Oct. 1946): 50.

Marovitz, Sanford. "Aldous Huxley and the Visual Arts." *Papers on Language and Literature* 9 (Spring 1973): 174.

Meckier, Jerome. *Aldous Huxley: Satire & Structure*. London: Chatto, 1969.

————. "Our Ford, Our Freud and the Behaviorist Conspiracy in Huxley's *Brave New World*." *Thalia: Studies in Literary Humor* 1.1 (1978).

————. "A Private Waste Land of the Thirties: Aldous Huxley's *Arabia Infelix* and *The Cicadas*." *Forum for Modern Language Studies* 23 (1987): 210.

Prescott, Orville. *Yale Review* 34 (Autumn 1944): 189.

Underhill, Evelyn. *Mysticism*. New York: Dutton, 1961.

Watt, Donald, ed. *Aldous Huxley: The Critical Heritage*. London: Routledge, 1975. (*AH*)

————. "The Meditative Poetry of Aldous Huxley." *Modern Poetry Studies* 6 (1975): 116–17.

————. "Vision and Symbol in Aldous Huxley's *Island*. In Robert E. Kuehn, ed., *Aldous Huxley: A Collection of Critical Views*. Englewood Cliffs, N.J.: Prentice-Hall, 1974.

Zaehner, Robert Charles. *Drugs, Mysticism and Make-Believe*. London: Collins, 1972.

JEROME MECKIER

Aldous Huxley's Modern Myth: "Leda" and the Poetry of Ideas

Aldous Huxley sent his brother a copy of "Leda" in response to Julian's letter announcing his engagement to Juliette Baillot. Technically the story of an adultery, it made an odd engagement present. As a poem about recurring disillusionment, however, it can be construed as indirect advice to an elder brother and a prospective sister-in-law not to expect too much. The newly engaged pair missed the poem's central point completely. Julian later surmised that their "euphoric state" caused this obtuseness, "for when Juliette wrote a note of glowing praise to Aldous, he replied [on 22 January 1919] with the following snub":

> 22.1.19 ... I am glad you liked Leda—though I fear your critical faculty may have been a little warped by your personal feelings! For you seem hardly conscious of the profound and painful irony which is the thread on which all its beauty is strung. You must read it again later. It is certainly very good!—but perhaps not so good as your feelings.[1]

One must determine "the profound and painful irony" serving as the poem's unifying "thread" because "Leda" is an important work in which Huxley formulated his first myth for modern times. This parody of the *epyllion* or

From *ELH* 58, (1991) © 1991 by The Johns Hopkins University Press.

short epic on an erotic theme was a brilliantly wicked declaration of the meaninglessness of contemporary existence. Paradoxically, its non-explanation of the dichotomous, self-contradictory nature of things—pointlessness as life's only point—seemed to account for the human condition following World War I. The negative explanatory hypothesis set forth in "Leda" governed Huxley's writing for the next ten years.

The title poem of the *Leda* volume (1920), Huxley's third major collection in five years, marks the twenty-six-year-old future novelist's high-watermark as a poet. Looking backward and forward simultaneously with a "strange mixture of pure beauty and irony" that Huxley boasted would "beggar description," it summed up the irreverent, anti-traditional poetry he had been perfecting since 1916; yet it also prepared him for the novel of ideas and ushered in the first entirely modern decade by helping to set its tone: bright, ironic, but with undercurrents of desperation and despair born of defeat.[2] Joyce and T. S. Eliot to the contrary, Huxley's finest poem of ideas benefited from a mythical method two years before *Ulysses* and *The Waste Land* were published.

Rough drafts of "Leda" occupied Huxley for the better part of a year, as indicated by his letters to Baillot between 5 February and 10 October 1918 (*L*, 143, 165).[3] By January 1919 he had completed part one, which was all he eventually decided to print. Reporting to Dorothy Brett on the first day of December 1918, Huxley wrote that he had "only just come to the point where the Swan approaches and does his worst" (*L*, 172). The intentional facetiousness, an unmistakable clue to satiric intent, was a reaction to the gravity and discretion of Dr. John Lemprière's *Classical Dictionary* (1788). In Huxley's novel *Crome Yellow* (1921), Mr. Scogan advises Denis Stone, a poet in search of worthwhile subjects, to read this work closely. Scogan relishes the Doctor's account of "how Jupiter, disguised as a swan, was 'enabled to avail himself of the situation' *vis-a-vis* to Leda."[4] The intriguing circumlocution inspired Huxley's cynical use of the brevity of copulation as a metaphor for modern philosophy's failure to produce a lasting synthesis.

Had the poem continued, its second part, as Huxley explained to Brett, would have wrestled with "the hideous problems of parentage which arise on Leda's production (do you think she cackled?) of the two eggs" (*L*, 172). Part two would have made the poet's Rabelaisian tendencies more apparent, but this additional segment might also have ruined the parody; it could have crudely reduced a self-refuting mixture of beauty and irony to vulgar farce. Wisely, Huxley stopped where he did; "the decision of the medical men of the period" on the parentage problem, which Huxley also mentioned to Julian (*L*, 174), was dropped from his plans for the poem.

Despite being kept posted on the progress of "Leda," Julian's fiancee forgot the hints she had been given by the time the finished poem arrived. Without those hints, Middleton Murry did worse: he objected that the poem's "reconciliation of opposites"—beauty and ugliness, for example—was "unreal," although this was precisely Huxley's satiric point, not just about these two concepts but about all previous philosophical and poetic reconciliations.[5] Murry correctly termed "Leda" a "retrogression" from Keats's "Endymion" but failed to see that it was deliberate. Similarly, Douglas Bush noted the unusual conjunction of a Keatsian style with attitudes allegedly borrowed from Krafft-Ebing; he relished Huxley's "original combination of conventional mythological romanticism with animal and tropical heat and exotic color," but regretted that the clash of "romantic idealism" and "modern sensuality" resulted in a failure of resolution. Such a standoff is actually the anti-aesthetic goal in Huxley's contrapuntal verse, but Bush decided that it prevented the poem from being more than a mediocre treatment of the Leda myth.[6]

Other readers have ignored the poem's counterpoints by siding with Jove or Leda. Alexander Henderson concluded that the union yields "satisfactory results for Jove," while John Vickery read the poem as the story of a dissatisfied wife finding fulfillment outside marriage—that is, as a myth reworked to favor women's liberation and permissive morals.[7] Critics have also disagreed when assessing the poem's morality: Stuart Mais praised its "sensuous beauty," but George Woodcock found it "notably decadent," a poem Aubrey Beardsley might have illustrated.[8]

Woodcock favored an allegorical interpretation; he considered the "one sharp sound" (98) Leda utters to end the poem a "metaphysical description of the mystic's unitive ecstasy."[9] This is the most misleading thing ever written about a much-misunderstood parody; Leda and Jove find a lesser amount of lasting gratification than either the subversive poet or the disappointed reader. The poet cannot fashion a positive myth for the modern era; instead, having realized his incapability, he must subtly, perhaps cruelly, disabuse himself and his readers of the hope that such a myth might still be possible. Although he does this by stringing his poem's beauty on a thread of irony, gullible readers who try to adopt an exclusively Keatsian-Shelleyan approach, who respond (like Julian and Juliette) to the poem's attractions without also savoring the cynicism undercutting them, become the satiric poet's ultimate target.

Leda and the swan must be read as contraries: she is mortal, he divine; she is real yet seems to fulfill his ideal of beauty; despite being real or fleshly, he suits her conception of an ideal, godlike lover; she is the body his mind longs for, and he the superior mind her flesh yearns to satisfy. The central irony is that the coupling of swan and heroine—the poem's lushly described main event—is a philosophical failure for all parties. The beautiful unity achieved in a moment of sexual climax is ultimately deceptive; this fusion of opposites, Huxley implies, can last only as long as the moment of intercourse. An exercise in disedification, "Leda" celebrates the sensual union of its male and female protagonists while actually restating, in aggravated form for modern times, the invincibility of perennial dualisms. The poem employs a supremely sensual moment as an ironic metaphor for the inevitably temporary, hence illusory, resolution of life's multiple divisions—which is all that a modern sensibility believes that sudden inspiration, whether poetical or philosophical, can provide. An elaborate metaphysical joke, Huxley's most enticing poem equates the swiftness of copulation with the lack of permanence in moments of apparent intellectual synthesis or imagined spiritual visitation. Such flights of mind and spirit, including the insights they supposedly bring, have never led to genuine breakthroughs, Huxley opined. Fundamental oppositions quickly reassert themselves; only they endure.

I

"Leda" can be divided into three unequal sections. The first ends with the unhappy heroine entering one of Eurotas's pools to bathe (83–86). Jove's "bull-like agony" occupies the longer second section (86–91); his anguish starts to subside when he spies Leda and thinks of a seducer's stratagem. Very much the novelist in these first two sections, Huxley clarifies the motivation of both characters. Events leading to the climax and then the event itself, which is extremely brief yet both sexual and melodramatic, constitute the longest section of the poem—almost seven pages in Watt's edition (91–98). The result is a mock-Hegelian structure: antithesis (Jove's lust) follows thesis (Leda's beauty), but the union in section three produces no positive synthesis of lasting conviction.[10]

From the outset, Huxley presents Leda as an ideal, a paragon of beauty. Called the "first star" (83), she is "far / Lovelier than any nymph of wood or green," her "sheer beauty and subtly moving grace" making her "the fairest" of mortals: in motion or at rest, "she was never less / … than perfect loveliness" (85). After one week of marriage to Tyndarus, however, Leda has yet to find *her* ideal. Significantly, "her mind" is "still virgin, still unwed," although her "body was her own no more" (83). The perfection of earthly, physical beauty in search of an ideal mate, Leda yearns for a lover who can satisfy her mind as thoroughly as she can satisfy his flesh; her goal is the pacification—both within her person and through union with another—of the passion-versus-reason counterpoint, a principal cause of self-division in an age the modern poet finds devoid of unifiers.

As Leda and her handmaidens prepare to bathe, they discuss love and marriage. One handmaiden wants "to live a virgin life / Alone" (84). A second would be wife if she can avoid motherhood, for she despises "bestial teeming" yet longs for "Love's rare delight." Quiet until now, Leda reveals herself to be a disappointed idealist. Although "queen / To the most royal king the world has seen," she objects to the word "delight": "Love to me has brought / Nothing but pain and a world of shameful thought. / When they say love is sweet, the poets lie." As does the would-be epic poet, Leda suspects the West's idealist poetic tradition.

Typical of much of the poem, the opening section is remarkable for smoothness and grace, virtues Huxley's verse eschews almost everywhere else.[11] A sensual, Keatsian richness, discernible throughout, seems especially evident in the passage describing Leda preparing for her bath:

> So proud
> A queen she stood, that all her maidens bowed
> In trembling fear and scarcely dared approach
> To do her bidding. But at last the brooch
> Pinned at her shoulder is undone, the wide
> Girdle of silk beneath her breasts untied;
> The tunic falls about her feet, and she
> Steps from the crocus folds of drapery,
> Dazzlingly naked, into the warm sun.
> God-like she stood: then broke into a run,
> Leaping and laughing in the light, as though
> Life through her veins coursed with so swift a flow
> Of generous blood and fire that to remain
> Too long in statued queenliness were pain
> To that quick soul, avid of speed and joy.
> She ran, easily bounding, like a boy,
> Narrow of haunch and slim and firm of breast.
> Lovelier she seemed in motion than at rest,
> If that might be, when she was never less,
> Moving or still, than perfect loveliness.
>
> (85)

Equally mellifluous in the next section are the couplets in which she dries herself in the sun:

> Stretched all her length, arms under head, she lay
> In the deep grass, while the sun kissed away
> The drops that sleeked her skin. Slender and fine
> As those old images of the gods that shine
> With smooth-worn silver, polished through the years
> By the touching lips of countless worshippers,
> Her body was; and the sun's golden heat
> Clothed her in softest flame from head to feet
> And was her mantle, that she scarcely knew
> The conscious sense of nakedness.
>
> (94)

With the switch to Jove comes a perceptible coarsening of tone.[12] But this contrapuntal relationship between sections one and two does not prevent each of Huxley's protagonists from standing for more than one idea. Jove's contradictory qualities are the consequence of the different roles he plays in the multiple dualisms he and Leda are asked to represent. Jove is both reality seeking ideal beauty and, from Leda's viewpoint, the ideal lover or superior mind being sought. He personifies the godlike half of the transitory union of natural and supernatural, time and eternity; yet he is also a rake and rapist, more human and less pure than Leda in both habits and thoughts—in short, he personifies the sordid truths her beauty cannot belie. Though father of the gods, Jove forms the unpleasant half of the contrast between love and lust, beauty and the beast. A very down-to-earth deity, he at times notices the "smell of his own sweat" (86). He is the epitome of imperfect, fragmented man, whose gross desires compel him to appreciate the ideal by sullying it.

Like Leda, Jove is full of longing, but his desires are blatantly physical: "His fevered head / Swarmed with a thousand fancies" that ruled out sleep: "O Love in Idleness! how celibate / He felt! Libido like a nemesis / Scourged him with itching memories of bliss" (86–87). Identifying the "Libido" as Jove's "nemesis," Huxley imitates Elizabethan poets who consciously employed anachronisms for humorous effect in their minor epics.[13] Yet Jove's downfall is also man's: the libido stands for unsatisfied desire, the longed-for ideal, the soul's need for consummate love. Never faltering regardless of Jove's grandeur, this nemesis prevents its victim from finding permanent satisfaction. "Itching memories of bliss" propel Jove toward Leda but suggest that none of his adventures has allayed his desires or ever will. A recurrently lustful Jove, craving physical union with the world's most beautiful women, is Huxley's mock-Faustian archetype for modern man's inability to locate a durable philosophy, one that the importunities of reality, including the perversity of man's own conduct, will not quickly spoil.

Jove's diligent search for beauty reveals how rare a quality it has become in Huxley's world. The god sweats and moans in his bed but cannot "still the pulses of his burning brain" (87); he pines to have his faith in life restored—that is, for a woman who "can medicinably give / Ease with her beauty to the Thunderer's pain" (89). But when the god peers through the clouds, the scene he beholds is appalling; it establishes a sharp modulation in mood and mode from the beauty surrounding Leda so that a tonal counterpoint of beauty and ugliness in sections one and two matches the thematic opposition of those ideas. Ugliness, the modern epic poet argues, is not only as true as beauty but seemingly inseparable from it, if not attracted by it; together, they constitute a fundamental dualism, a flaw in the nature of things.

Jove is horrified by the antics of savages who are "not men so much as bastardy of apes," and his disgust culminates when he demands:

> This world so vast, so variously foul—
> Who can have made its ugliness? In what
> Revolting fancy were the Forms begot
> Of all these monsters?
> What strange deity—
> So barbarously not a Greek!—was he
> Who could mismake such beings in his
> Distorted image.
>
> (89)

Although voiced by Jove, the moral outrage belongs to the countrapuntist poet who is puzzled aesthetically and philosophically—indeed, he is repulsed by the irreconcilable division he must posit between Leda's charms and the monstrous simians. An Olympian perspective merely discloses life's bewildering multiplicity—"so vast, so variously foul"—and Jove blames it on an unnamed deity stranger than himself. Ironically, although Jove shares the poet's dislike for the counterpoint of beauty and ugliness, he will defile the world further by seducing Leda in pursuit of a perfect antidote for life's manifold foulness.

The light of Jove's "living eyes" (90), Huxley states, arouses in women a "strange desire" that leaves them "longing and terrified," whether the god grapples with them or not. The woman upon whom Jove's glance falls is never the same afterwards:

> For never, never from this day forth will she
> In earth's poor passion find felicity,
> Or love of mortal man. A god's desire
> Has searched her soul; nought but the same strong fire
> Can kindle the dead ash to life again,
> And all her years will be a lonely pain.
>
>   (90)

Clearly, Leda's encounter with her ideal lover (or perfect mind) is as foredoomed as Jove's momentary union with her surpassingly beautiful body. He will make reality henceforth forever unacceptable to her, even though, unlike the woman in the passage above, she experiences more than just his passing glance. Leda stands for the inability to settle for less than the imagined ideal once it has been fleetingly comprehended. Just as she cannot gratify Jove's desires forever, he can only increase her sense of life's inadequacies. Part of the poem's profoundly "painful irony" is the reader's gradual realization that by temporarily satisfying each other, Leda and Jove condemn themselves to a continuation, perhaps an exacerbation, of their different but interconnected plights. Just as beauty seems to demand ugliness, that is, to summon its opposite, gratification and frustration emerge as yet another inevitably contrapuntal sequence.

Although "conscious of" Jove's "hungry glance" early in the poem (91), Leda must languish until Huxley outlines the plan the god will use to assuage his lust. It is closely interwoven with his idealism; hunger for the "longed-for loveliness" makes him wonder: has "beauty fled, and was there nothing fair / Under the moon?" (91). He is fascinated by "that almost spiritual grace / Which is her body" and impressed with the "purity" of her "soul's inward light." Jove's heart holds "but one thought: he must possess / That perfect form or die—possess or die." Unfortunately, even momentary possession is a form of death; it signals the end of the desire for a specific object by bringing the "perfect form" out of the world of ideas into the real world, in effect tarnishing it. What the idealist wants, therefore, can only result in a self-defeating, ultimately contrapuntal process, another indication of life's capacity for diametric contradictions that double in perversity as unpleasant ironies. In the person of Leda, Jove has enjoyed a glimpse of the

Idea of Beauty but cannot leave it at that: "she was the whole world now; have her he must, he must ..." (92).

With Aphrodite's aid, Jove invents a ruse to enlist Leda's sympathy: he transforms himself into a "splendid swan," a creature "dazzlingly white" (95). The word "dazzling" recurs to describe Leda and Jove both individually and as a love-making pair, but that which dazzles overpowers with light. Jove overpowers Leda and "Leda" is itself fulgent; its deceptive brilliance, especially at the climactic moment, blinds one to its ironies yet cannot permanently conceal them. Huxley encouraged this state of affairs to suggest that many of the West's greatest poems, which seem to have hit upon solutions to inherent contraries, are mostly poetic razzle-dazzle. The epic poet (new style) does not rule out beauty but will not allow it to achieve supremacy—that is, to reign unopposed and thus lessen the tenacity of perennial dualisms. Once Jove has been transformed into a white swan, Aphrodite changes into a "tawny and black" eagle. The color contrast is also deceptive, a matter of appearance versus reality, for the competing birds actually unite against Leda.

The ensuing suspenseful chase is not unlike aerial dogfights from World War I. Jove must convince Leda to grant him the protection of her embrace and thereby rescue him from the marauding eagle: he slants down toward the safety of her arms while the eagle drops from heaven like a hurled javelin. Huxley juxtaposes Leda's frightened cries—"she could not see him die, / Her lovely, helpless swan" (96)—and the cynical conversations between swan and eagle as the latter mounts his final simulated attack. Explicitly phallic, the swan's approach also carries a mischievous suggestion of target practice: he flies "like a winged spear, / Outstretching his long neck, rigid and straight, / Aimed at where Leda on the bank did wait" (97). This is followed by the most remarkable landing in aviation history: "The great swan fluttered slowly down to rest / And sweet security on Leda's breast."

As the poet confesses that he is impressed by the "dazzling pair" (97), Leda presses to her side the swan's "proud-arching opulent loveliness" (97). But the lines appear to parody the Annunciation by also describing Jove and Leda in Old Testament terms as Eve and the serpent. Leda's "teeth / Grated on edge; for there was something strange / And snake-like in the touch" (97–98). This suggestion is sufficient to temper the attractiveness of the scene. After all, Jove is no angelic messenger but "the sombre bird / Of rage and rapine" (96).

He leaves the imprint of his beak on Leda's breast, cheek, and arms as the poem builds to a literal, physical climax that is both explicit and effective: "Closer he nestled, mingling with the slim / Austerity of virgin flank and limb / His curved and florid beauty, till she felt / That downy warmth strike through her flesh and melt / The bones and marrow of her strength away" (98). This is one of the best passages Huxley wrote as a poet, but it is typical of him that its beauty cannot be trusted. Should instantaneous copulation be called fusion? Not, says Huxley, when Leda and her swan become an elaborate, fantastic conceit: if the duration of the sexual act indicates the evanescent validity of sudden moments of expanded awareness, this fleeting intersection of real and ideal merely re-establishes discontinuity as the primary natural law, the only modern equivalent to bygone absolutes. For the opposites that Jove and Leda represent to achieve genuine resolution, the poet implies, nothing short of continuous copulation will do; clothed in some of the most ornate poetry Huxley ever wrote, the excruciating irony underlying these beautiful lines is that the unification of life's contraries seems as unlikely to the modern poet as perpetual orgasm.

Only if one responds contrapuntally, acknowledging the negative thread that holds the poem's attractions together, can the ending be explained: "Hushed lay the earth and the wide, careless sky. / Then one sharp sound, that might have been a cry / Of utmost pleasure or of utmost pain, / Broke sobbing forth, and all was still again" (98). Leda's outcry encompasses both extremes simultaneously because the conclusion accentuates what an epiphanic poet generally avoids: the precise, contrapuntal moment of transition from gain to loss, from attainment to dissolution—not just the moment of breakthrough but also of unavoidable breakdown, when the temporary coming together begins to come apart. "Leda" does not end but rather falls silent, as does its eponymous heroine. The poem stops the instant the lovers' union is over, for neither can hold together longer.

Ironically beautiful, "Leda" achieves fusion subversively—by synthesizing, in one symbolic relationship, all the counterpoints preventing a lasting synthesis. The theme of this "most luscious poem," as Huxley called it, is the futility of combination itself. Only an act part seduction, part rape can momentarily join the incommensurable ideas that beauty and beast personify. Separation—"The irony of being two"—is the rule even for impassioned lovers because unbridgeable divisions underlie, perhaps cause, life's chaotic diversity.[14] A "charming story ... susceptible of perfectly serious and perfectly ironic treatment at one and the same time" (*L*, 143), "Leda" traps the reader in a contrapuntal bind: like the Jove who idolizes and desecrates a Leda who seems in ecstasy and agony, the reader is caught between conflicting responses; these illustrate life's penchant for creating self-division by imposing diverse laws simultaneously.

II

Yeats knew "Leda" and borrowed from it when devising "Leda and the Swan" (1924), his myth to explain the way new eras dawn. Both poets use "shudder," and Huxley's vision of "the folded glory of [Jove's] wings" (98) probably inspired "the feathered glory" in Yeats.[15] Nevertheless, the Irish poet either chose to ignore the English one in order to reinstate epiphanic breakthroughs, or else he misread Huxley's poem entirely. Yeats interpreted the Leda story as the classical equivalent of the Annunciation; it signaled the start of a new cycle, the period immediately preceding the Christian era. The poem argues that the eternal (Zeus) requires the temporal (Leda), that the human (Leda) requires the animal (Zeus), and that God and Nature require each other—and all of these requirements are met within the poem. At its structural center, John Unterecker has stated, "a kind of communion takes place," so that Leda, although terrified, may have gained a compensatory insight from her supernatural encounter.[16] The "one sharp sound" coming at the end in Huxley's poem remains ambiguous at best, but the Irish poet can ask, almost rhetorically, whether Leda, struggling in her brutal admirer's grasp, "put on his knowledge with his power."[17] Huxley's Leda myth turns the instant of extra perception against itself, silencing it so that "all was still again" (98) at the conclusion. Using epiphany parodically at the poem's climax, instead of at its structural center, Huxley breaks down the idea of breakthroughs, one of the final obstacles to an ultraskeptical world view embracing meaningless standoffs as life's only discernible pattern.

"Leda and the Swan" is harsh and violent, beginning with a "sudden blow"; Jove's wings are "great," and the "staggering" girl clearly a rape victim. "Dark webs" caressing her thighs and the bill catching "her nape" have a sinister aspect. But surprisingly, Yeats's myth is not pessimistic, whereas Huxley's sensual treatment of the identical incident definitely is. Lovemaking in "Leda" is an elegant event "whose different grace in union was a birth / Of unimagined beauty on the earth" (97), but "unimagined" connotes the unimaginable, and the prolongation of "grace in union" for life's opposites is precisely the phenomenon the poem cannot manage. Intercourse becomes a misnomer, a sharper realization than before of life as a series of dead ends, the same blank wall of separateness reached over and over, not the inauguration of a new era. Huxley negated that possibility by omitting the egg hatching (Castor and Pollux from one egg, Helen of Troy from the other) that Yeats carefully included.

According to William York Tindall, Yeats decided "that a poet needs a philosophy, a religion, in order to excite his passions": failing to "discover a suitable myth in modern Europe, he turned inventor. His system was to him what theology was to Dante."[18] But Huxley had already written a "Leda" poem to insist that poets could no longer invent positive myths to explain God's ways and justify the nature of things. The myth for a fragmented age short on absolutes but abounding in contradictions (the multiple contraries Jove and Leda personify) must contradict itself; it must have a resolution more apparent than real. Commenting on Yeats's sonnet, Tindall emphasized myth's usefulness as "an instrument of integration."[19] Huxley's anti-myth parodies that very idea. Subverting the mythmaking process, redefining "suitable myth" as the systematization of obstacles to harmonious coordination, explaining that things remain inexplicable unless viewed negatively as inexplicable phenomena—such were the modern satirical poet's thoroughly ironic yet oddly viable substitutes for Dante's theology.

Were Sturge Moore's poems better known or simply better, it would be worth detailing how subtly "Leda" parodied a mode poets were still using. Moore's "Danaë" (1893), for example, tells the story of King Acrisius's daughter, whose son, according to an oracle in the temple of Zeus, was destined to slay her father; to prevent this, Acrisius imprisoned the girl in a tower of brass where she would never know love. But Moore's Zeus is "the Will that is Love" and "the Power that is Light," a quasi-religious conception very different from Huxley's Jove.[20] Consequently, when Zeus penetrates the tower in the form of sunlight and gives Danaë a child, the story overcomes its tragic possibilities in order to celebrate love's power to surmount obstacles, a theme traditional to the *epyllion*.

Moore habitually recycled Greek legends, reinterpreting them from a Platonic viewpoint; he has been called a primary instance of the poet as a moral mythologist, and was consequently the obligatory target for Huxley's parody since Yeats's poem was not yet available.[21] "If Mr. Sturge Moore had flourished three hundred years ago instead of at the present day," Huxley commented, "his 'Danaë' would now be occupying a modest but honorable place" alongside "those rather indefinite narratives, shot through with fancy and reflection" that the Caroline poets churned out: "Pharonnida," "Gondibert," "Cupid and Psyche," and "Thealma and Clearchus."[22] In short, Moore was the epitome of an anachronism. His misuse of "fancy and reflection" was as intolerable to a genuinely modern poet of ideas as Dante's theology was useless. Moore's quaintness could be made to stand for the ineffectualness of the artistic process, especially for the epic-writing, myth-making poet's bygone utility as a sage, a serious provider of values.

The central myth offensive to Huxley in Moore's poems was his benevolent resolution of the struggle between limited earthly perfection and the true, timeless ideal. Moore regularly presented this conflict as an attraction to both a heavenly and an earthly Aphrodite; rival goddesses symbolized the opposing principles fighting for man's soul, the contradictory laws to which he seems to be subjected simultaneously or by turns. In Huxley's opinion, Moore's myths unthinkingly reasserted the potential unity of love, truth, beauty, time, and eternity, a unity it was now clear that past poets had either been wrong about or had deliberately falsified. Invariably, Moore's protagonists elected to strive for the ineffable ideal; Uranos, for instance, chooses Nemesis over Ge in *The Powers of the Air* (1920). Even worse, Moore's "Ode to Leda" (1904) equated being impregnated by Zeus with contacting a higher ideal. Legends about Zeus's affairs with mortal women were revamped throughout Moore's poetry to make sense of the world—that is, to proclaim, as does traditional religious belief, the unification of the temporal and the timeless, not just their interpenetration.

Although Moore's poetry would have faded without help from Huxley, the modern poet dissected it to puncture Western literary tradition in several other places as well. Through Moore's lifeless imitations, Huxley also struck at seventeenth-century Ovidian love poems, thereby silencing their paler nineteenth- and twentieth-century imitations at the source. Besides ridiculing "Danaë" and "Ode to Leda," Huxley questioned the validity of such forebears as Keats's "Endymion" and Marlowe's "Hero and Leander." The Romantic poet's hero attained a fellowship with essence when he perceived a unity transcending the flux of the temporal world. Unlike Moore's Uranos, who selected the heavenly Aphrodite over the earthly one, however, Endymion chose a real girl, Peona, but found in her his Phoebe, the ideal. No poem written in homage to Keats, Huxley objected, no facile mythologizing in which pairings off symbolize life's susceptibility to unity and synthesis, could work any longer; such wishful thinking could not serve as the direction-giving, mind-forming philosophical poem of ideas for a modern period that was characterized not by consensus, but by conflicting attitudes toward life and by multiple voices declaiming them.

The *epyllion* often ended disastrously, but its catastrophes confirmed the value of love, which gave life continuing significance. Huxley maliciously inverted this paradox. Marlowe proclaimed love's supremacy, allowing passion to break down the defenses of both Hero and Leander even though neither survives long enough to savor its delights to the fullest.[23] In contrast, "Leda" seemingly concludes with the protagonists enjoying erotic bliss, but the efficacy of their encounter is much in doubt. Marlowe, Chapman, and

Marston laced their sensuous passages with wit; each appended a moral to his Ovidian tales in order to realign them with accepted morality. But Huxley undermined his sensuousness with irony and deliberately baffled the reader's desire for a comforting resolution. Just as Jove and Leda embody more than one set of counterpoints, they also parody several love-affirming couples (Hero and Leander, Endymion and Peona-Phoebe, Uranos and Nemesis). Huxley's deceptively refulgent pair turn out to be doubly subversive: a challenge to Moore's reuse of the Jove-Leda legend and a barrier to Yeats's.

III

In "The Subject Matter of Poetry," his 1920 *ars poetica*, Huxley concluded that no modern poet of real consequence had surfaced; "the twentieth century," he lamented, "still awaits its Lucretius, awaits its own philosophical Dante, its new Goethe, its Donne, even its up-to-date Laforgue. Will they appear?" he asked, "or are we to go on producing a poetry in which there is no more than the dimmest reflection" of the age's "incessant intellectual life?"[24] The implied answer was not affirmative because the period's "distinguishing mark," euphemized as constant mental activity, was actually its intellectual confusion, the Babel of conflicting ideas and viewpoints that Huxley accused modern poetry of either avoiding or foolishly trying to resolve. Only by poets can "the life of any epoch be synthesized," Huxley later admitted, but "one may venture to doubt," he added, if "even Dante's abilities" would "suffice to inform our vast and swiftly changing chaos, to build it up into a harmonious composition.... There is too much raw material, of too many kinds."[25]

The problem facing Huxley in 1920, as he issued his third collection, was how to emulate the great poet-philosophers of the past, sage-like figures who had justified God's ways to men—that is, revealed the nature of things, unveiled the way life worked, and recommended methods for keeping one's self in harmony with forces natural and divine.[26] How, Huxley pondered, does one become the directing mind or formative poetic intelligence for a shapeless age that would have stumped Dante? His answer: one does so in jest, parodically, in a fashion self-consciously irreverent and yet self-deprecating. One assumes the voice of a sage whose sagacity does not extend beyond a knowledge of his own inadequacies; this sage expresses a sense of defeat when confronted with demands for "a harmonious composition," a positive, reassuring synthesis; while savoring the ironies involved, he proffers instead a negative synthesis.

Eventually, Huxley would attempt to become seriously what at first he only felt qualified to try ironically. He would formulate a salvationary hypothesis in *The Perennial Philosophy* (1946) and bring it to life as society's first principle on the Pala of *Island* (1962). But in "Leda," he is the sage as a highly sophisticated jester, a prototype for the "amused, Pyrrhonic aesthete" who authors the early novels; this poetic modern Pyrrho's skepticism extends to the viability of his own artistic enterprise, which he uses to undermine itself. For such a persona, the lack of a positive explanation seems to be the only acceptable explanation for the human condition; thus the incorporation of life's major counterpoints within a single frame was the only plausible modern synthesis. The "Leda" poet jokes in earnest as a mock-epical, parodic mythmaker who substitutes absolute ironies for bygone absolutes. Aesthetically impressive, his short epic is designed to emancipate readers from a futile search for significance—but only at the cost of significance itself. What Huxley called "the apparent pointlessness of modern life," the result of vitiating counterpoints, became the point; the "lack of significance and purpose" was the only explanatory hypothesis fitting all the facts.[27]

"The philosophy of meaninglessness," as Huxley phrased it, worked only too well as "an instrument of liberation" (*EM*, 273) from outmoded political and economic schemes and from all systems of morality. But when Lucretius wrote "to relieve people of religious fears," especially of punishment after death, he posited a scientific universe independent of divine interventions—in his opinion, a more likable, more livable place.[28] As the twentieth-century's parodic Lucretius, Huxley deprived the universe of all supernatural and scientific purposiveness; unlike his Roman antecedent, this devilish deliverer could not redirect life, much less adopt a positive outlook regarding it. Too much of a Pierrot to rival Dante or Goethe, the "Leda" poet was closer to an updated Laforgue: having set out to explain everything, he found that he could only do so by explaining nothing. He had to "deny that the world had any meaning whatsoever" (*EM*, 273).[29] Such was the profoundly painful, virtually self-silencing irony that "Leda," Huxley's modernized *De rerum natura*, brought forward as what should be called his first "Minimum Working Hypothesis."[30]

"There are passages in *Point Counter Point*," André Maurois later observed, "which remind us that [Huxley] has in him the elements of a great poet, and that he might well write the *De Rerum Natura* of our day."[31] Actually, Huxley made several subversive attempts at it, "Leda" being his maiden effort and *Point Counter Point* (at age thirty-four) the next. The negative solution to art's and the modern world's dilemma was to frame the discordant multi-verse in terms of the contradictions that appeared to be its only universals. Compounding the impediments to combination allowed the "Leda" poet to achieve his objective not just parodically but also paradoxically—that is, in spite of himself.

Inasmuch as Huxley finally strove to become legitimately the maker of syntheses whom he had parodied in "Leda," he discovered his ultimate vocation while writing a contrapuntal poetry of breakdowns and standoffs between 1916 and 1920. First he sabotaged the dramatic lyric in "The Walk," a parody of "Tintern Abbey" that concluded *The Burning Wheel* (1916). Then in "The Defeat of Youth" (1918), the title poem for his second collection, he discredited the sonnet sequence. In "Leda," he assailed the minor epic. The major poems from his first three collections subverted the stages through which great poets have usually passed en route to Parnassus. Since the modern era was the first to suspect that life is too self-contradictory for solutions, Huxley felt obligated to parody the time-honored pattern (or myth) of a poet's growth from short outbursts of insight to sustained philosophical statement; this pattern had to be exposed as another pointless process.

Huxley's career as a poet was not a progress but a progressive canceling, an iconoclastic series of increasingly ambitious parodies. His poetic development at the expense of shopworn formats and stale ideals could only emulate the maturation of a poet's mind by reenacting it ironically as a housecleaning process, which briefly prolonged the phenomenon of growth only by subverting it. Since there were no answers and artists were not entitled to fabricate them, only the artist who ventured to explain why solutions had become obsolete and why poets and formats expounding them deserved to be censored still had the right to speak, even if he did so mainly to silence peers, predecessors and, ultimately, poetry itself.

IV

According to Richard Chase, myth "reaffirms" the world's "dynamism and vibrancy."[32] But Huxley's negative myth preserved mythmaking at the price of its traditional mission, exposing the tradition as obsolescent rather than dynamic. Huxley's myth became one to the embarrassment of mythmaking itself. "Leda" is a synthetic anti-synthesis by a poet-synthesizer functioning as a parodist of the synthesizing process. Myths, Chase argued, dramatize life's "disharmonies" poetically; "reconciling" the "clash" between the "inward and outward forces" affecting human nature, the mythmaker "performs a profoundly beneficial and life-giving act."[33] In an ironic reversal of this process, "Leda" employs the "life-giving act," sexual intercourse, to record the triumphant persistence of disharmony, a sense of disunion going to the core of things and even informing union itself. As disjunctions turn out to be the rule, they acquire a perverse and painful beauty of their own, and it is their "vibrancy" and "dynamism" that the mythmaking poet finds himself underlining. Huxley's parody of the *epyllion* elevated the dualisms his poetry had been exploring since 1916 to the status of myth; in their modernized guises as ruinous irreconcilables, such conflicts as body against mind, ugliness against beauty, and love against lust were revealed to be as timeless as Leda and Jove. The modern myth, Huxley decreed, had to be contrapuntal, both a myth and a parody of mythmaking, both a statement and a counter-statement, art perpetuating itself only by turning against itself through a synthesis cleverly fashioned out of dichotomy. Consequently, T. S. Eliot's refusal "to show any enthusiasm" for Huxley's verse when *Leda and Other Poems* was "submitted for [his] opinion" is not surprising.[34] Yet it seems inconsistent with his praise, not long afterward, for Joyce's use of the mythical method in *Ulysses* and for his own variations on the method throughout *The Waste Land*.

Eliot's inconsistency may have been self-serving: in parodying Marlowe and upending Sturge Moore, Huxley not only anticipated the mythmaking aspirations of Joyce, Eliot, and Yeats but precluded the positive impetus underlying their efforts. Inventing parallels between antiquity and the contemporary world, Huxley implied in "Leda," is unconscionable if it means that the artist sincerely tries to give modern life's chaotic materials more shape and significance than they merit. Such activity can only be an illegitimate substitute for the creation of a new order. Despite a deliberate spuriousness, indeed, because it subtly and reflexively acknowledged that spuriousness, "Leda" pronounced itself the only honest alternative to the sort of genuinely positive outlook it deemed inconceivable; in contrast, *Ulysses* and *The Waste Land* took themselves too seriously as saviors of modern art.

The poet is not allowed to invent his own mythology just because credible myths do not exist to soften life's dichotomies; it follows that he cannot seriously reuse positive myths from the past to contain negative materials in the present—not if he has read "Leda" correctly. But Joyce's reconstruction of Homer's *Odyssey*, in which Bloom is both a new Ulysses and a good-natured parody of the wily Greek, resembles Eliot's allusions to fertility myths and the Grail legend: both impart to the modern predicament not only a semblance of pattern and direction, but a sense of connectedness with the dilemmas of the past, and hence a pretense of hope. Unlike

Huxley's, these mythical methodologies were essentially an *affirmative* structural technique, in which form was asked to go beyond theme—in fact, it often does in all sincerity what theme honestly cannot. No matter how parodic Joyce and Eliot initially seem, they can be said to be trying to revitalize traditional materials: they find them reusable as positive ordering devices. In contrast, Huxley repeatedly reused the West's most revered formats in order to do them in, the new state of affairs fitting into an aesthetically attractive envelope only to incriminate previous proponents of the form. The difference is between form rescuing matter and matter challenging form—only the latter, in Huxley's opinion, a modern phenomenon: the achievement of form at the expense of a traditional form, indeed at the expense of the traditional idea of form.

The mythical method, as Eliot described it, was essentially a positive response to a negative situation: "a way of controlling, of ordering, of giving a shape and a significance to the immense panorama of futility and anarchy which is contemporary history." *Ulysses* overwhelmed Eliot in 1922 because he deemed it a step toward "order and form," a step "toward making the modern world possible for art."[35] To an age without beliefs, he could proffer what I. A. Richards called "a form for unbelief," which translates into a method for doing what poets have always done, even when it can be done no longer.[36] In contrast, Huxley's idea of an extension is closer to extermination, a negative response to a negative situation. In "Leda," he suggested the impossibility of a modern art except in self-scrutinizing testimonials to its failures—to its own futility, not just to contemporary history's. In Huxley's best pre-novel poetry climaxing with "Leda," art's self-preservation comes ironically through self-cancelation and lasts only as long as a specific poem does, only until the final line. The format for the *epyllion*—and for the epic in general—both survives and perishes in the composition process; it is put to use one more time in order to be declared unfit for future use; it emerges as another instance and yet its collapse constitutes a decisive termination.

Ulysses and *The Waste Land* can be said to camouflage life's formlessness, its resistance to ordering, with a form that counters this resistance. Neither the Ulysses story nor the fertility myth works as it once did, but each still functions adequately, as if on a lower frequency. Neither is made to turn entirely against itself so as to testify to its own obsolescence by confessing that its chief goal is to warn readers that it can no longer accomplish its goal. Both of these myths were designed to resuscitate the artistic process, to get things going again. For Joyce's mythical method, Eliot wrote, "the horoscope is auspicious."[37] But Huxley's forms are simultaneously anti-forms, and his parodic use of them is an elaboration of his satiric message. His better efforts are about counterpoints, such modern phenomena as standoffs, stalemates, breakdowns, and collapse. These poems fail to achieve traditional resolution because they are designed to convey a sense of loss: the loss of forms and formality structurally reflects the disintegrating values that comprise their negative themes. Instead of "controlling," "ordering," giving "shape" and "significance," they synthesize only to corroborate modern life's loss of coherence, to emphasize its collapse through irresolution into a state of permanent oppositions that one can equate with meaninglessness.

That poetry must depict, not defray, the intellectual confusion resulting from an unprecedented large-scale fragmentation is clear from Huxley's definition of the modern spirit, which he delivered almost in the same breath as "Leda." He began by describing the twenties:

> We live today in a world that is socially and morally wrecked. Between them, the war and the new psychology have smashed most of the institutions, traditions, creeds and spiritual values that supported us in the past. Dada denies everything, even art itself, that last idol which we all tried so pathetically hard to keep standing when everything else—the soul, morality, patriotism, religion—has been laid low.[38]

Here, surely, is Eliot's "immense panorama of futility," the world that Huxley's early poetry and subsequent novels portray.[39] Although he was no follower of Tristan Tzara, his parodic poems of ideas can be said to work against themselves long before poststructuralism and Derrida. They epitomize the "modern spirit" by denying everything except the phenomenon of collapse and the inevitability of a consequent nothingness. They challenge not only the tenets of philosophy and logic but even the repository value of "art itself," the very medium for message sending and, therefore, civilization's "last idol," which both Joyce and Eliot, misguided modernists in this regard, strove to keep standing.

Having defined the current social wreckage, Huxley went on to speculate about the immediate future, in which the artist's most pressing obligation was to record not only the world's wreck but the smash of its last remaining idol:

> The question still hangs over us. What is the new artistic synthesis going to be?... The new synthesis that will reassemble, in an artistic whole, the shattered values of our post-war world,

the synthesis that will reflect the disintegration in an artistic
unity, will surely be a comic synthesis. The social tragedy of these
last years has gone too far and in its nature and origin is too
profoundly stupid to be represented tragically. And the same is
true of the equally complicated and devastating mental tragedy of
the break-up of old traditions and values. The only possible
synthesis is the enormous farcical buffoonery of a Rabelais or an
Aristophanes, a buffoonery which, it is important to note, is
capable of being as beautiful and as grandiose as tragedy. ("MS,"
55)

Just as the letters to Juliette Baillot emphasized the simultaneity of beauty
and irony in "Leda," this new synthesis was to feature tragic farce,
"beautiful" buffoonery—Huxley stressed the paradoxes. The pyrrhonic
synthesizer working in this modern mode had to reflect the postwar
disintegration and yet create from it an artistic unity. "One of these days,"
Huxley concluded, "we shall see the new Rabelais putting all the broken bits
together in an enormous whole" ("MS," 55).[40]

Huxley's call in 1922 for a "comic synthesis" should be read in
conjunction with his search two years earlier for a poet-philosopher to
succeed Dante, Goethe, and Lucretius. The later statement, although
prognostic, applies to a contrapuntal "Leda" as surely as it anticipated *Point
Counter Point*. In 1928, "all the broken bits" came together in an "enormous
comic whole" worthy of a modern Rabelais: the human race was compared
to a noisy fugue of "eighteen hundred million parts," all in competition, each
contributing to futility's panorama by insisting on being the main melody.[41]
In "Leda," however, the mythmaking poet had also performed as "the new
Rabelais." The new Lucretius in Huxley revealed that pointlessness was the
nature of things while the updated Laforgue in him made poetry out of his
own sense of failure, his inability to mythologize affirmatively. But both of
these roles depended on a Rabelaisian conceit: perpetual copulation. For the
modern era's "shattered" state, its "devastating mental tragedy" caused by the
innumerable breakups of values and traditions, a myth about a rapacious bird
and the ancient world's most beautiful woman might have provided "the only
possible synthesis" if they could have fornicated indefinitely.

Rabelais, Aristophanes, Lucretius, Dante, Goethe, Laforgue—the
Huxley who wrote "The Subject Matter of Poetry," "Leda," and, eventually,
Point Counter Point was not name-dropping. Instead, he was forging a
modern artistic personality, derived in part from all of the above. Once again,
T. S. Eliot's actions—Huxley seems to be imitating Eliot parodically—supply

the analogue. Through a parodic forging of the conscience of his race, Huxley aligned himself with poet-philosophers searching for a coordinating hypothesis. He defined his individual talent in light of one of the West's most prestigious literary traditions, but employed the former to announce the latter's bankruptcy. From one point of view, he invented a novel way to affix his name to the list of poet-sages and proclaim himself the mind for his generation; from another viewpoint, however, he undermined his own achievement because "Leda" substantiated the judgment that the short "list of the great poets of thought comes to an end" after Lucretius, Dante, and Goethe ("SMP," 34); the poet had only joined their ranks by mythologizing his own failure to duplicate their achievements in a positive manner. Paradoxically, the list did not really expand despite an addition.

The Arnoldian in Eliot considered Goethe and Lucretius less fortunate than Dante: the Italian poet was able to absorb a philosophy, whereas Goethe and Lucretius had to invent one. "Dante had the benefit of a mythology and a theology which had undergone a more complete absorption into life than those of Lucretius."[42] Given "a framework of accepted and traditional ideas," Dante was not required to philosophize; he could concentrate on being poetical (*SW*, 157–58). According to Eliot, a poet should never do the kind of thinking a philosopher does: a poetry that discusses ideas, he decreed, is inferior to one that realizes them. *The Divine Comedy* surpassed *De rerum natura* because it was penetrated by a philosophical idea that had seeped into the life of the period. In an era with a viable philosophy, therefore, a great poet readily expresses the mind of his age because, thanks to a corporate ideology, his thinking has been done for him by others, and his task is to give that thinking a magisterial utterance.

Huxley disagreed. He drew no sharp distinctions between Dante and Lucretius. The real difference, he discovered, was between poets who were given a philosophical idea or could concoct one, and those who, modern like himself, received no mythology, knew it was dishonest to contrive one, and had to undeceive readers who thought otherwise. Eliot succumbed to his nostalgia for a certain kind of poet who was no longer feasible and then resorted to the mythical method as a substitute for a controlling philosophical idea; it took the place of Dante's "framework of traditional and accepted ideas." Instead of circumventing the modern situation, Huxley acknowledged its newness fully, despite a sense of loss; adopting the lack of controlling ideas as his controlling idea, he plunged into the newness resolutely, no matter how deplorable this only legitimate recourse.

If a period has no overview to temper life's counterpoints, as happened in Huxley's modern multiverse, then contradiction and impossibility, not wishful thinking (that is, envy of Dante's Catholicism), must become the poet-philosopher's themes. Once pointlessness was recognized as the major discernible pattern, then so-called more "fortunate" poets, those who had an agreed-upon framework of ideas to work with, suddenly seemed to have been wrong—a possibility that Eliot, anxious to exalt them, had overlooked. To the newly undeceived modern, Dante appears to have shared, and Goethe to have fashioned, a corporate delusion, a way of approaching the world that had become inapplicable, hence false, not just difficult to emulate. The author of "The Subject Matter of Poetry" bemoaned the chronic shortage of poet-sages and taunted Yeats, Noyes, Aiken and others for not remedying the deficit. But having failed to mimic Dante and Lucretius except through mockery, the "Leda" poet went on to suggest that the modern mythical method, parodic and subversive, must confirm the end of the line for art, not art's artificial resumption. Inventors of sense-making frameworks and nondestructive reusers of famous myths and legends in frame-like fashion were anachronisms. Sappers, experts at termination including the art of self-termination, were the real innovators; they were the only truth-tellers.

When Huxley later formulated his "Minimum Working Hypothesis" in the epilogue to *Time Must Have a Stop* (1945), he replaced the idea of pointlessness with a salvationary hypothesis containing six positive tenets. He could justify this seemingly hypocritical turnabout with the assertion that he had dived into nothingness unflinchingly and had found it wanting. More so than Joyce or Eliot who drew back prematurely, he had delved to the bottom, eventually establishing, one might say, the pointlessness of pointlessness itself, before turning back. Only after attempting to live with nothingness and to write negatively without an agenda, only after making art by silencing many of the West's major traditional forms for belief, did Huxley prove to himself the futility of such a course: it was another dead end. Having tested the merits of constant repudiation and disavowal, he reached, in effect, the outer limits of this avenue of modernism. That his theorem of sheer but subtle negation had been absorbed by then into the life of the period became clear when, ironically, most readers and critics missed the beginnings of a turnaround in *Brave New World* (1932); thus they felt betrayed by the solution-offering author of *Eyeless in Gaza* (1936) and *After Many a Summer Dies the Swan* (1939).

V

One can discover twentieth-century life in its art, Huxley conceded, "but precious little of its mind" ("SMP," 36). The fault lay with poetry's "curiously narrow range of subject-matter" ("SMP," 26). Given the era's intellectual uncertainty, it was time for "enlarging the bounds of poetry" ("SMP," 31) by improving "relations between poetry and that vast world of abstractions and ideas—science and philosophy—into which so few poets have ever penetrated" ("SMP," 27). In short, there was a need for a poetry of ideas. As it grappled with the modern condition, it had to measure up scientifically: its conclusions could not go contrary to the changes in world view demanded by recent scientific discoveries. Huxley specifically criticized Yeats for ignoring the implications of Einstein's theories; the Irish poet should step "out of the Celtic twilight" and "give us ... his lyrics of relativity" ("SMP," 30).

Similarly, Huxley decried Louis Untermeyer's *Anthology of Modern American Poetry*; despite boasting of its "newness," its return from "jewelled exquisiteness" to "ordinary life," it lacked "a satisfactory artistic method for dealing with abstractions" ("SMP," 31–33). Carl Sandburg, Alfred Noyes, Conrad Aiken—none of these amounted to a poet "in whose mind ideas are a passion and a personal moving force" ("SMP," 33). Aiken was "perhaps... the most successful exponent in poetry of contemporary ideas," but although "all his emotions are tinged with his ideas," he lacked a satiric edge; unlike the "Leda" poet, he frequently surrendered to an "intellectual sentimentality," his verses becoming too "fluent," too "highly coloured" ("SMP," 37).

Clearly, Huxley aspired to be one of those rare poets "who do feel passionately about abstractions, the men to whom ideas are as persons— moving and disquietingly alive" ("SMP," 29), as are the modernized versions of life's counterpoints in "Leda." In Huxley's contrapuntal poetry of ideas, the use of satiric structures—parodic subversions of traditional formats— became a virtual idea supporting the themes of breakdown, stalemate, and collapse, modernity's hallmarks. As Huxley improved his satiric poetry over the five-year period from 1916 to 1920, he grew increasingly desirous "to express himself with that passionate apprehension of ideas and that passionate curiosity ... that characterize the man of science and the philosopher" ("SMP," 30), no matter how parodically he first realized his lifelong goal. Huxley believed that an abstract idea "must be felt with a kind of passion," until it became "as immediate and important to the poet as a personal relationship" ("SMP," 28): for the consummate poet-philosopher, one must repeat, "ideas are as persons" ("SMP," 29). Both pronouncements can be applied directly to "Leda," as well as to Huxley's subsequent fiction. The commingling of swan and heroine, which turns out to be more like a collision, anticipates the many discussion scenes in the novels, such as the debate in which John Savage and Mustapha Mond present their opposing viewpoints at the climax of *Brave New World*. Just as the conflicting ideas and competing planes that Jove and Leda represent cannot come together permanently, so liberty and happiness, personified by a Lawrentian primitive and a Wellsian World-Controller, remain counterpoints; the would-be utopist can choose either but not both.

Whether jokingly as a Pyrrhonist or seriously as the perennial philosopher, Huxley aspired to fuse again the roles of poet, philosopher, and scientist. His concept of a unified sensibility, implicit in his veneration of the poet-philosopher, emanates from the unusual emphasis he placed on the "passionate apprehension of ideas" ("SMP," 33). Like T. S. Eliot, he felt that it would "not be unprofitable to compare the literary situation in this early twentieth century of ours with the literary situation of the early seventeenth century" ("SMP," 35). The later period has only "minor poets," but the earlier was blessed with "a single poet of genius, John Donne," not quite the equal of Dante or Lucretius but still able to "put the whole life and the whole mind of his age into poetry" ("SMP," 36).

Essentially contrapuntal, Donne's "intensely lyrical poetry" could "skip from the heights of scholastic philosophy to the heights of carnal passion, from the contemplation of divinity to the contemplation of a flea" ("SMP," 36). Eight years later, Philip Quarles applied this process of rapid alternation in tone and subject to Huxley's novels, calling it "the musicalization of fiction" (*PCP*, 408). But in 1920, intellectuals like Huxley had to consider themselves "metaphysicals without our Donne" ("SMP," 36–37). Indeed, Huxley parodied Donne more than he resembled him, for the movement in "Leda" is not "from philosophical heights to carnal heights" but to the depths of both. Huxley became a modern metaphysical by explaining that poets could not issue positive metaphysical statements concerning the nature of things because there was nothing supernatural to believe in.

The "Leda" poet demonstrates the importance of a unifying sensibility by becoming a deliberate parody of it. Having compared the poet's mind to a "receptacle" for feelings, phrases, and images, Eliot defined poetry as a process of "combination," the key being the "intensity," the "pressure," under which the "fusion" of "all the particles" in the poet's mind-receptacle "takes place" (*SW*, 55). In "Leda," Huxley strove to become a "combination ... of poet and philosopher" ("SMP," 30), but the fusion necessary for both this persona and his poem, although acute, was extraordinarily shortlived because it involved combining a swan and a king's wife, thereby symbolizing the unlikely or merely momentary reconciliation of life's counterpoints.

After Chapman, Middleton, Webster, Tourneur, and Donne, Eliot pontificated, "we end a period when the intellect was immediately at the tips of the senses" (SW, 129). Donne and Chapman "had a quality of sensuous thought, or of thinking through the senses, or of the senses thinking" (SW, 23). Unlike Eliot, whose point got weaker with each qualification, the author of "The Subject Matter of Poetry" insisted upon reunification the other way round: not thinking through the senses but passionate thinking, for it was the "mind" of the age that he failed to locate in modern poetry. How better to realize this kind of unity, Huxley jested, than in a short epic on an erotic theme, a sensuous poem of ideas in which conflicting ideas converged in a passionate embrace? The coming together and falling apart of Leda and her lover reminded readers of life's resistance to reconcilements: the real disunifications lay in the nature of things, not in the modern poet's sensibility; improving the "receptacle," the poet's fusion chamber, could not remedy an existential situation.

As happens subsequently with characters in Huxley's novels, Jove and Leda are fleshly projections of the author's apprehension of ideas: they are ideas taking on flesh and persons tending to become ideas. They were meant to illustrate what modern art needed most: a plausible method for handling abstractions, for relating poetry to the world of ideas. Jove and Leda do not merely bring to life opposing principles; throughout their clash and convergence, the male/female dichotomy—all the world's divisions in microcosm—is handled with the adroitness of a psychological novelist. In 1920, Huxley's poetic use of contrapuntal male/female pairings—"He" and "She" in "The Walk," the youth and his girl in "The Defeat of Youth"— reached its apotheosis.

Unfortunately, the poem best exemplifying Huxley's innovative poetry of ideas nearly exhausted it. A work that simultaneously met the criteria for a satiric poem of ideas yet strained them to their limits seems tantamount to a dead end: the success of "Leda" was virtually a self-silencing akin to parody's carrying matters to excess. As Jove and Leda personified one set of counterpoints after another, the contrapuntal poem of ideas approached its saturation point, and the novel of ideas beckoned. In Point Counter Point, for instance, Huxley could animate life's contraries by setting in motion not only a series of couples to personify them but also several sets of parents and their offspring. He could use the marriage of Philip and Elinor Quarles to illustrate one dichotomy while comparing them with several other couples;

at the same time, he could employ Philip and Sidney Quarles, father and son, and Elinor and John Bidlake, father and daughter, as additional embodiments (individually and in tandem) of life's dualisms. Shifting from contrapuntal poems to contrapuntal novels of ideas was both a logical development and a quantum leap forward.

VI

"Leda," one must reiterate, was hardly a reincarnation of "the old smooth, mythological world, consecrated by a thousand poets."[43] Its publication was not a sign that another Dante or a new Goethe had miraculously appeared; nor did it mean that one of their "lesser assistants—Donne, for example" ("SMP," 34), had suddenly found his voice. "Leda" did not seek to revive or to justify Sturge Moore's simplistic mythmaking, and it was definitely not a harbinger of the kind of mythical vision perfected shortly thereafter by Eliot, Yeats, and Joyce.

Ulysses, Richard Ellman decided, "had isolated what was affirmable in existence, and had affirmed that."[44] So, ironically, did "Leda," even if it isolated dualism and dichotomy, thereby affirming the philosophy of pointlessness, a negative philosophy predicated on the collapse of values and forms, and hence on the impossibility of traditional affirmations. The argument of Ulysses is that the act of love is the basic act of both art and nature, and that the "highest form" of love is "sexual love."[45] But the use of copulation as a metaphor for the impermanence of visionary moments and philosophical syntheses challenged such notions in advance.

"Leda" is about acceptance, which is more difficult than affirmation. "If we accept the universe," Huxley insisted, "we must accept it" for contrapuntal reasons, "for its divinely appalling and divinely beautiful inhumanity, or, in other words, because, by our standards, it is utterly unacceptable."[46] As an explanation of why no explanations will be forthcoming, "Leda" was designed to be "beautiful" and "appalling," "acceptable" and "unacceptable," "perfectly serious" and "perfectly ironic"— like modern life itself. Just as its beauty proves ironic, its irony can be considered beautiful: although disappointing and disillusioning, the poem is an aesthetically pleasing rendition of life's "inhumanity," its failure to respond to mankind's moral and metaphysical requirements, which in 1920 thus came to seem irrelevant.

This cancelation of expectations brought an inescapable liberation; it was an ironic act of mercy, a sort of gift after all: one that was necessary but not necessarily wanted. The dazzling yet ironic engagement of Leda and her swan was a problematic present not just for Julian and Juliette but for modern art and the newly arrived modern epoch. In 1920, the era's self-appointed, self-deprecating spokesman synthesized the postwar age; trustworthy despite being subversive and parodic, he raised the modern period's lack of a plausible overview to the level of myth.

NOTES

1. Julian Huxley, *Memories* (New York: Harper and Row, 1970), 120–21; all quotations from Huxley's "Leda" come from Donald Watt, ed., *The Collected Poetry of Aldous Huxley* (London: Chatto & Windus, 1971) and will be cited hereafter in the text by page number.

2. For Huxley's boast, see his letter to Juliette Baillot for 10 October 1918 in Grover Smith, ed., *Letters of Aldous Huxley* (London: Chatto & Windus, 1969), 165; cited hereafter as *L*.

3. Besides containing several poems not collected in Watt, Huxley's letters provide the best clues to his intentions for specific poems, but for none more clearly than for "Leda."

4. Aldous Huxley, *Crome Yellow* (London: Chatto & Windus, 1921), 149. In Lemprière's *Classical Dictionary of Proper Names Mentioned in Ancient Authors*, ed. F. A. Wright (Routledge and Kegan Paul, 1949), Leda is already pregnant when Jove arrives. She later gives birth to two eggs, from one of which come Pollux and Helena and from the other Castor and Clytemnestra. Lemprière writes: "The caresses with which the naked Leda received the swan, enabled Jupiter to avail himself of his situation" (323).

5. See Middleton Murry's review in the *Athenaeum*, 28 May 1920, 699–700.

6. See Douglas Bush, *Mythology and the Romantic Tradition in English Poetry* (1937; reprint, New York: Norton, 1963), 478. Following Bush, William York Tindall decided that Huxley merely wanted to "retell ancient myth with baroque improvements." See *Forces in Modern British Literature 1885–1956* (New York: Vintage, 1956), 312.

7. Alexander Henderson, *Aldous Huxley* (New York: Russell and Russell, 1964), 234; John Vickery, "Three Modes and a Myth," *Western Humanities Review* 12 (1958): 371–78. Vickery deprives Huxley's poem of "mythistorical interest," reducing it to a purely sociological treatment of the "issue of sex" beneath "the shifting character of such social institutions as marriage and the

family." Huxley's theme is "the erotic puzzle," whether the act of intercourse is pleasurable or painful to the woman.

8. Stuart Mais, "The Poems of Aldous Huxley" in *Why We Should Read* (New York: Dodd, Mead, 1921), 91; George Woodcock, *Dawn and the Darkest Hour: A Study of Aldous Huxley* (New York: Viking, 1972), 54.

9. Woodcock (note 8), 59.

10. Huxley may have profited from Conrad Aiken's essay on "Counterpoint and Implication," *Poetry* 14 (June 1919): 152–59. Aiken's interest in "symphonic form," his desire for "an architectural structure in poetry analogous to that of music," and his intention to put "contrapuntal effects" into poetry make him sound like a poet-forerunner of the novelist Philip Quarles. By June 1919, however, Huxley had already completed "Leda" and none of Aiken's poems resembles it technically.

11. The reviewer in the *Sunday Times*, 23 May 1920, 5, called the lyrics in *Leda* "violently ugly."

12. Aiken (note 10) suggested that the contrapuntist regard each part of his poem as an "emotion-mass," a musical unity having its distinctive "tone quality" (157); Huxley added that each part should have its own ideas and attitudes as well.

13. Elizabeth Donno discussed the characteristics of the *epyllion* or minor epic in her introduction to *Elizabethan Minor Epics* (New York: Columbia Univ. Press, 1963); see especially 18.

14. This "irony" is the opening line of "Sympathy," a minor effort in the *Leda* volume (note 1); see 100.

15. These and other similarities are mentioned briefly by Giorgio Melchiori in *The Whole Mystery of Art* (New York: Macmillan, 1961), 150n.

16. John Unterecker, *A Readers's Guide to William Butler Yeats* (New York: Farrar, Straus and Giroux, 1959), 187–89.

17. *The Collected Poems of W. B. Yeats* (New York: Macmillan, 1956), 212.

18. William York Tindall, "Transcendentalism in Contemporary Literature," *The Asian Legacy and American Life*, ed. Arthur E. Christy (New York: John Day, 1942), 183.

19. Tindall, *Forces in Modern British Literature* (note 6), 315.

20. Moore employed both of these phrases in his prose account of "The Story" preceding his poem; see *The Poems of T. Sturge Moore*, 2 vols. (London: Macmillan, 1931), 1:195.

21. Frederick Gwynn, *Sturge Moore and the Life of Art* (Lawrence: Univ. of Kansas Press, 1951), 116. Bush praised Moore's "Platonic gospel of

beauty" at length in *Mythology and the Romantic Tradition* ([note 6], 434–56), ranking Moore first among modern poets who work with myth.

22. See "Mr. Sturge Moore's Poetry," *Athenaeum*, 15 October 1920, 515. Huxley referred to William Chamberlayne's *Pharonnida* (1659); Sir William Davenant's unfinished *Gondibert* (1651), in which the poet said he "intended ... to strip Nature naked and clothe her again in the perfect shape of Virtue"; Shakerley Marmion's *Cupid and Psyche* (1637); and John Chalkhill's incomplete "Thealma and Clearchus" (1683). Albert C. Baugh's *A Literary History of England* (New York: Appleton-Century-Crofts, 1948) quoted Davenant's statement of intention, dubbed his poem "an epic on a very modern plan" (672), and called Marmion's a "fine mythological poem" (584).

23. The tale of Hero and Leander has been judged "one of the most beautifully sensuous stories in all the pagan literature of Greece and the treatment Marlowe gives it is one of the purest things in Elizabethan poetry" (Baugh [note 22], 514).

24. Aldous Huxley, "The Subject Matter of Poetry" in *On the Margin* (London: Chatto & Windus, 1923), 38; hereafter cited as "SMP." This essay originally appeared in *The Chapbook* 2 (March 1920): 11–16.

25. Aldous Huxley, *Texts and Pretexts* (1933; reprint, New York: Norton, 1962), 4.

26. "Who are we? What is our destiny? How can the often frightful ways of God be justified?" Huxley asked. "Before the rise of science, the only answers to these questions came from the philosopher-poets and poet-philosophers." See *Literature and Science* (New York: Harper and Row, 1963), 82. Many ideas first stated forty years earlier in "The Subject Matter of Poetry" are reaffirmed and expanded in this book.

27. Huxley discussed the philosophy of meaninglessness in *Ends and Means* (London: Chatto & Windus, 1937), 123–24; cited hereafter as *EM*. An "amused, Pyrrhonic aesthete" was Huxley's description of himself in his 1946 foreword to *Brave New World* in the Collected Edition of his works (London: Chatto & Windus, 1950), viii.

28. C. H. Sisson described the poem's purpose this way in the introduction to his translation of *De rerum natura* (Manchester, Eng.: Carcanet New Press, 1976), 8.

29. Martin Green and John Swain have analyzed the Pierrot sensibility (self-irony, self-conflict, self-parody, self-fragmentation); they assert that for Laforgue "parody and irony are not modes of disengagement from an idea; indeed they are modes of engagement with it." See *The Triumph of Pierrot:*

The Commedia dell'arte and the Modern Imagination (New York: Macmillan, 1986), 29.

30. When Huxley submits his recipe for redemption, Sebastian Barnack emphasizes its tentative, evolving nature in contrast to rigid, "excessive working hypotheses"; see *Time Must Have A Stop* (London: Chatto & Windus, 1945), 289.

31. Typical of critics since the 1930s, André Maurois wrote as if Huxley was not a poet who had become a novelist; see his *Prophets and Poets* (London: Cassell, 1936), 208.

32. See Richard Chase, "Myth as Literature" in James E. Miller, ed., *Myth and Method* (Nebraska: Univ. of Nebraska Press, 1960), 138.

33. Chase (note 32), 143.

34. It was forty years afterward when Eliot recalled this incident; see Julian Huxley, ed., *Aldous Huxley 1894–1963: A Memorial Volume* (New York: Harper and Row, 1965), 30.

35. Elizabeth Drew quotes at length from the crucial final paragraph of Eliot's review essay, which appeared in *The Dial* in November 1923; Eliot, Drew argues, had "Mythical Vision." See *T. S. Eliot: The Design of His Poetry* (New York: Charles Scribner's Sons, 1949), 1–5.

36. I. A. Richards quoted in Fred D. Crawford, *Mixing Memory and Desire: The Waste Land and British Novels* (University Park: Pennsylvania State Univ. Press, 1982), xviii.

37. T. S. Eliot, "Ulysses, Order, and Myth," *The Dial*, November 1923, 483.

38. Aldous Huxley, "The Modern Spirit and A Family Party," *Vanity Fair* 18 (August 1922): 55; cited hereafter as "MS."

39. Eliot, "Ulysses," (note 37), 483.

40. Rabelais was frequently on Huxley's mind in 1922–23: in chapter 9 of *Antic Hay* (London: Chatto & Windus, 1923), Gumbril, Jr. becomes Toto, "the complete Rabelaisian man" (118).

41. Aldous Huxley, *Point Counter Point* (London: Chatto & Windus, 1928), 32; cited hereafter as *PCP*.

42. T. S. Eliot, *The Sacred Wood* (1920; reprint, New York: Barnes and Noble, 1960), 162; cited hereafter as *SW*. Eliot called Dante "a classic," whereas Blake, another inventor of his own mythology, was merely ingenious, a "poet of genius" (158).

43. Desmond MacCarthy's statement appears in a review for the *New Statesman* 15 (1920), 595–97.

44. Richard Ellman, *Ulysses on the Liffey* (New York: Oxford Univ. Press, 1972), 185.

45. Ellman (note 44), 174–75.

46. Aldous Huxley, *Music at Night* (London: Chatto & Windus, 1931), 95.

JEROME MECKIER

Aldous Huxley, Satiric Sonneteer:
The Defeat of Youth

"The Decameron" in Aldous Huxley's *The Defeat of Youth* (1918) deserves reconsideration as a minor masterpiece in which principles for achieving counterpoint, later formulated by Philip Quarles in *Point Counter Point*, already operate with sophistication. This short poem previews the anti-Garsington satire in *Crome Yellow*. It also brings to a climax an attack upon the sonnet form begun two years earlier in *The Burning Wheel*. Most important, "The Decameron" ties in with the full-scale parody of the sonnet sequence that gives Huxley's second collection its title.

Intensely contrapuntal, "The Decameron" anticipates Quarles's insistence upon a "multiplicity of eyes and multiplicity of aspects seen" (266), for the plague is viewed from three vantage points: the victims,' the storytellers,' and the omniscient satirical poet's:

> Noon with a depth of shadow beneath the trees
> Shakes in the heat, quivers to the sound of lutes:
> Half shaded, half sunlit, a great bowl of fruits
> Glistens purple and golden: the flasks of wine
> Cool in their panniers of snow: silks muffle and shine:
> Dim velvet, where through the leaves a sunbeam shoots,

From *Contemporary Literature* 29, 4 © 1988 by the Board of Regents of the University of Wisconsin System.

Rifts in a pane of scarlet: fingers tapping the roots
Keep languid time to the music's soft slow decline.

Suddenly from the gate rises up a cry,
Hideous broken laughter, scarce human in sound;
Gaunt clawed hands, thrust through the bars despairingly,
Clutch fast at the scented air, while on the ground
Lie the poor plague-stricken carrions, who have found
Strength to crawl forth and curse the sunshine and die.

(Collected Poetry 67)

Huxley discusses the plague in terms of its contradictory results: a work of art for Boccaccio, at the cost of widespread death. Perceiving an event simultaneously from different angles, Quarles decides, produces a "very queer picture indeed" (266), puzzlement about the nature of things rather than explanations. Although set in fourteenth-century Fiesole, "The Decameron" reveals what the satirical modern poet contends the life process is like always and everywhere, if seen from a sufficiently inclusive point of view: life and death, beauty and ugliness, the magnificence of art and the sordidness of reality, pleasure and disaster—these constantly coexist and alternate, point counter point, to defy the theorizer whose philosophy would encompass them all. They embarrass the artist who tries to preserve unity of mood or employs a single mode. The greater one's overview, Huxley implies, the more contradictory life appears, the more artificially limited the respected works and traditional formats of great artists and thinkers become.

The orchestration of Huxley's poem proceeds in accord with Quarles's recipe for the "musicalization of fiction." It depends on "changes of mood … abrupt transitions" (408). Quarles stipulates that emphasis fall on "variations" that will uncover unexpected contrasts and similarities, such as similar people solving different problems or, as initially happens here, dissimilar people facing the same problem (the plague, death) in different ways. The inexplicable strangeness of life, Quarles contends, its "astonishingness" (266), results from a realization that "while Jones is murdering a wife, Smith is wheeling the perambulator in the park" (408).

In *Point Counter Point*, as in "The Decameron," life makes sense chiefly as a constant source of amazement for the savorer of its cruel ironies. Quarles attends a concert while his son is struck down with meningitis; as Elinor hastens to little Phil, Webley arrives at Philip's to carry her off but is ambushed and murdered by Spandrell and Illidge. Similarly, the Italian Renaissance blossoms and Boccaccio pens his masterpiece while, despite the era's art and refinement, thousands die of plague. No single philosophy or generic mode can readily explain both events or do full justice to the exquisite yet unsettling ironies their contrapuntal simultaneity produces. The artist who ignores either type of event—*Decameron* or plague— decreases the "astonishingness"; he falsifies what Huxley later calls life's "pluralistic mystery" ("Shakespeare and Religion" 172), its refusal to be comprehensible except as counterpoint.

The satiric contrapuntist maintains that life is a bundle of contradictions. This becomes clear whenever one manages to look at it correctly. He knows that he cannot untie the bundle. His challenge is that no reader, no philosopher, can reconcile Boccaccio's masterwork with the plague or justify the irony whereby the second was the gestation period for the first. Most art, the poet implies, is like *The Decameron:* woefully partial, incomplete, much too sanguine, owing to the lack of a theory to fit all the facts. The satiric sonneteer pursues inclusiveness by underlining divisions as the essence of life. He elects to capture the inexplicability of the life process by showing the baffling quality its incongruities acquire when juxtaposed. On the larger canvas *Point Counter Point* later supplies, Huxley can show the dismayed reader a better picture of the macrocosm in which the pattern for any given moment is made up of countless juxtapositionings like the one in this sonnet.

Huxley's satire in "The Decameron" is also topical, thanks to a placing side by side of past and present. In a letter to Lady Ottoline Morrell in late June or early July of 1915, D. H. Lawrence proposed that he, Bertrand Russell, and their associates establish at Garsington the seat of a new community destined to save England. "Garsington," he wrote,

> must be the retreat where we come together and knit ourselves together. Garsington is wonderful for that. It is like the Boccaccio place where they told all the Decamerone. That won-derful lawn, under the ilex trees, with the old house and its exquisite old front—it is *so* remote, so perfectly a small world to itself, where one *can* get away from the temporal things to consider the big things. (243)

Reference to "the Boccaccio place" is the tip-off. Huxley's poem is in part an expression of guilt cloaked in satire against the pretentious escapism of his friends. They travel to a kind of rustic Bloomsbury to avoid reality and live the life of the mind. Garsingtonians, Huxley charges, undeservingly idealize themselves as a private, superior world. Using a historical analogy,

"The Decameron" attacks the irresponsible eccentricity of some of the century's most prominent intellectuals, who talked while the world burned. Recalling his own visits to Garsington during the war, Huxley condemns it as an unjustifiable refuge from the military conflicts plaguing Europe.

Quarles would regard Fiesole as a "diaphonous" spot (342) through which the story of the universe can be seen. The modern satirical poet senses a parallel between Garsingtonians, safely away from the war, and Boccaccio's storytellers, who try to leave the plague behind. It is a case of similar people, centuries apart, solving different forms of the same problem. Both groups sadly illustrate the apparent uselessness of art and intellectuals in times of natural disaster or national crisis, events which are staples of the unsatisfactory nature of things.

Physically unfit to fight and by temperament destined for pacifism, Huxley is nevertheless discomforted by a war that ravaged Europe while he studied at Oxford and visited the Morrells. In "The Decameron" he visualizes himself and his friends from a hostile point of view, from outside the gates of the estate as well as from within. The omniscient poet's vantage point enables him to relish the counterpoint of art for some and death for others. At the same time, however, he addresses, through art, an uneasiness about his own participation in Lady Ottoline's coterie. He expresses the guilt he feels as a modern, ineffectual storyteller in a new period of plague. Indirectly, the poet vents feelings of helplessness and self-loathing while exploring an intriguing historical parallel on the theme of artistic irresponsibility. He raises doubts about art's ability to construe the human condition but also identifies the inexplicable diversity that makes man's condition so difficult to explain. The modern, postwar sonneteer is truthful about life's incommensurabilities and harsh upon escapists yet just as powerless as Boccaccio to remedy one or avoid the other.

Getting away from "temporal things" to consider the "big things" strikes Huxley as a philosophical blunder. It is precisely the "temporal things" Lawrence wishes to push aside that call the reality of most "big things" into question. One's overview must somehow embrace both, or it will be as useless in times of adversity as the "small world" Lawrence idolizes, an enclave that foreshadows the many private worlds Huxley's egotists try to sustain everywhere in his novels. Storytellers in "The Decameron" spin elegant, naughty tales that exclude the eyesore reality of the plague victims. Lawrence suggests a similar "retreat," even if the quality of discussion he envisions would be higher. Such exclusion separates art from life. It is this kind of contrapuntal separation that Huxley's sonnet considers one of the "big things" or important ideas worth worrying and writing about.

"Men on leave from the front," Paul Fussell writes, "were not comforted to hear of things like Philip and Lady Ottoline Morrell's farm, Garsington Manor, near Oxford, where, after conscription was introduced in January, 1916, numerous Bloomsbury essayists harbored as conscientious objectors performing 'agricultural work'" (86). Soldiers on furlough, who found Lady Ottoline's farm an affront, relied nonetheless on literature to explain reality. It was, after all, a literary war, fought, in many instances, by poets who were soldiers and by soldiers who still believed in poetry. They believed in the "curious literariness" of real life, the reciprocal process whereby life feeds literature so that literature, read attentively, enables one to confer form upon life (Fussell ix). "The Decameron" is satirically intricate enough to refute this position, too. Huxley subverts a reciprocal process which the soldiers who condemned Garsington farm foolishly relied on. At the same time, he continues the process ironically in that his sonnet attacks "literariness" as sharply as real life had been doing since 1914. Life feeds literature in Huxley's satirical poem but also discredits it.

Fighters in the Great War soon learned that politicians, clergymen, and newspapers had lied about its nature, purpose, and duration. Still, many infantrymen carried the *Oxford Book of English Verse* as a reliable guide. Although never truly a war poet, Huxley does his bit: he drives a wedge between the *Oxford Book* and modern realities. The Western literary tradition, the poet's satirical sonnet suggests, must take some of the blame for the war because it has too often been an escape, a pernicious illusion. Huxley explodes such repositories of wisdom as the *Oxford Book* and a literary masterpiece like *The Decameron*. But in the process he preserves a role for his own topical, contrapuntal artistry as a formative clarifier of, among other things, the status of traditional forms, in this case the sonnet.

In ten sonnets in *The Burning Wheel* (nine Italian), one sees Huxley working toward "The Decameron." A need for loveliness in the octave of "The Canal" (*Collected Poetry* 26) is filled by the swan that swims past in the sestet. In "The Ideal Found Wanting" (27), however, a Pierrot decides in the octave that he is "sick of clownery." But in the sestet, the audience finds his attempts to "break a window" through his "prison" a new phase in his comic routine. The octave of "Misplaced Love" (27) is a list of romantic clichés at the poet's disposal (red wine, shell of pearl, naked petals, gold memories, Ariel's wings). In the sestet, the poet places these "treasured things" upon a pyre, ignites them, and awaits the "Phoenix" that will arise as proof of the romantic tradition's continuing vitality. But, laments the poet, "there was naught but ashes at the last," for the props of a degenerate movement disintegrate under stress from the critical intelligence, symbolized by the pyre.

Different poetic voices in these three poems compete contrapuntally. Breakdowns in "The Ideal Found Wanting" and "Misplaced Love" refute "The Canal." Whether the modern artist tries to revitalize his role at the expense of the medium he practices or to reconstitute art as a rich inheritance, he fails. The sonnet format's refusal to cooperate makes each poet's inability to achieve his intentions more emphatic. Yet failure seems artistically appropriate since concessions of defeat are what must be conveyed. The poet of "The Decameron" outstrips his less fortunate predecessors by deliberately cultivating the betrayal by format to which they succumb.

No precursor in *The Burning Wheel*, therefore, is as good as "The Decameron." The poet contrasts the "sound of lutes" with the "scarce human ... sound" of plague victims. The slow, rich assurance of the octave is interrupted by clamorous grasping in the sestet. Huxley connects two groups while placing them in stark opposition. The poem unveils the heights and depths life is arbitrarily capable of: diverse fates bring riches and luxurious comfort for some, disease and death to others. One group basks in sunshine, the other curses it and dies. The counterpoint of octave and sestet, abruptly introduced by "Suddenly" in the poem's pivotal shortest line, becomes a formal extension of the clash between incompatibles, such as life's ugliness and man's desire to create beauty.

Huxley exposes Boccaccio as a writer whose vision was not broad enough to express the life of an age. In the sestet of the modernized *Decameron*, reality intrudes upon the ideal, life breaks in brutally upon art, the real world fails to meet literary standards. Ironically, the storytellers, destined to be immortalized, are "languid," while the plague victims exhibit "strength" as they expire. The sonnet generates lasting tension between the heartless complexities of life and the simplifying falsity of art. Since the calmness and beauty of the octave are as true as hysteria and horror in the sestet, only a contrapuntal sonnet, devoted in theme and structure to permanent opposition rather than resolution, can hold these two realities together.

Storytellers in the first eight lines cannot escape from the sufferers in part two; nor can sufferers exonerate the storytellers. The two groups and the contrasting conditions they represent remain unalterably opposed: the first beautiful but irresponsible, the second real yet terrible. Plague victims compromise the aesthetics and morality of the privileged party that has shut them out. Their exclusion, the poet sardonically suggests, is part of the price one frequently pays for art. Readers unwilling to accept the sonnet's contrapuntal stand-off as an end in itself are the ultimate victims. If Huxley's intentionally diabolic sonnet builds to a dead end, an irreducible irony, readers cannot continue to argue that life makes sense, with art as its mirror. They must replace their own outlook with the poet's, resolution with counterpoint and contradiction.

A poet intent on emphasizing dichotomies, Huxley was bound to discover contrapuntal possibilities in the Italian sonnet. Its octave and sestet fall naturally into the kinds of opposition his modern sensibility was anxious to explore. Normally, the octave bears the burden (a doubt, problem, desire, or hoped for vision); then the sestet eases the burden by resolving doubt, solacing desire, or realizing the vision. But Huxley's better Italian sonnets are parodies of the form. Reversing the roles of octave and sestet so that the latter challenges the former, Huxley uses the Italian sonnet against itself. Either he shows the form betraying poets or impersonates a poet sabotaging the form. The resulting anti-sonnets reflect a world of contrary urges, militant contradictions. Sestets destroy the calm of their octaves or confess failure to settle issues raised there. Such poems frustrate expectations; they introduce readers to modernity by posing insoluble problems instead of resolving them.

Form becomes a kind of subject matter in Huxley's finest poems, as it does later in his modern satirical novels. Irreverent use of structure, in poetry or prose, amounts to satiric restatement of theme. It not only discredits the values of the writer's parental and artistic antecedents but recapitulates the modern collapse into chaos of unifiers and absolutes. For a "Pyrrhonic aesthete"[1] skeptical about everything, including the efficacy of art, the Italian sonnet makes the perfect target. Essentially a solution-finding form, it is possibly the most resolution-oriented poetic structure.

If modern life affords few comfortable conclusions, says Huxley, art must follow suit. Parodying Petrarch's format and Boccaccio's masterwork enables him to strike at the roots of the West's literary tradition, which began with infusions of poetry from the Italian Renaissance. An artist, Huxley later wrote, strives to "perceive the forms inherent in nature and to find a symbolic equivalence for these forms which he then imposes upon the world in order to produce the order which he feels to be so supremely important" (*Human Situation* 183), even if disorder or disintegration is the only pattern he can legitimately impose. The forms inherent in nature, as Huxley perceived them in the postwar world, had to be contrapuntal, cacophonous, and collapsing. Anti-Petrarchan sonnets are among the earliest manifestations of modernism's tendency to dissociate itself from the intellectual assumptions of a dead past, especially as they appear in moribund literary forms.

T. S. Eliot measured our devitalized age against a more attractive bygone era. In his quatrain poems, for example, modern perceptions, no matter how recondite or alarming, are kept under control by the poet's faultless use of an orthodox form that accentuates the superiority of past over present. The Pyrrhonic aesthete implies that an age without an accepted myth or consoling dogmas is seeing life's formlessness clearly for the first time. Recent events (namely, World War I) have called into question an inapplicable tradition. So Huxley creates contrapuntal conflicts between modern subject matter and conventional verse structures. Pouring new wine into old skins, he watches them take on unpleasant shapes: the wineskins prove lamentably porous, the wine tastes like gall. Huxley exposes the barrenness of the present by casting doubt on assurances poets embraced in the past. That their certitudes no longer have currency in the modern wasteland is abundantly clear. No less critical is the suggestion that assurances in respected poetic forms were always misjudgments, now finally being detected by a parodic poet-philosopher for whom detection must serve as an end or art in itself.

In "The Defeat of Youth" (*Collected Poetry* 41–50), Huxley produced the century's most successful sonnet sequence, better than Auden's or Edna St. Vincent Millay's. One thinks of the sequence as a Renaissance form, compared with which nineteenth-century variations—*The House of Life*, *Sonnets from the Portuguese*—seem inferior in zest and scope. Short sequences the Georgians published—Harold Monro's "Week-End," Masefield's seven untitled sonnets in volume two of *Georgian Poetry*, Drinkwater's "Persuasion" in volume five—now appear silly and banal. But "The Defeat of Youth" is both sonnet sequence and a highly original subversion of that traditional form. Paradoxically, only parody, Huxley argues, can still confer vitality when old value systems and the formats sacred to them no longer function; satire prolongs the lives of both temporarily, even as it deals the *coup de grâce*. In this way, art continues in spite of itself as the poet makes art at art's expense.

Instead of concentrating on the wooing of the Laura figure, as did Petrarch, Huxley anatomizes the disastrous inner turmoil of the would-be lover. The youth's failure at love becomes a pervasive metaphor for the downfall of idealism, the defeat of false or exalted notions that had taken place throughout Europe by 1918. Movement within the modernized sequence is from the protagonist's sense of love's marvelousness to his chilling realization of libidinousness. Neither life nor the youth himself is as good as he originally thought. This parallels the disillusionment of European youth, a change from confident heroism and belief in mission to the suspicion of futility not just at the front but at the heart of the life process generally. Huxley's young man is undone by his growing awareness of life's dichotomies. The poet indulges in few parodies of the sonnet form per se,[2] but he reverses the direction of the traditional sequence: his hero starts in bliss and ends in misery. Structurally, this is a large-scale equivalent of pitting sestet against octave.

By contrast with Petrarch's 317 sonnets, Sidney's 108, and Spenser's 89, Huxley needs only 22 to suggest the rapid collapse under stress of his protagonist's romantic philosophy. Huxley's young man experiences a breakdown of the past. He ends as a modern, thoroughly alienated, plagued by self-doubt. Inevitable disillusionment, given the nature of the world and divisions within the self, becomes the poem's real theme, not love's splendor as a verification of man's aspiring spirit. "The Defeat of Youth" is the only sequence in literary history to terminate with its protagonist's apparent suicide. It must be told in the third person by an omniscient satiric sonneteer.

The introductory sonnet depicts a well-meaning romantic day-dreamer who pursues "phantoms" and "ghost things" (I). In *Epipsychidion*, Shelley seeks a "soul out of my soul," the "one form resembling hers, / In which she might have masked herself from me." A voice finally informs him that "the phantom" he seeks is beside him. The ideal woman for Huxley's youth is "formless still, without identity, / Not one she seemed, not clear, but many and dim." Therefore, the poet calls her an "Indifferent mystery ... / Something still uncreated, incomplete." But her materialization will not bring the millennial satisfaction Shelley found. When Huxley's youth discovers his soul personified, he cannot unify the ideal and the profane, art and reality, as readily as Stephen Dedalus does upon encountering the wading girl. Thanks to the arousal of unexpectedly physical desires, the ideal within the youth's mind and the person embodying it become counterpoints. An epiphanic experience, a spot in time, is gradually ruined by the girl's unwillingness to remain on a pedestal and the youth's growing desire to take her from it.

Huxley's sonnet sequence occasionally resembles a short story told in verse: some sonnets merely establish time and place. "Under the Trees" in the "long hot days" of "heavy summer," a little group "is deep / In laughing talk" (II). The sestet's description of alternating shadow and sunlight, the initial instance of Manichean chiaroscuro, suggests deeper divisions to come. The "shadow as it flows" not only "dims the lustre of a rose"; it also "Quenches the bright clear gold of hair ... / ... and life seems faint." But when the "light / Swings back," the rose takes fire and hair is "aflame."

Similarly, shadows of lust fall across romantic love. Unfortunately, there will be no swing back.

Sonnets III through V are emphatically antidualistic. Scoffing at the idea of life as counterpoint, they reject dualism as the human condition. In III the youth catches first sight of the girl who becomes the catalyst for all his troubles; immediately, he falls in love. Her turning toward him is like "a door / Suddenly opened on some desolate place / With a burst of light and music." This explosion of beauty occurs in the third of twenty-two sonnets, too early to be conclusive.

Sonnet IV is strongly Wordsworthian in content. The poet consciously overdoes it so that one suspects him of describing the youth's feelings without sharing his euphoria. Romantic poets perceive the ideal in the real, divine in mortal. This sonnet acknowledges that "Men see their god ... / Smile through the curve of flesh or moulded clay, / In bare ploughed lands that go sloping away / To meet the sky in one clean exquisite line." But the poet implies that this is folly. The verb "Smile" seems chosen for its lack of high seriousness. "Out of the short-seen dawns of ecstasy," the sonnet continues, now Shelleyan in manner, men "draw new beauty, whence new thoughts are born." How far the "short-seen" differs from the short-sighted remains an open question. The sonnet recognizes no counterpoint of body and mind or beauty and ugliness. It expresses the youth's naive state of mind when it contends that "Out of earthly seeds / Springs the aerial flower."

The fourth sonnet sags beneath the weight of its facile optimism. Its conclusion blends Wordsworthian spirituality with belief in inevitable progress:

> One spirit proceeds
> Through change, the same in body and in soul—
> The spirit of life and love that triumphs still
> In its slow struggle towards some far-off goal
> Through lust and death and the bitterness of will.

This echoes the resolution of *In Memoriam* and Tennyson's belief in "One God, one law, one element, / And one far-off divine event, / To which the whole creation moves." Positive conclusions romantic and Victorian poets struggled toward, Huxley suggests, were more satisfying than real, applicable solely within the poems themselves. These poets began in uncertainty and self-doubt, then pushed through to a more sanguine outlook that met the demands of the moment. Subsequent poets, however, cannot safely begin where they left off, as though their resolutions were scientifically verified. To adopt so affirmative a stance in the third poem of a sequence, as Huxley's protagonist does, is sheer bravado.

The youth does not prove to be "the same in body and in soul." The contrapuntal halves of his being clash violently when obstacles sonnet IV blithely dismisses return to torment him. "Lust," "bitterness of will," and finally "death" turn out to be stages in the youth's defeat. Huxley's poem begins with resolution, then problems start. Affirmations of previous poets crumble when subjected to new tests. "One spirit" or "One God, one law, one element"—the youth who brings such precepts to the modern world finds no corroborative unity. The struggle from uncertainty to qualified optimism and sometimes faith itself can be called the archetypal pattern in nineteenth-century poetry. "The Defeat of Youth" reverses and parodies it.

A hymn to harmony, sonnet V is more extravagant than its predecessors. Continuing the "One spirit" theme, it finds it stirring all minds, shaking all trees, singing in all music. The mind-body dichotomy—passion against reason—quickly vanishes. The youth decides that the spiritual and the physical, often synonymous in Huxley with ideals versus reality, are providentially unified: "the soul is wrought / Of one stuff with the body—matter and mind / Woven together in so close a mesh." The real mesh is the one Huxley weaves for readers who mistake parody for imitation. No matter how drugged by the complacency of the Georgians, some readers must have suspected the sincerity of "flesh / May strangely teach the loveliest holiest things." Back-to-back superlatives and the conjunction of "flesh" and holiness, one feels, are not permissible exaggerations, even for a lover.

Sonneteers traditionally claim that love ennobles. The youth hints that it can actually sanctify. Keats's "Ode on a Grecian Urn" probably inspired the inept declaration that concludes this sonnet and the first section of Huxley's sequence: "Truth is brought to birth / Not in some vacant heaven: its beauty springs / From the dear bosom of material earth." The alleged partnership of truth and beauty is tempered by the realization that bosoms do not produce offspring.

The next pair of sonnets, section two, take place "In the Hay-loft" and build to comic anticlimax. Glaring sunlight from "Under the Trees" yields in VI to "darkness in the loft." The counterpoint of light and darkness, running throughout the poem, creates a world of opposing forces which the gushing youth at first cannot perceive, much less explain. "Perched mountain-high" atop the hay, Huxley's couple are still not safe from life's contraries since the storm that drove them indoors makes the sky an illustration of dualism. The distance seems "close and clear," but the sky "at hand is cloud." Distant clearness, Huxley ominously notes, may be like the "brightness of dreams / Unrealisable, yet seen so clear."

When VII begins, the couple feel the presence of "Mysterious powers," for the storm is internal as well as external. Unfortunately, the youth is hesitancy personified. A more than genuine Petrarchan, he idealizes his lady to the point where he fears vulgar contact. Perhaps, he speculates, "he could kiss her face, / Could kiss her hair!" On the other hand, she may be "pedestalled above the touch / Of his desire." To dare to kiss her seems both "little" and "infinitely much." As he vacillates, the girl makes up her own mind: "suddenly she kissed him on the cheek." The mood is temporarily one of comedy as the Laura figure seizes the initiative. The girl in Huxley's sequence is driven by the youth's timidity to make the first move.

Securing the first kiss is both ritual and milestone in most Renaissance sonnet sequences. Spenser does not achieve this breakthrough until sonnet 64 of the *Amoretti*, while Sidney's Astrophel has to wait until sonnet 79. In both cases, the poet is agent, not recipient. Huxley's young lady temporarily resolves the youth's indecision whether to possess her or place her on a pedestal. By her action, she asserts her full-blooded reality and becomes a challenge to the overly sensitive young man, whose indecisiveness betrays an unhealthy preference for untested, abstract ideals over troublesome realities.

The first kiss is no prelude to additional favors. When section three, entitled "Mountains," begins, the youth has moved from the "mountain-high" hayloft to more traditional romantic scenery. His climbing of an actual mountain is a pathetic physical attempt to transcend his problems. The setting in VIII is frightening, not sublime. Huxley strongly suggests a comparison between the abyss beneath the ascending youth and the darkness newly discovered within. As if Wordsworth or Shelley scaling Mont Blanc, the youth is wreathed in clouds and mist; but a gust of wind catches a cloud "and twists / A spindle of rifted darkness through its heart." The cloud's heart, one suspects, represents the youth's.

Through this "gash in the damp grey" mists comes a momentary revelation of "black depths" below, out of which the youth is desperately trying to climb, literally and symbolically. His hayloft encounter with the girl has triggered unexpected tensions between his notion of the ideal, a Laura figure, and an undeniably real girl. This tension is also between the two halves of himself that draw him simultaneously toward idolizing and seducing her. Love and lust not only divide the youth but have external causes in what strikes him as the girl's dual aspect: she makes an appeal both to mind and body, to the youth's ability to appreciate beauty and his desire to possess and sully it.

As he "strains on upwards," the youth wonders what would happen if he simply "let go":

> What would he find down there, down there below
> The curtain of the mist? What would he find
> Beyond the dim and stifling now and here,
> Beneath the unsettled turmoil of his mind?
> Oh, there were nameless depths: he shrank with fear.

Obviously terrified, the youth remains slightly absurd, his fright as excessive as his former optimism. The "nameless depths" refer to the abyss beneath the mountain and darker aspects of his own soul, neither of which he has ever carefully examined. He is afraid to "let go," to plunge into the recesses of self, because he might learn that he is Manichean, not Shelleyan. Huxley's youth, a modern schizophrenic, is a would-be idealist whose romantic Western upbringing renders him unable to cope with his complicated self. He is an intellectual surprised by a reality less cooperative than he was conditioned to expect by the best literature of the preceding hundred years.

The modern world and the dictates of one's imagination, Huxley contends, are invariably at odds, perhaps to an unprecedented degree. His poetry conveys disappointment that the real world persistently lets one down and his fury that poet-philosophers have continued to see there what can only be found among constructs of the mind. "The Defeat of Youth" begins doing something Malcolm Cowley claims Huxley did not manage before "Leda": contrapuntally, it "measures the traditional precepts into which one has been educated against the immoral realities of experience" (73).

Mountains in IX offer provisional solace to bring this section of the sequence to a satisfactory conclusion. A "sense of blessed release / From wilful strife" overtakes the youth once he has climbed high enough. Calling his surroundings "Mountains of vision, calm above fate and will," he decides that they "hold the promise of the freer life." But his climbing is futile and the peace he finds atop the mountains escapist and illusory, not at all on a par with Calamy's at the end of *Those Barren Leaves* seven years later. Consequently, the next section of seven sonnets takes place "In the Little Room," a cheerful place in autumn but claustrophobic by contrast with the mountains. The counterpoint of inside and outside settings, like that between light and darkness, proves detrimental to the youth's idealism, his belief in unities. These seven sonnets record the youth's actual defeat, and the remainder of the sequence deals with vain attempts at recovery.

Sonnet X sets the new scene. Again Huxley underlines a contrast of light and darkness, the "cheerfulness of fire and lamp" inside as opposed to the menacing "darkness" outside. Awaiting the girl, Huxley's youth, in sonnet XI, spies on her wall "Rich coloured plates of beauties that appeal / Less to the sense of sight than to the feel, / So moistly satin are their breasts." Hanging alongside is his gift to her: the "silken breastplate of a mandarin," symbolic of the youth's attempts at intellectual detachment. It gives no defense against those "moistly satin" breasts and the thoughts that they, like the girl, arouse.

Halfway through the sequence, in sonnet XII, the youth tries to freeze the passing moment, to make midpoint and counterpoint into still point. "In silence and as though expectantly," the girl "crouches at his feet." The youth's fingers, as they touch her hair, are "lightdrawn," as if moths in search of flame. Formerly overconfident of life's unity, the youth now feebly wishes to separate thought from action. He wants the passing moment to linger indefinitely. He muses:

So to exist,
    Poised 'twixt the deep of thought where spirits drown
    Life in a void impalpable nothingness,
    And, on the other side, the pain and stress
    Of clamorous action and the gnawing fire
    Of will, focal upon a point of earth—even thus
    To sit, eternally without desire
    And yet self-known, were happiness for us.

Thought and action, another counterpoint in the poem, become the youth's Scylla and Charybdis. Afraid of both, he desires to exist between them, as if there were neutral ground between counterpoints, a place where one is fully known to oneself ("self-known") yet spared the pull in opposite directions. But the urge toward the "void impalpable nothingness," Huxley's unflattering description of the world of thought, and the contrary pull toward "the gnawing fire," his unpleasant symbol for feverish yet ineffective action, admit no middle course.

In sonnet XII, the youth appears to desire a place on Keats's urn. Becoming part of that art work's embroidery offers a means of escape. He would avoid life's dichotomies by stopping time a moment or so before they appear, before thought demands action or action requires more thought. The youth's egoism prompts him to speak of "happiness for us," but it is unlikely the girl would choose a condition so sterile.

Sonnet XII is especially interesting because its turning point appears to come in line seven, thereby almost forming a sestet-octave sonnet. This structural peculiarity occurs at a most appropriate point, the halfway marker. Despite elongation, the efficiency of the solution-finding segment does not improve. Sonnets XIII and XIV are variations on the fantasy of existing between thought and act. In no other sonnet sequence is the girl so forthrightly anxious to begin serious lovemaking and the male so reluctant. Her attitude in XIII is one of "glad surrender." Her refrain in XIV is "'I give you all; would that I might give more.'" But her prospective partner has become a would-be urn-dweller; he finds art well wrought, not full of contradictory impulses, as is modern man and contemporary life.

The youth's second attempt to preserve the status quo touches off the sharpest counterpoint in the sequence. In XIV the youth persuades himself that holding the girl and gently kissing "her brow and hair and eyes" is "love perfected." In XV, however, the young man's "passion … / Comes forth to dance … / His satyr's dance." He is initiated into a dualistic world where body and mind, lust and love, are at odds. Opposition between them is a variant form of conflicts between reality and ideals, ugliness and beauty, life and art.

Calling passion "a hoofed obscenity" is not Huxley's opinion but an expression of the youth's distressing realization that life's dichotomies can be personal and internal. He experiences a betrayal of his better self by baser instincts. On the national level, European civilizations had just made similar discoveries about themselves. The youth finds that he harbors "Love's rebel servant" within, as if he were simultaneously Adam and the serpent. His physical nature, not his proud mind, echoes Dedalus's *"non serviam."* Huxley's reluctant Lucifer surmises that romance and idealism have survived by pretending that one can separate love from lust (good from evil).

Fatally attracted by the girl's "inward flame" in XIII, the youth is closer to paralysis than apotheosis. "In full tide / Life halts within him, suddenly stupefied." Discovery of his physical feelings for the girl is described in terms of blindness and thunderbolts: "Sight blackness, lightning-struck; but blindly tender / He draws her up to meet him." Petrarch was confident his love for Laura would lead to contemplation of the supreme good. Astrophel's difficulties stem largely from the frustrations of nonattainment. But Huxley's aroused youth cannot pursue the girl with the ardor Spenser expended courting Elizabeth Boyle. Epiphany seems to put out the lights.

Sonnet sequences from the past, the poet attests, have inadequately prepared the youth to come to terms with himself. He expects "love perfected" to mean being "templed high and white / Against the calm of golden autumn skies, / And shining quenchlessly with vestal light" (XIV). If the girl is an "aerial shrine," lust should have no place there. But the youth is "ambushed" even in this shrine, for opposite calls to opposite and the astonished youth hears "The maddening quick dry rhythm of goatish feet / Even in the sanctuary" (XV).

When the youth, frightened of himself, "thrusts her from him" in sonnet XVI, he is intelligence rejecting limitations imposed by the flesh; he is disappointed idealism repulsing reality. "Was lust the end of what so pure had seemed?" the youth demands. As he does so, he also voices youth's displeasure with another recent outcome, the war just ended having betrayed the high ideals with which it started. The sonnet sequence ceases to work as a traditional vehicle for the celebration of love and as the medium for the successful drive of ardent spirit toward the mind's desire. This theme lacks relevance for modern times unless presented satirically as an impossibility.

Huxley's sequence begins to break down as its protagonist succumbs to the counterpoints taking over as its themes. The young man is defeated first as a lover, then as a philosopher. Inability to make love to the girl, "glad in the promise of her sacrifice" (XV), signals his failure to explain himself and his world. This inability is more than a squeamish refusal to accept life as it is. Unprepared for what he learns about himself, unschooled in the wearisome divisions that constitute man's plight, the youth speaks for a generation that is grievously disappointed, philosophically lost. The poem's title and development are Huxley's description of the major psychological event of his era: the disappearance of dependable guidelines. Disorienting loss of belief involves not just existing ideals but ideals themselves. Not just a particular generation has been defeated, Huxley contends, but all youth, optimism, and intellectual confidence once and forever. He doubts whether life or literature can ever be the same again.

The next three sonnets, titled "In the Park," are a debate. The girl does not desire an argument but is forced to share in the youth's defeat, for the title of the sequence pertains to them both. Having realized too late the youth's lamentable state of mind, the girl tries to reimpose a romantic view of life. But the youth elegiacally records the disintegration of one traditional poetic prop after another. Now that the roles of wooer and wooed are reversed, the lady must revive her despairing suitor, even though her refusals were not what depressed him. In this section, certain ways of viewing the world—Marvell's, Milton's, Keats's—no longer work in the modern situation.

The girl speaks in XVII and XVIII, and the youth replies in XIX. Her efforts seem ill-fated because the youth has trouble seeing her clearly. To him she is "like some wild wood-thing / Caught unawares" (XIV). But he also fears her as a succubus that can "body forth in palpable shame / Those dreams and longings that his blood, aflame / Through the hot dark of summer nights, had dreamed / And longed" (XVI). She cannot resolve the conflict between inflated idealism and man's natural desires because she cannot cease to play a twofold role in her lover's imagination. Counterpoints at the heart of life, the poet reveals, appear to be just as fundamental within human nature. The young woman embodies a previously unsubstantial image that turns out to have existed in the youth's untamed blood, not in his mind and soul.

In XVII the girl attempts to transform the park they have entered into a "green world," poetic and idyllic. "'The Park,'" she claims, "'Has turned the garden of a symbolist,'" and she can recognize in it "'Those ancient gardens mirrored by the eyes / Of poets that hate the world of common folks.'" She wishes to convince the youth that they have found a retreat all their own. Perhaps she has in mind the second stanza of Marvell's "The Garden," which begins, "Fair Quiet, have I found thee here, / And Innocence, thy sister dear!" and ends, "Society is all but rude, / To this delicious solitude." If so, she speaks from sound intuitions, for the youth badly needs a respite where, as Marvell contends, "the mind, from pleasures less, / Withdraws into its happiness."

Regrettably, the girl has forgotten Marvell's eighth stanza in which the "happy garden-state" remains so only "While man there walked without a mate." Marvell concludes that "Two paradises 'twere in one / To live in paradise alone." Huxley's youth would also prefer being solitary in paradise if he could regain his former innocence and peace of mind. Presence of an Eve has awakened what he interprets as the serpent within himself. The girl's talk of gardens recalls the Fall and expulsion from Eden, a catastrophe the youth seems to be reliving psychologically. The modern fall, however, is the loss of idealism, a forfeiting of respect for one's own human nature and all creation.

The girl's second analogy, which connects the garden with the scene on Keats's urn, is even less fortunate. She intends no irony by describing this "'garden of escape'" as "'still the bride / Of quietness, although an imminent rape / Roars ceaselessly about on every side.'" She refers, no doubt, to passers-by whose lack of sensibility threatens the park's continued existence. But Keats's poem and its time-free figures have been haunting the youth since sonnet XII. Like Marvell's garden, the urn is a symbol of repose the youth no longer expects to attain. Instead of working a cure, the setting becomes an extension of the youth's inner state: about to be overrun by encircling urbanization, the threatened park mirrors the youth's turbulent mind and becomes the garden of a symbolist after all.

Her remarks in XVII, the girl states, were "lightly said," not intended to be disquieting. After speaking, she was "without a thought" and "all content," unaware of her effect on the youth. Ironically, her innocence blinds her to his deepening despair and so she aggravates it. The romantic lament she delivers for "transient beauty" in XVIII works equally well as an elegy for the idealist. Both can be imagined speeding "Out of eternal darkness into time," where they are "doomed ... / To fade, a meteor, paying for the crime / Of living glorious in the denser air / Of our material earth." From here on, the poet reveals increased sympathy for the youth. His tragic aspects still coexist with traits comic and absurd, but the girl's reference to "youth's feebleness" has pathetic connotations.

In his reply in sonnet XIX, the youth condemns places of escape as poetic delusions. The girl recalls how he "spoke abrupt across [her] dream." "'Dear Garden,'" the youth begins, "'A stranger to your magic peace, I stand / Beyond your walls, lost in a fevered land / Of stones and fire.'" Hero and heroine see two different realities: her haven is his hell. The youth's place, he now realizes, is in the modern ideological wasteland outside the garden, a refuge which exists only to confirm his sense of loss.

Milton's providential world view is impossible for Huxley's youth, who understands the loss of paradise but does not expect to regain it. He still has "'yearning glimpses of a life at rest / In perfect beauty.'" These visions are interrupted, unfortunately, by the reality of "'putrid alleys'" and the "'sickening heart-beat of desire'" within himself. Outside the garden, the youth realizes, "'the wind / Of scattering passion blows.'" Milton's pair experienced lust *after* an act of disobedience. For Huxley's youth, desire itself constitutes a fall. It makes the youth disloyal to his romantic view of himself and the world. The garden is several things at once: actual place, unworkable poetic convention from a discredited past, peaceful internal states that have been lost, and an illusion.

"Self-Torment" is an appropriate title for sonnets XX and XXI. The youth becomes the personification of passion against reason. His "high love" and "fair desire" degenerate into "dull rancorous fire." The last romantic prop fails when he finds no restoration of peace in solitude or country places. Huxley likens his protagonist to "a man born blind." Upon opening his eyes "from lovely dreams," such a man perceives "a desert and men's larval faces / So hateful" that he longs to recover "darkness and his old chimeric sight / Of beauties inward." The youth undergoes a miracle in reverse. He relives the "Immortality Ode" with a modern, ironic twist. Wordsworth complained of the gradual loss of a kind of special vision, but Huxley's youth would gladly sacrifice newly acquired insights to regain his former blindness. The idealist, it appears, is the blind man, an eccentric inhabitant of a private, imaginary world, for whom epiphany is always dangerous; a glimpse of reality deprives him of his visions.

When mountain climbing, the youth feared "black depths" (VIII). As the contrast of light and dark resumes, the youth, thoroughly undeceived, prefers the darkness of the blind, a particularly poignant choice in view of Huxley's partial recovery in 1911 from almost total blindness. The youth recognizes what he has always been: an "island-point, measureless gulfs apart / From other lives." This is the human condition Huxley's novels explore. In later poems, blindness stands for sterility of soul. Here it symbolizes the blissful ignorance of romantic idealism. Movement toward clarity of vision has been downward, away from transcendence; the poet switches from the vantage point of a mountaintop to an island so isolated its separateness is "measureless," an ironic confrontation with infinity.

The title of the concluding sonnet, "The Quarry in the Wood," is deliberately ambiguous. It refers to the excavation pit into which the despairing youth, a modern Empedocles, plunges. As such, the quarry is a literal extension of the abyss he sensed below and within himself in sonnet VIII. Throughout the sequence, Huxley employs external scenery as a projection of inner states. The pit becomes at once a real and a psychological place. Sadly, external realities never correspond to the youth's ideals, only to internal doubts and confusion, which makes for another reversal of romantic practice. The title of the final sonnet also suggests the object of a chase. One can see the youth as the prey of his own desires, the victim of his upbringing.

At the start of XXII, the youth revisits the copse where he first saw the girl. Contrast between then and now sets off a thoroughly negative epiphany of despair. Huxley expects the reader to juxtapose the message and mood of the premature affirmations in sonnets III–V and the final lines of XXII:

> The world a candle shuddering to its death,
> And life a darkness, blind and utterly void
> Of any love or goodness: all deceit,
> This friendship and this God: all shams destroyed,
> And truth seen now.
>   Earth fails beneath his feet.

Macbeth's "brief candle" becomes the youth's final metaphor for life. It shudders feebly against the potent darkness of a truly Manichean world view. Imagery of light-darkness concludes in paradox: the youth sees "truth" clearly but it is synonymous with "darkness." Formerly naive, sightless, unaware, the youth now perceives that life itself is "blind" to "love" and "goodness," indifferent to ideals. When the youth finally sees, it is life's emptiness he must contemplate. Destruction of "shams" and "deceit" lead to his own. Life has nothing to do with beauty. Division of thoughts into lines manages to make "all deceit" stand on its own as a sort of summary while also serving as predicate for "This friendship and this God." The moment of complete insight is one of total extinction, a climax too intense for even the most ardent romantic.

The traditional sonneteer generally insists that he will die if he cannot obtain his lady's favor. Huxley's youth perishes because he could have had the girl but could not face what he learned about himself and the modern world. Raised an optimistic idealist on poets like Keats and Shelley, he cannot survive as the modern he must become. His final fall is captured typographically by the two-level concluding line. The choice of "Earth fails" over "Earth falls" underscores the failure of reality to meet the young man's ideals.

Normally, the Petrarchan sonnet sequence is an eloquent attempt at seduction in which the reader, taken into the poet's confidence, participates vicariously. In "The Defeat of Youth," the youth is seduced, diverted from optimistic idealism, by an uncooperative world and his own divided self. The counterpoint of ideal and real, art and life, intensifies throughout the poem; it is reinforced by the contrast between past and present, between traditional sonnet sequences and Huxley's parody of them.

"The Defeat of Youth" is not entirely successful. The third-person point of view, necessary to an ironic stance, fits clumsily in places, encouraging critics to confuse poet with protagonist. Throughout the early poetry, Richard Church decides, the "conflict in [Huxley's] personality was not yet fully abated, and I suspect it has been the disturbing element in his writings … which prevents them from possessing the simplicity and hardness of perfect form" (11). One ought not to protest that Huxley's inner conflicts are reflected but unresolved in his art; formulation without resolution is the point, not a sign of aesthetic immaturity. Life's contraries, newly rampant under modern circumstances, are perennial dualisms updated; they are not peculiar to the poet. Huxley's better poems seldom resolve oppositions because irresolution is the statement they make, just as breakdown is the goal in reusing traditional formats parodically. Irresolution and collapse give

Huxley's major efforts toughness, originality, and honesty. Their "disturbing element," articulation of discords that mar "perfect form," is the desired terminus.

What weakens "The Defeat of Youth" is one's inability to grieve as seriously as Huxley does. The youth is superb as a parodic rendition of Petrarch, but his suicide borders on tragedy rather than farce. Failure to maintain consistency of mood in the closing sonnets can be attributed to parallels between the youth's death and the suicide, in 1914, of Aldous's favorite brother, Trevenen. He apparently took his life after becoming involved with a servant girl whom he felt society would not allow him to marry. This situation differs from the one in Huxley's poem, but his interpretation of it for Gervas Huxley in August 1914 does not:

> There is—apart from the sheer grief of the loss—an added pain in the cynicism of the situation. It is just the highest and best in Trev—his ideals—which have driven him to his death—while there are thousands, who shelter their weakness from the same fate by a cynical, unidealistic outlook on life. Trev was not strong, but he had the courage to face life with ideals—and his ideals were too much for him. (*Letters* 61–62)

"The Defeat of Youth" starts as a poem about "the cynicism of the situation." The youth's idealism, like the patriotism the war called forth, seems quixotic, a projection of the romantic ego. But the youth's suicide reminds Huxley too strongly of "the sheer grief" of losing his brother. Reference to "thousands" who take refuge in "a cynical, unidealistic outlook on life," Huxley's solution and the vantage point from which the sequence is written, sounds like self-disparagement. On one hand, Huxley indulges vicariously in the sort of self-pity that produced a cult of youth in the twenties. Ironically, a similar morbidity was later used to excuse a generation's hedonistic excess. On the other, the poet indicts himself as he did when attacking Garsington in "The Decameron." Toward the climax of the sequence, use of a youth's demise to stand for the death of ideals yields to the poet's painful personal recollections. Nevertheless, the youth is the prototype for the defeated heroes and unsuccessful poets in Huxley's early fiction. Indeed, defeated heroes proliferate in literature, both British and American, during the twenties and thirties. Figures such as Jay Gatsby, Nick Carraway, Jake Barnes, Frederic Henry, Paul Pennyfeather, and Tony Last owe their existence, in part, to Huxley's frustrated, anonymous, yet seminal youth.

Harsh conflicts between love and lust seem less relevant in the 1980s, now that sexual attitudes resemble those in *Brave New World*. The youth's failure as a lover, a metaphor for the triumph of matter over mind, forfeits its immediacy and some of its credibility. At the same time, however, the implication that love in the postwar world is not a realizable ideal or sufficient reason for living identifies "The Defeat of Youth" as one of the earliest modern announcements of the death of romantic love, a subject Hemingway and Lawrence would not discover until the next decade.[3]

The girl's thematic role poses another problem. Despite the damage she causes, this unnamed damsel seems sensible and healthy, a personification of the intuitive world of emotion and feeling. But if the male-female dichotomy is to turn into a conflict between untenable ideals and disillusioning postwar realities, the girl must be a femme fatale, a symbol for a material world that attracts only to disappoint. Although she triggers the youth's downward slide, she retains a positive charge that interferes with her performance as a destructive siren. Huxley never ascertains the full impact the youth's suicide has upon her. He wants the girl to do double duty as a cause for defeat and another instance of youth defeated but lacks the skill to bring it off.

Imperfectly adumbrated in the heroine of "The Defeat of Youth" are the more memorable male-devouring females of Huxley's subsequent novels. A partial list includes Myra Viveash (*Antic Hay*) and Lucy Tantamount (*Point Counter Point*). If Huxley's youth is a seminal creation, his Loreleis prove equally inspiring to creators of the bewitching bitches for whom novels of the twenties remain famous: Hemingway's Brett Ashley, Fitzgerald's Daisy Buchanan, and Waugh's Margot Beste-Chetwynde.

For the title poem of his second collection, Huxley coins the most apt phrase ever devised for a beleaguered generation's intellectual disappointments. "The Defeat of Youth" is hardly a war poem, yet it makes broader statements about a greater calamity stemming from that conflict: it pinpoints disillusionment, the collapse of ideals, as the only suitable response to a series of oppositions found to be inherent in the system of things. The poet and his peers, whether combatants or not, suffered this collapse during the war years and did not come to terms with it for at least a decade thereafter. The theme of Huxley's most intrepid parody prior to the twenties suits the postwar years better than the thesis from Spengler's *Decline of the West*, which appeared in German the same year. The idea of a defeat for youth, a routing of its aspirations, seems more traumatic than a pattern of inevitable descent that overtakes all civilizations. Huxley's idea better describes what actually happened than Gertrude Stein's notion of *"une génération perdue."*

The Defeat of Youth is conceived contrapuntally in terms of variations on the idea of defeat. Defeatism, however, reveals itself to be an exceptionally fertile stance, not just the only approach Huxley felt he could honestly adopt. The poet occasionally writes without irony in 1918, but these mediocre effusions are quickly overwhelmed by the poems surrounding them. In some cases, he assumes the personality of the traditional poet who seems not to realize times have changed. Thematically and formally, this poet experiences defeat: in spite of his struggles to churn out conventional pieces, he writes parodic subversions of formerly credible poems and formats. In other cases, characters the poet writes about are unaware of changed times; then the poet of defeats records their disappointments. Behind even the unintentional Pierrot stands Huxley manipulating the fool's role. In the act of failing to substantiate themes and forms the past respected, the would-be traditionalist becomes a skilled demolisher through whom Huxley fashions surprisingly good poetry. The satiric sonneteer of "The Decameron" and "The Defeat of Youth" is a deliberate saboteur. But he and the persona-poet with good intentions owe their confrontations with defeat to the counterpoints Huxley installs as the troublesome core of modern life.

NOTES

1. An "amused, Pyrrhonic aesthete" is Huxley's description of his earlier self in the 1946 foreword to *Brave New World* (viii).

2. On the other hand, Huxley's rhyme scheme helps him to parody traditional sonnet sequences. Sidney's favorite scheme was *abba abba cdcd ee*. He also employed *abab abab cdcd ee* and *abba abba cdcd ee*, while Spenser preferred *abab bcbc ccdc ee*. Huxley uses either *abba cddc ee fgfg* or *abab cdcd ee fgfg*. In both he systematically avoids the closed effect Sidney and Spenser achieved in lines 13–14. The *ee* section customarily occupies lines 8–9 in Huxley, the crucial turning point where octave becomes sestet. His sonnets therefore seem to move away from resolution in lines 10–14.

3. See Mark Spilka's "The Death of Love in *The Sun Also Rises*," 127.

WORKS CITED

Church, Richard. Introduction. *The Collected Poetry of Aldous Huxley*. 7–12.

Cowley, Malcolm. Rev. of *Leda*, by Aldous Huxley. *The Dial* 70 (1921): 73–76.

Fussell, Paul. *The Great War and Modern Memory*. New York: Oxford UP, 1975.

Huxley, Aldous. *Brave New World*. London: Chatto, 1950.

———. *The Collected Poetry of Aldous Huxley*. Ed. Donald Watt. London: Chatto, 1971.

———. *The Human Situation: Lectures at Santa Barbara, 1959*. Ed. Piero Ferrucci. 1959. New York: Harper, 1977.

———. *Letters of Aldous Huxley*. Ed. Grover Smith. London: Chatto, 1969.

———. *Point Counter Point*. London: Chatto, 1928.

———. "Shakespeare and Religion." *Aldous Huxley, 1894–1963: A Memorial Volume*. Ed. Julian Huxley. New York: Harper, 1966.

Lawrence, D. H. *The Letters of D. H. Lawrence*. Ed. Aldous Huxley. New York: Viking, 1932.

Marvell, Andrew. "The Garden." *Andrew Marvell: The Complete Poems*. Ed. Elizabeth Story Donno. Harmondsworth, Eng.: Penguin, 1972. 100–102.

Shelley, Percy Bysshe. *Epipsychidion. The Complete Poetical Works of Percy Bysshe Shelley*. Ed. Thomas Hutchinson. London: Oxford UP, 1943. 411–30.

Spilka, Mark. "The Death of Love in *The Sun Also Rises*." *Hemingway: A Collection of Critical Essays*. Ed. Robert P. Weeks. Englewood Cliffs, NJ: Prentice, 1962. 127–38.

Tennyson, Alfred, Lord. *In Memoriam A. H. H. The Poems of Tennyson*. Ed. Christopher Ricks. London: Longmans, 1969. 853–988.

NINA DIAKONOVA

Aldous Huxley in Russia

The story of Huxley's reputation, at home and abroad, during his own
lifetime and in the years following his death in 1963 has been adequately
described. But little attention has been paid to one aspect of the problem—his
standing among Huxley's Russian readers and critics. For the six decades since
he was first heard of in what used to be the Soviet Union, that spirit, more
often than not, was critical and hostile. Their evolution, however, is revealing.

Huxley's name found its way to Moscow about ten years after it had
become fairly familiar to West–European, to say nothing of English readers.
The cause was the general break–up of cultural relations after the October
Revolution of 1917: very few English books, if any, reached Soviet Russia.
When they did, it was only to take their place at the best libraries of Moscow
and Leningrad.

The first translation of a novel by Huxley was published in Moscow in
1930, as the title heading of *Point Counter Point* was rendered as *Through
Different Lenses (Skvoz' raznye stekla)*—an attempt to interpret the meaning of
the novel. The second translation of the same book remained true to
Huxley's title, *Kontrapunkt* (Moscow, 1936). His earlier novel, *Antic Hay*
(Shutovskoi Khorovod), appeared almost simultaneously, while the still earlier
Crome Yellow was represented by an extract about the three lovely Lapiths in
an *English Literary Reader for Secondary Schools*, compiled by Anna Jacobson

From *The Journal of Modern Literature* 21, 1 (Fall 1997) © 1997 by the Foundation for Modern
Literature.

and Marianna Kuznets (Leningrad, 1935). In their brief introduction to the text, the editors severely criticized Huxley for incurable bourgeois ideology, for devotion to psychoanalysis, and for pessimism unrelieved by respect for humanity and its future. The same type of criticism was adopted in the courses of lectures on English Literature at philological departments of Russian universities and teachers' colleges, as well as in most succinct references to Huxley in every encyclopedia of the period.

Unflattering as these references were, they became possible only after Huxley had participated in the anti–fascist Congress for the Defense of Culture held in Paris in the summer of 1935. In his new capacity as a liberal public figure, Huxley was judged worthy of public attention. This accounts for the sensational appearance of four chapters of *Brave New World* in Number 8 for 1935 of the highly popular magazine *Foreign Literature* (*Inostrannaya Literatura*);[1] the same magazine published an anti–fascist chapter from *Eyeless in Gaza* in Number 9 for 1936. In addition, several critical essays on Huxley's work were offered to the general reader.

One of these (by A. Leites) was published in the official newspaper of the Communist Party of the Soviet Union (*Pravda*) on 15 August 1935 and approved of Huxley's new "leftist" views. Two surveys (of *Antic Hay* and *Point Counter Point*, respectively) were contributed by L. Borovoi. The latter (characteristically called "The Club of Highbrows") appeared in Number 12 of the journal *Literaturnyi Critic* for 1936; another reviewer of the same novel was more severe: A. Startsev called his notes in the *Literaturnaya Gazeta* for 20 October 1936 "The New Decadence." There were at least two additional surveys of *Point Counter Point*: V. Dmitrievski's in the *Literaturnaya Gazeta* for 10 July 1936 and M. Levidov's in the journal *Literary Review* (*Literaturnoye Obozreniye*), Number 15 for 1936.

The best by far of all the essays dealing with *Point Counter Point* was the introduction to the novel written by D. Mirskii, a highly erudite critic who had spent many years in England and was a good judge of the world recreated by Huxley. Mirskii later became one of the many victims of the tragic purges of the time. The atmosphere of the Great Terror was not exactly conducive to admiration of Huxley's art, and in the later 1930s, after a sketch of his life and work published by I. Zvavich in Number 5 of *Inostrannaya Literatura* for 1937, there was silence. It lasted throughout the war of 1939–1945—a time hardly favorable to disinterested scholarly analysis–and was broken only in 1948–1950 by the burst of indignation brought on by Huxley's *Ape and Essence*. The previewers were furious: "Flunkeys as Philosophers of Reaction" (*Culture and Life—Kultura i zhizn*, for 30 September 1948); "The Arm–Bearer of Warmongers" (*Literaturnaya*

Gazeta, July 1949); "The Philosophy of the Ape" (*The Banner–Znamya*, Number 5, 1949); "Literary Predecessors" (*The Star—Zvezda*, Number 3, 1950). The official *Pravda* published two very fierce papers: one entitled "Enemies of Mankind" (12 May 1950), the other more amiably and gently called "Modern Malthusians" (28 May 1950), nonetheless savagely attacked both Aldous and Julian Huxley.

A belated echo of the anti–Huxley campaign was an article by the well–known critic D. Zaslavskyi entitled "The Mystical Voyage of Professor Huxley" (*Pravda*, 5 July 1954). This was a very coarse, not to say brutal, assault upon Huxley's *The Doors of Perception*. The method displayed in this, as well as in the earlier articles, uniformly was misrepresentation and vulgar simplification, *reductio ad absurdum*.

Then again came silence until the end of Stalin's reign and the denunciation of its atrocities by Khrushchev. In the later 1950s, it gradually became obvious to intelligent readers that Soviet knowledge of European culture should be broader and not be limited to those authors whom it was customary to call progressive. The necessity of serious and systematic studies of foreign literature led, *inter alia*, to the preparation of a many–volumed *History of English Literature* (*Istoriya Angliiskoi Literatury*) published in Moscow. Its final volume, containing a review of twentieth–century events, appeared in 1958. The author of the chapter on the novel, D.G. Zhantieva, devotes a few pages to Huxley's novels and endeavors to do him justice. The novelist is praised for his wit, his satirical thrusts at modern civilization, but strongly rebuked for the bleak view which he takes of human nature, for his departure from realism and for yielding to mysticism in his later productions, starting with *Eyeless in Gaza*. Zhantieva expands her arguments in her book on the English twentieth–century novel (*Angliiskyi Roman XX veka*, Moscow, 1965), and again in a paper entitled, "Collision of Ideas in English Criticism" ("Ideologicheskaya bor'ba v literature i estetike," Moscow, 1972). Huxley also drew the attention of A.A. Anikst, the author of many books and essays on the history of European Literature (*Istoriya Angliiskoi Literatury*, 1956).

Along with books concentrated entirely on English studies, the 1950s and 1960s witnessed a variety of Russian publications on European and American literatures. In most of these, the author of paragraphs (never actually chapters) devoted to Huxley is V.V. Ivasheva. She insists on Huxley's break with realism and humanism after *Brave New World*, on the hopelessness of his skepticism and pessimism ("Istoriya zarubezhnoi literatury posle oktyabr'skoi revolyutsii," Moscow, 1969). The same is true of professor Ivasheva's brief remarks on Huxley made in the *History of Foreign Literature*, published in Moscow by L.G. Andreyev in 1980 (*Istoriya Zarubezhnoi Literatury XX veka*).

In addition to short descriptive sketches of Huxley's works in textbooks, two important papers were published in the 1960's. The first, "Death of a Satirist," was written by P. Palievskiy and published both in a popular literary journal (*Voprosy Literatury*, Number 7, 1961) and in a collection of his papers: *Gibel' satirika* (*Sovremennaya literatura za rubezhom*, 1961). The author most eloquently accuses Huxley of having sacrificed talent and satire for the sake of an escape into mysticism caused by his mortal disgust with humanity. He denounces Huxley for abandoning himself to complete degradation and for his falsification of Marxism.

A far fairer treatment was given to Huxley by V. Shestakov in a paper, "The Social Anti–Utopia of Aldous Huxley," published in the magazine *The New World* (*Noviy Mir*, Number 7, 1969), for which the critic was sharply reprimanded by Zhantieva in her 1972 article.

In the 1970s, the first symptoms appeared of a favorable change in the critical treatment of Huxley (along with other European and American writers who had not had the luck to be recognized as politically safe), with greater respect and penetration than previously. A good example of that attitude is to be found in the essay of A.K. Savurenok, "Faulkner and Huxley" (*Sravnitel'noye izucheniye literatur*, Leningrad, 1976). Only a little earlier, I had written a paper for *Voprosy literatury*, in an effort to break away from the clichés of Soviet Huxley criticism and to present his literary career as an earnest quest for truth. The article was accepted, but at the last moment, when the proofs were out, the type was broken up and the author mildly reproached for her non–Party attitude. However, this paper was published in English in the *Transactions of Tartu University* for 1979 under the heading "Aldous Huxley and the Tradition of the English Novel" (*Acta at Commentationes Universitatis Tartuensis*, Number 480). Huxley's importance for his contemporaries and followers is regarded as a proof of the Importance of Being Aldous.

A few years earlier than this, I had published a paper on "Music in Huxley's Novel *Point Counter Point*," in a collection of Leningrad University essays, *Literatura i muzyka*, 1975. And finally, in the 1990s, there were two other essays of mine, "Aldous Huxley and the Genre of the Intellectual Novel" (*Mezhvuzovskiy Sbornik Nauchnykh Trudov*, in *Tipologiya zhanrov i literaturniy protses*, St. Petersburg, 1994), and "Time and Space in the Works of Aldous Huxley," an enlarged version of a public lecture at the University of Durham in 1992 (Number 1 of the joint Russian—British *Journal of Philosophy and Philology, RuBriCa Russko-britanskaya Cathedra*, Moscow, 1996).

Although not much critical attention was given Huxley in Russia in the 1970s, the general tone of reviewers changed for the better in accordance with the more civilized tendencies of Soviet criticism that were slowly developing after the downright rudeness of the ideological censure of the 1930s and the 1940s. This is even to be felt in the style of accepted text—books, as well as—and even more so—in the short notes on Huxley in the *Literary Encyclopedia* (volume 8, 1978). To give but one more example, the three pages devoted to Huxley in the much used text—book on English literature by G.V. Anikin and N.P. Mikhalskaya (1975) are politely critical and objective.

Very cautiously, then, Huxley's books began gradually to be used for the study of the English language: his stories appeared as sections of readers designed for students, and his first novel, *Crome Yellow*, was published in English in 1976 and then again in 1979, with a prefatory note by G.A. Andzhaparidze. (In co—authorship with A. Martina, Andzhaparidze introduced and published a Russian translation of the book in 1987).

A new stage of Huxley studies can be observed in the mid—1980s, partly preceding but mostly succeeding the great *perestroika* started in 1985. Characteristically, several theses on his art written for what we here call "Candidate of Philology"—more or less equivalent to the American Ph.D.— were presented and successfully defended at Russian universities, most often in Moscow and Leningrad. These works can be divided roughly into two categories, the first dealing with linguistic and the second with literary aspects of Huxley's prose.

The linguistic approach to Huxley's work is also demonstrated in many articles published by different Russian universities. To give but a few examples: A.A. Zhivoglyadov, "Proper names in Literary Texts" (*Khudozhestvennyi tekst*, Krasnoyarsk, 1987); A.U. Podgornaya. "Adverbials of Quality in English Prose," (*Moskovskiy pedagogicheskiy institute inostrannykh yazykov*, Moscow, 1984); M.P. Karp, "The Role of the Linguistic Expression of Emotions in Satirical Novels" (*Tekst kak ob'ekt kompleksnogo analiza v vuze*, Leningrad, 1984).

The literary aspect of Huxley's art, not unnaturally, became the subject of far more numerous theses and studies, among them L.D. Rebicova, *Aldous Huxley's Early Novels*, Leningrad, 1986; N.K. Il'ina, *Aldous Huxley and the English Short Story of the 1920s*, Leningrad, 1987; V.S. Rabinovich, *The Moral and the Aesthetic Quest of Aldous Huxley (1920s–1930s)*, Moscow, 1992. In each case, these dissertations were followed by articles illustrative of their central ideas.

These examples show that towards the end of the 1980s there was a great upsurge of interest in Huxley's books in Russia, a veritable Huxley revival. This is confirmed by a striking number of papers on his life and work: M. Kazantsev, "A Comparative Analysis of *Brave New World*, by Huxley, and E. Zamyatin's *We*" (*Aktual'nye problemy filosofii*, Sverdlovsk, 1989); U. Kagarlitskii, "Wells, Darwin, Huxley" (*Nauchnaya fantastica*, vyp. 15, 1989); A.V. Tolkacheva and L.D. Bogdetskaya, "Reminiscences from Shakespeare in the Works of Aldous Huxley" (*Shekspir i mirovaya literatura*, Bishkek, 1993). This list by no means exhausts the studies dedicated to Huxley in the later 1980s and the 1990s. It seems as if the Russian people feel that they had been too long from knowledge and truth and can at long last discuss what for years and years had been forbidden fruit.

More important still than special studies intended for a more or less narrow range of readers, there came a perfect downpour of new translations of Huxley's works. Starved readers seemed ready for anything. Along with a new version of the previously translated *Point Counter Point* (published in Leningrad in 1990, together with some of Huxley's short stories), new materials were made available. *Brave New World*, of which only four chapters had previously been available, now appeared in a complete edition that was immediately reproduced by eager publishers. After it was enjoyed by the readers of Number 4 of *Inostrannaya Literatura* for 1988, there were at least six editions in many thousands of copies (1989, 1990, 1991). As often as not, *Brave New World* was offered in company with other anti—utopias—those of Wells, Orwell, Zamyatin, and once with Huxley's own *Ape and Essence*, (as in the Moscow "Progress" edition of 1990). *Ape and Essence* was also published in the magazine *Aurora* (Numbers 3 and 4 for 1991).

After Many a Summer Dies the Swan and *The Genius and the Goddess*—which had been charged, along with *Ape and Essence*, with stimulating the bleakest pessimism and hatred of man against man—were similarly translated and repeatedly published in the 1990s. They were taken up by *Inostrannaya Literatura* (Number 5 for 1991 and Number 4 for 1993) and by the Moscow Progress publishers (1994) and introduced by A. Shishkin. A Russian translation of *Island* was published in Kiev in 1995.

All of these publications were much read and gave rise to many sensitive and well—informed reviews, as, for instance: A.F. Lyubimova, "The Dialectics of the Social and Universal in Huxley's *Brave New World* and Zamyatin's *We*" (*Traditsii i vzaimodeistviya v zarubejnoi literature*, Perm,' 1990); O. Lazarenko, "Those Looking Ahead: On the Antiutopias of Huxley, Orwell, Platonov" (*Pod'em*, 1991, Number 9).

Huxley's short stories had been largely unknown to Russian readers until the mid–1980s. There had been exceptions, of course.[2] "The Claxtons," appeared in Number 1 of the magazine *Literaturnyi Sovremenik* as early as 1936; "Half–Holiday" had made up part of a reader intended for foreign trade workers in 1941 (Moscow), while "The Fairy Godmother" had been included in a collection of English short stories (*Angliiskaya Novella*) published in Leningrad in 1961.

The first fairly representative selection of Huxley's stories was published and introduced by this writer in 1985 (*Oldos Haksli: Novelli*, Leningrad, 1985). After that, short stories repeatedly appeared as addenda to novels (for instance, to the *Point Counter Point* translation of 1990) and in other publications, sometimes most unexpected ones. To give but one example, "The Portrait" saw the light in a collection entitled *Agatha Christie and* ..., published in 1990 by the Moscow Headquarters of the International Association of Detectives (*Moskovskaya Shtabkvartira Mezhdunarodnoi Assotsiatsii Detectivov*) and in 1992 in a perfectly serious, academic edition under the heading *Art and Artists in Foreign Twentieth Century Short Stories* (*Iskustvo i Khudozhnik v Zarubezhnoi Novelle XX veka*, St. Petersburg). The story of Gioconda's fatal smile appeared in at least five or six different selections, ranging from those that go in for detective stories to those that concentrate on legal problems (*Sovetskaya Yustitsia*, Moscow, 1993).

I regret to say that less attention has been paid to what seems Huxley's supreme art—his art as an essayist. No collection of his essays has found its way to Russian readers, either in English or in Russian; only a few individual essays have become part of various anthologies: "The Jesting Pilate," in *Freedom to Oppress* (*Svoboda ugnetat*,' Moscow, 1986); "Edward Lear," in *Writers of England on Literature* (*Pisateli Anglii o literature XIX–XX vekov*, Moscow, 1981). My suggestion to compile a book of Huxley's choicest essays has not been accepted by Russian publishers. During the past two or three years, Huxley seems to be less popular than previously; new editions appear to be waiting for their time.

This short survey of the evolution of Huxley's reputation in Russia was preceded by a brief and erudite paper published not long ago in one of the leading philological journals of this country, in *Voprosy Literatury* (Number 5, 1995, pp. 211–228). The author is Mikhail Landor, critic and historian. His article is called "Aldous Huxley. Attempting Dialogue with the Soviet Side" (*Popytka ialoga s 'ovetskoi 'toronoi*). Not content with a review of Russian Huxley criticism, Lander has much to say on the writer's attitude toward the Soviet Union and Russian culture. He also points out certain parallels between *Brave New World* and the satirical trends in the works of two fine modern Russian writers, Yirii Olesha and Andrei Platonov. These parallels should become a matter of special studies and are too significant for superficial remarks.

While laying a heavy stress on Huxley's profound lifelong admiration of Russia's great writers, Tolstoy and Dostoyevsky, Landor makes it quite clear that he was constant in his interest in the Soviet Union as a country both of high artistic achievement and of daring social experiment. If he had any illusions about its nature and success in his early days, he soon did away with them and in *Brave New World* plainly showed what he thought of Soviet socialism. There was a certain rapprochement between Huxley and this country in 1935–1936 in connection with his anti–fascist activities, but it soon passed. He was horrified not only by Stalin's political terror, but also by his later destructive methods in dealing with biology, about which he knew only too well from his brother, Julian. Landor says that shortly before his death, in the period of Khrushchev's liberal thaw, Huxley resumed his interest in Russia and was on the point of traveling there; this was prevented by bureaucratic procedures that made the writer put off his journey until it was too late.

I think that this visit would not have been a success. The time for mutual understanding had not come yet. Huxley had been fiercely rejected by critics who embodied the official opinion. The greater part of his books (practically all those that came after the 1920s, "Brief Candles" being really the last one) were not available even to readers of the best libraries of Leningrad and Moscow, for they were all kept under special control (subordinate to the KGB) and given only to those who proved themselves worthy of political trust.

It was only in the 1970s and 1980s that the complexities of Huxley's art and thought began to be revealed to the public, but the mode of speaking about him remained severely critical. Very few scholars ventured to study the Huxley enigma in context. The rise of his reputation in the 1980s and 1990s, the striking number of publications—both of his works and analytical studies of these works—proved how stimulating his thought was to those who in the last decades of the millennium shook off the control of feeling and intelligence imposed by the former socialist state. In their striving for freedom of thought, these readers were keen to study the workings of an alert mind passionately involved in intellectual quest for moral values, even if that quest, as Huxley himself was well aware, did not prove to be successful and satisfying: his failure to open new vistas to those who for decades were deprived of the sacred right to think for themselves.

The intelligentsia of Russia are sensitive to Huxley's appeal to men of letters and science "to advance together further and further into the ever expanding region of the unknown." These last words of the writer's last complete essay ("Literature and Science," New York and London, 1993) mean a great deal to his Russian audience.

NOTES

1. The political effect of this satire against a totalitarian state, in which even thinking is regulated, was neutralized by its being accompanied by an essay (M. Levidov's) under the formidable heading of "An Orgy of Pessimism," intended to warn the reader against a whole–hearted admiration of Huxley's power as a satirist.

2. "After Many a Summer Dies the Swan" was even translated twice, once by A. Zverev, an outstanding critic and historian of literature. He rendered the title as *And After Many a Spring* (*I posle mnogikh vesen. Moscow, Izdatel'stvo im. Sabashnikovykh*, 1992).

JAMES R. BAKER

Golding and Huxley: The Fables
of Demonic Possession

Surely we have heard enough about William Golding's *Lord of the Flies*. Published in 1954, it rapidly gained popularity in England, then in America, then in translation throughout Europe, Russia, and Asia, until it became one of the most familiar and studied tales of the century. In the 1960s it was rated an instant classic in the literature of disillusionment that grew out of the latest great war, and we felt certain it was the perfect fable (more fable than fiction) that spelled out what had gone wrong in that dark and stormy time and what might devastate our future.

But in the postwar generation a new spirit was rising, a new wind blowing on campus, a new politics forming to oppose the old establishment and its failures. Golding, proclaimed "Lord of the Campus" by *Time* magazine (64) in 1962, was soon found wanting—an antique tragedian, a pessimist, a Christian moralist who would not let us transcend original sin and the disastrous history of the last 50 years. Many "activist" academics came to feel his gloomy allegory was better left to secondary or even primary schools, where a supposedly transparent text (now put down as lacking in intellectual sophistication and contemporary relevance) might serve to exercise apprentice readers. It remained appropriate to read Orwell, *Animal Farm* or *Nineteen Eighty-four*, because he was a political novelist writing in behalf of what he called political freedom, whereas Golding was apolitical

From *Twentieth Century Literature* 46, 3 (Fall 2000) © 2001 by Hofstra University.

and seemingly without faith in political means. The Nobel poet Wislawa Szymborska describes the fashionable attitude, the movement itself, in her "Children of Our Age" (1986):

> We are children of our age,
> it's a political age.
> All day long, all through the night,
> all affairs—yours, ours, theirs—
> are political affairs.
>
> Whether you like it or not,
> your genes have a political past,
> your skin, a political cast,
> your eyes, a political slant.
>
> Whatever you say reverberates,
> whatever you don't say speaks for itself,
> So either way you're talking politics.
>
> Even when you take to the woods,
> you're taking political steps
> on political grounds.
>
> Apolitical poems are also political,
> and above us shines a moon
> no longer purely lunar.
> To be or not to be, that is the question,
> And though it troubles the digestion
> it's a question, as always, of politics.
>
> To acquire a political meaning
> you don't even have to be human,
> Raw material will do,
> or protein feed, or crude oil,
>
> or a conference table whose shape
> was quarreled over for months:
> Should we arbitrate life and death at
> a round table or a square one.

Meanwhile, people perished,
animals died
houses burned,
and the fields ran wild
just as in times immemorial
and less political.   (149–50)

The identity assigned to Golding during these years was not substantially altered by his later work. *The Inheritors* (1955) and *Pincher Martin* (1956), two more fables on the limitations of "rational man," confirmed the prevailing judgment; the later attempts at social comedy, *The Pyramid* (1967) and *The Paper Men* (1984), or the long holiday from contemporary reality in the eighteenth-century sea trilogy, *Rites of Passage* (1980), *Close Quarters* (1987), *Fire Down Below* (1989), failed to efface the original image. He remained the man who wrote *Lord of the Flies*, the man who felt he had to protest his designation as pessimist even in his Nobel speech of 1983 (Nobel Lecture 149–50). Have we been entirely fair? Golding's reputation, like that of any artist, was created not simply by what he wrote or intended but also by the prevailing mentality of his readership, and often a single work will be selected by that readership as characteristic or definitive. Writer and reader conspire to sketch a portrait of the artist that may or may not endure. In "Fable," a 1962 lecture at the University of California at Los Angeles, Golding acknowledged that in *Lord of the Flies* he was acting as fabulist and moralist, as one who might as well say he accepted the theology of original sin and fallen man; and on other occasions during his rise to fame he acknowledged that for a time after the war he read almost exclusively in Greek tragedy and history. Such statements contributed to his identity as philosophical antiquarian and served to condition his reception by critics and millions of readers. Yet something was lost, something important obscured that must be recovered—or discovered—to amend our reading of *Lord of the Flies* (in spite of the attention lavished upon it) and our estimate of Golding's total accomplishment. Most critical judgments on the famous fable are locked into the clichés established soon after its appearance.

In 1962 I began correspondence with Golding in preparation for a book on his work (*William Golding: A Critical Study*). My thesis, foreshadowed in an essay published in 1963 ("Why It's No Go"), was that the structure and spirit of *Lord of the Flies* were modeled on Euripidean tragedy, specifically *The Bacchae*, and that the later novels also borrowed character and structure from the ancient tragedians. Golding's response to the book was positive, kinder than I expected, but it carried a hint I did not immediately understand:

With regard to Greek, you are quite right that I go to that
literature for its profound engagement with first and last things.
But though a few years ago it was true I'd read little but Greek
for twenty years, it's true no longer. The Greek is still there and
I go back to it when I feel like that; now I must get in touch with
the contemporary scene, and not necessarily the literary one; the
scientific one perhaps.

(Baker and Golding, letter 12 August 1965)

Science? What could he mean? *Lord of the Flies* and *The Inheritors*, as many
readers recognized, had displayed a broad knowledge of anthropological
literature. *Pincher Martin*, the third novel, was not such an obvious case, but
it did focus on an arrogant rationalist who repudiated any belief in a god and
claimed for himself the god-like power to create his own world, his own
virtual reality. *Free Fall* (1959) had more obviously employed scientific
metaphor—the state of free fall or freedom from gravitational law—to
describe the moral drift and lawlessness of the narrator, Sammy Mountjoy;
and his mentor, the science teacher Nick Shales, is found in Sammy's
retrospective search for pattern in his life to be an incredibly one-sided and
naive man. And the little comic play, *The Brass Butterfly* (1958), satirized the
ancient Greek scientist Phanocles, a brilliant but dangerously destructive
inventor who specializes in explosive devices. Was Piggy, the precocious
protoscientist of *Lord of the Flies*, first in this series of negative and satirical
portraits? At the urging of his father, a devotee of science, Golding had gone
up to Oxford in 1930 to study science, but after two years he threw it over to
study literature. Some of the student poems written at Oxford, published in
1934, mock the rationalist's faith that order rules our experience, and these
seem to evidence that turning point. Years later he wrote a humorous
autobiographical sketch, "The Ladder and the Tree" (1965), recalling the
conflict that had troubled him as he prepared to enter the university. The
voice of his father joined with Einstein and Sir James Jeans (and no doubt the
authors of all those scientific classics found in the household), while the voice
of Edgar Allan Poe, advocate for darkness and mystery, urged him to choose
the alternative path.

When I interviewed Golding in 1982 I was determined to question
him about this early confrontation with the two cultures. Had there been a
"classic revolt," I asked, against his father's scientific point of view? After
some defense of the father's complexity of mind, the conclusion was clear:
"But I do think that during the formative years I did feel myself to be in a
sort of rationalist atmosphere against which I kicked" (130). I also asked

whether he felt he belonged to the long line of English writers who, especially since Darwin, had taken scientists and the scientific account of things into their own work—a line running from Tennyson and including among others Hardy, Wells, Huxley, Snow, Durrell, and Fowles. And Golding? His reply was oblique, equivocal, and we hurried on to other matters. In 1988 I tried to sum up what had been achieved and what needed to be done:

> We need more work on the role of science in Golding's fiction
> (perhaps beginning with the impact of Poe on the formation of
> his attitudes) and we need to reassess his accomplishment in the
> larger context made up of his contemporaries.
>
> ("William Golding" 11)

No scholar has responded. Since Golding's death in 1993 his work has gone into partial eclipse, as he himself predicted. While we wait for recovery, if it ever comes, we should adjust our accounts. We shall find that much of the fiction was oriented and directly influenced by his knowledge of science and that there is an evolution from the extreme negativism of *Lord of the Flies* toward greater respect for the scientist and scientific inquiry. The much discussed sources for the dark fable lie in Golding's experience of the war, in his connection with Lord Cherwell's research into explosives, in the use of the atomic bombs on Japan, in the postwar revelations of the Holocaust and the horrors of Stalinist Russia—quite enough to bring on the sense of tragic denouement and, as he said in "A Moving Target" (163), "grief, sheer grief" as inspiration, if that is the proper word.

Was there a contemporary literary source or precedent on which he could build his own account of the failure of humanity and the likelihood of atomic apocalypse? There have been a few unfruitful forays into this question. Craig Raine, for example, finds occasional stylistic parallels in Golding with Huxley (*Antic Hay, Eyeless in Gaza*) as well as Dostoyevsky, Henry James, and Kipling but concludes that these or others that might be hunted down are not "real sources" (108) worthy of serious attention. We get more specific guidance from Golding himself. In an address titled "Utopias and Antiutopias" he comes, inevitably, to Aldous Huxley:

> As the war clouds darkened over Europe he and some of our most
> notable poets removed themselves to the new world.... There
> Huxley continued to create what we may call antiutopias and
> utopias with the same gusto, apparently, for both kinds. One

antiutopia is certainly a disgusting job and best forgotten.... Yet I
owe his writings much myself, I've had much enjoyment from
them—in particular release from a certain starry-eyed optimism
which stemmed from the optimistic rationalism of the nineteenth
century. The last utopia he attempted which was technically and
strictly a utopia and ideal state, *Island* (1962), is one for which I
have a considerable liking and respect.   (181)

Huxley arrived in America in 1937, toured part of the country, then wrote
most of *Ends and Means* (1937) at the Frieda Lawrence ranch in New Mexico,
and settled in Los Angeles that fall. He wrote only two books in the genre
Golding discusses before his death in 1963, *Island* and an earlier antiutopia—
undoubtedly the "disgusting job ... best forgotten"—*Ape and Essence* (1948).
Golding's harsh judgment on this book (shared by several reviewers and
critics) may reflect disappointment in a literary idol. Again there is talk of
Huxley in one of the last interviews, "William Golding Talks to John Carey,"
when the interviewer asks about the four novels the apprentice Golding tried
to write. He abandoned all of them (they have never come to light) because
they were merely imitations, "examples of other people's work":

JC. Huxley was one of the influences on the earlier attempts,
wasn't he?

WG. I took him very neat, you know. I was fascinated by him.
And he was, I think superb—but *clever*; it was cleverness raised to
a very high power indeed. Never what Lawrence can sometimes
produce—never that mantic, inspired ... I don't think Huxley was
even inspired; almost too clear-sighted to be inspired.   (189)

Huxley was the near-contemporary (17 years separated them) so much
admired in the early stage of Golding's efforts, and he was quite like
Golding—knowledgeable about science and scientists, yet dedicated to
literature, intent upon spiritual experience and a search for an acceptable
religious faith. Huxley's skeptical views were an update on H. G. Wells and
his rather quaint "scientific humanism," a faith fading in Huxley's mind and
lost to Golding and many of his generation.

   The California years were often difficult for Huxley. After the war
began he was privileged to find himself in the company of one of the most
extraordinary gatherings of intellectuals ever assembled in the United
States—including exiles Mann, Brecht, Stravinsky, Schoenberg, Isherwood,

and Heard, and Americans Faulkner, Fitzgerald, Agee, and West—some of them writing for money at the studios as Huxley was to do. On the negative side, he was attacked by his countrymen for his pacificism, his eyesight failed further, he was often short of money, and the anxious quest for spiritual sustenance drove him constantly. These personal problems were intensified by the events of the war, the ugly alliance of the scientific and military communities, the bombing of Japan, the emergence of the cold war. Inevitably, he was subject to bouts of depression and despair over the behavior of men and nations. David King Dunaway sums up the effect of these burdens: "In the fall of 1946, Aldous Huxley turned a dark corner and found himself in a hallway of desperation; *Ape* was at the end of that long dark corridor" (214). Back in England, Golding had entered upon a similar period of doubt and reorientation; at the end of his trial he would write *Lord of the Flies*.

We have long thought of Huxley as a "novelist of ideas"—and one who rarely effected a perfect marriage of art and idea. Some of the ideas in his mind as he began *Ape and Essence* are found in the long essay *Science, Liberty, and Peace* (1946), but the novel he planned was to be a darker affair altogether, with flashes of grotesque comedy serving only to enhance the power of darkness. Don't take this too seriously, it seems to suggest, but remember that you have already created in reality an obscene disaster which stands as preface to the future described in this fiction. Yet, experienced as he was, Huxley could not find the right narrative voice, so he abandoned the novelistic plan and turned to film scenario, a form in which he had enjoyed some success, notably with *Pride and Prejudice* and *Jane Eyre*. Nevertheless, most of Huxley's critics speak of *Ape and Essence* as a novel and judge it as a novel, ignoring the fact that it is an odd pastiche of scenario, dialogue, narrative, and verse. The scenario is indeed set up or framed by a Huxley-like narrator who recounts the discovery of a film script by an unknown, rejected writer, William Tallis. The setting for this discovery is a studio lot on 30 January 1948—"the day of Gandhi's assassination." Two Hollywood writers walk through the studio lot, one intent upon his own trivial affairs, the more serious narrator meditating upon the newspaper headlines and the fate of the saint in politics. Gandhi's mistake, he thinks, had been to get himself "involved in the sub-human mass-madness of nationalism, in the would-be superhuman, but actually diabolic, institutions of the nation state."[1] Alas, it is only from without "that the saint can cure our regimented insanity... our dream of Order" which always begets tyranny. He speaks to his companion of other martyred saints, some of them rejected candidates for film treatment, all of them participants in this repetitive tragic pattern. The headlines in the morning paper were "parables; the event they recorded, an allegory and a prophecy" (8–9). Here, in the abstract, is the outline for Golding's allegory of the boy saint, Simon, martyr to a "sub-human mass-madness." At this point the narrator stumbles upon the rejected manuscript. After reading it he goes in search of this strange man, Tallis, only to find that he had retreated from the world to the Mojave Desert, where he died six weeks before his scenario was rescued from the studio trash. The narrator decides to "print the text of 'Ape and Essence' as I found it, without change and without comment" (32).

The author takes his title from Shakespeare's *Measure for Measure* (2.2.118–23):

> But man, proud man,
> Dress'd in a little brief authority,
> Most ignorant of what he's most assur'd—
> His glassy essence—like an angry ape
> Plays such fantastic tricks before high heaven
> As makes the angels weep.

His method is to employ an omniscient narrator who introduces the dramatic scenes and follows them with moralizing or sardonic commentary. The setting is a ruined city, Los Angeles in the year 2108.[2] How did the city fall? We are given flash scenes of Einstein and Faraday, representatives of the great men of science we have so revered, enslaved by the ape king and made to serve in an apocalyptic bacteriological and atomic war which ends in "the ultimate and irremediable / Detumescence" (42) of modern civilization. The narrator comments on the ends and means that brought about this great fall:

> Surely it's obvious.
> Doesn't every schoolboy know it?
> Ends are ape-chosen; only the means are man's.
> Papio's[3] procurer, bursar to baboons,
> Reason comes running, eager to ratify;
> Comes, a catch-fart, with Philosophy,
>   truckling to tyrants;
> Comes, a Pimp for Prussia, with Hegel's
>   Patent History;
> Comes with Medicine to administer the
>   Ape-king's aphrodisiac;

Comes, with rhyming and with Rhetoric,
    to write his orations;
Comes with the Calculus to aim his rockets
Accurately at the orphanage across the ocean;
Comes, having aimed, with incense to impetrate
Our Lady devoutly for a direct hit.[4] (45)

Soulless reason provides a means to serve animal lusts, especially the lust for power; thus the man becomes the ape, the "beast."

In Golding's island society the man of reason, the scientist, is represented in the sickly, myopic child Piggy, the butt of schoolboy gibes, but unfortunately many readers and most critics have failed to understand his limitations and thus his function in the allegory. This may be explained, in part, by the uncritical adoration of the scientist in our society, but another factor is the misunderstanding found in the prestige introduction by E. M. Forster in the first American edition of *Lord of the Flies* and subsequently held before our eyes for 40 years. We are asked to "Meet three boys," Ralph, Jack, and Piggy. We do not meet Simon at all. Piggy is Forster's hero, he is "the brains of the party," "the wisdom of the heart," "the human spirit," and as for the author, "he is on the side of Piggy." In a final bit of advice we are admonished: "At the present moment (if I may speak personally) it is respect for Piggy that is most needed. I do not find it in our leaders" (ix–xii). Actually, rightly understood, Piggy is respected all too much by our leaders, for he provides the means whereby they wield and extend their powers. Jack must steal Piggy's glasses to gain the power of fire. Forster, of course, was the arch-humanist of his day and apparently a subscriber to the "scientific humanism" Golding wished to demean. Contrast Golding's remarks to Jack Biles, a friendly interviewer: "Piggy isn't wise. Piggy is short-sighted. He is rationalist. My great curse, you understand, rationalism—and, well he's that. He's naive, short-sighted and rationalist, like most scientists." Scientific advance, he continues, is useful, yet

it doesn't touch the human problem. Piggy never gets anywhere near coping with anything on that island. He dismisses the beast ... says there aren't such things as ghosts, not understanding that the whole of society is riddled with ghosts.... Piggy understands society less than almost anyone there at all.

Finally, Piggy is dismissed as a type, a clownish caricature who "ought to wear a white coat ... ending up at Los Alamos" (12–14). He is the soulless child who adores the science that blew up the cities and obliterated the technological society he idealizes.

Putting Forster aside, we have in Golding's Jack, the lusty hunter who instinctively pursues power, a diminutive version of Huxley's ape. In the silence of the forest Jack hunts but is momentarily frightened by the cry of a bird, "and for a minute became less a hunter than a furtive thing, ape-like among the trees" (62). He meets his adult counterpart when the boys find the dead airman on the mountaintop: "Before them, something like a great ape was sitting asleep with its head between its knees" (152). And, in his hour of triumph, he looks down from his castle rock on the defeated Ralph and Piggy: "Power lay in the brown swell of his forearms: authority sat on his shoulder and chattered in his ear like an ape" (185).

On a bright day in Huxley's February 2108, a sailing ship, the *Canterbury*, flying the flag of New Zealand and carrying the men and women of the "Re-discovery Expedition to North America," approaches the coastline near the ruined city of Los Angeles. New Zealand has been spared, and now radiation has diminished enough to allow this shipload of scientists of all kinds to explore the remains of civilization. It is a ship of fools rediscovering America from the west, and the biggest fool aboard is our antihero, "Dr. Alfred Poole, D.Sc." Poole is a parody figure of a man entirely removed from his bodily functions and his very soul, but he is the man to watch because Huxley (unlike Golding) builds into his dismal story a parable of redemption. But there is no redemption awaiting the city of fallen men and women. These survivors are deformed, regressive, bestial, and held in check by a repressive dictatorship that combines the authority of church and state. The gamma rays have effected a reversal or devolution in which humans, like the beasts, mate only in season and are incapable of enduring love. Dr. Poole is taken prisoner by these decadent Angelenos. Throughout his scenario, the narrator (Tallis) juxtaposes lyrical description of the sublimity of nature—the dawn, the sunset, the stars, each an "emblem of eternity"—with scenes from the fallen "City of the Angels," now only a "ghost town," a mass of "ruins in a wasteland" (62) inhabited by a desperate and savage race. This second discovery of America is black irony in which we see the ruination of a "promised land," the paradise given at the outset to the bold pioneers. One recalls the tropical enchantments given to Golding's castaways and the burning island "discovered" by the naive naval captain who is incapable of rescuing the ragged survivors. The two fictional societies have much in common, and even the history leading to their downfall is strikingly similar: parliaments fail, a third world war devastates the earth, and a new religion forms to recognize and honor the seemingly mysterious power manifested in this sequence.

The religion in Huxley's fable emerges with what its followers call "the Thing." This is not simply a reference to the bioatomic catastrophe but also to the psychopolitical dialectics that led to violent climax and apocalypse. The Chief, a rude master of the work crews that dig the graves of Hollywood Cemetery in search of manufactured goods, explains to his prisoner, Dr. Poole: "*The* Thing. You know—when He took over.... He won the battle and took possession of everybody. That was when they did all this" (71). There's no need to struggle for recognition here, since the future will resurrect a familiar idol known generically as the devil, though it is capable of assuming an interesting variety of forms. In a catechism offered by a "Satanic Science Practitioner" the children respond:

> "Belial has perverted and corrupted us in all the parts of our being. Therefore, we are, merely on account of that corruption, deservedly condemned by Belial."
>
> Their teacher nods approvingly.
>
> "Such," he squeaks unctuously, "is the inscrutable justice of the Lord of Flies." (94–95)

As the lessons continue we learn that woman is the "vessel of the Unholy Spirit," the source of deformities and therefore "the enemy of the race" (98). Annually, on Belial Day, mothers are publicly humiliated, punished, and their deformed babies killed. The purpose of this blood sacrifice is, of course, a vain attempt to purify the race, but more broadly the catechism reveals, "The chief end of man is to propitiate Belial, depreciate His enmity, and avoid destruction as long as possible" (93). Similarly, the little Christian boys on Golding's island bow down before a ubiquitous fear and soon spontaneously invent a blood ritual to purge this fear ("*Kill the beast! Cut his throat! Spill his blood!*" [187]) and a rite of propitiation to ensure their survival. The pig's head on the stick becomes a "gift" for the beast and an idol, an incarnation of ancient Beelzebub, Lord of Flies. Like Huxley's devotees they invert and parody the lost and more hopeful religion given to them by a forgotten savior.

On the day of propitiation in 2108 crowds mass in the Los Angeles Coliseum and we witness "the groundless faith, the sub-human excitement, the collective insanity which are the products of ceremonial religion" (108) as the ritual unfolds and chanting is heard from a great altar. The chorus mourns that all have fallen "Into the hands of living Evil, the Enemy of Man":

Semichorus I
Of the rebel against the Order of Things

Semichorus II
And we have conspired with him against ourselves

Semichorus I
Of the great Blowfly who is the Lord of Flies
Crawling in the heart ... (109)

The chorus curses woman, the mother, as "breeder of all deformities who is driven by the Blowfly," goaded "Like the soiled fitchew / Like the sow in her season" (112–13).

We know now that *Lord of the Flies* was not the title of the manuscript of a novel Golding sent to Faber in 1953. In a charming essay, Charles Monteith, who became editor of the manuscript, recalls the brief note attached: "I send you the typescript of my novel *Strangers from Within* which might be defined as an allegorical interpretation of a stock situation. I hope you will feel able to publish it" (57). Reader judgments were largely negative, much revision was demanded, the title was rejected, and a new one—*Lord of the Flies*—suggested by another editor at Faber. Golding readily agreed, as well he might have, for it was quite appropriate to give his devil a familiar name (Beelzebub, the fly lord, was present in the "buzz" of conflicting voices at the parliaments on the platform rock), and his theme of submission to evil remained intact. The original title, nevertheless, was no doubt deliberately chosen to reflect something built into the narrative progression—the gradual effacement of sane and civil behavior and the emergence of an alien power in the consciousness of the boys. The theme of demonic possession was most vital to Golding's purpose, and again it demonstrates the bond with Huxley.[5] When the Arch-Vicar delivers his talk on world history for Poole (all the while munching pig's trotters) he comes to a clear statement of his thesis on the downfall of civilization:

> [A]t a certain epoch, the overwhelming majority of human beings accepted beliefs and adopted courses of action that could not possibly result in anything but universal suffering, general degradation and wholesale destruction. The only plausible explanation is that they were inspired or possessed by an alien consciousness, a consciousness that willed their undoing and willed it more strongly than they were able to will their own happiness and survival.   (128)

This "alien consciousness" signifies the presence of Belial and the defeat of "the Other" (god) in the minds of human beings. It is a form of psychological regression that brings the ape, the beast, into power. In Golding's manuscript metaphor, consciousness is invaded by "strangers from within."

In both fables of possession we see how ritual motion and corybantic chanting bring about the psychological birth of the aliens. Huxley captures this perfectly in the antiphonal chant of the priests on Belial Day hailing that brief period in which mating is spontaneous and allowed:

Semichorus I
This is the time,

Semichorus II
For Belial is in your blood,

Semichorus I
Time for the birth in you

Semichorus II
Of the Others, the Aliens

Semichorus I
Of Itch, of Tetter

Semichorus II
Of tumid worm.

Semichorus I
This is the time,

Semichorus II
For Belial hates you,

Semichorus I
Time for the soul's death

Semichorus II
For the Person to perish

Semichorus I
Sentenced by craving,

Semichorus II
And pleasure is the hangman;

Semichorus I
Time for the Enemy's

Semichorus II
Total triumph,

Semichorus I
For the Baboon to be master,

Semichorus II
That monsters may be begotten.

Semichorus I
Not your will, but His

Semichorus II
That you may all be lost forever.   (142–44)

As individuals fall victim to collective hysteria, to possession, so too, the Arch-Vicar insists, do nations, entire civilizations. In his sketch of modern history (116–33), however, he offers some forceful arguments that go beyond theological platitude. He cites the failure of nations to curb population growth or to arrest environmental degradation (failures that would have resulted in world apocalypse even without "the Thing"), yet these and other negative policies were driven by the politics of "Progress and Nationalism" (125). The overarching myth of the age was "the theory that Utopia lies just ahead and that, since ideal ends justify the most abominable means" (125), ethical restraints collapse; in the scientific-technological society now defunct the "means" were extended beyond any power known to previous ages, the power to destroy the earth.

The growth of Alfred Poole, D.Sc. (known to his students and colleagues as "Stagnant Poole") to full manhood is the dubious subtext of Huxley's grim fantasy. Golding's harsh judgment on *Ape and Essence* in 1977 may be aimed primarily at this comedy of redemption. Young Alfred's psychological development has been stunted by a devoted and vampiric mother. It is tempting to compare this mother with Piggy's "auntie" and the life of self-indulgence she allowed, the diet of sweets and scientific fantasy. Poole is 38 when he arrives with the expedition in the company of a tweedy virgin, Miss Ethel Hook, "one of those amazingly efficient and intensely English girls" (57) who hopes to marry this incomplete man. His redemption begins when he is temporarily buried alive by the Chief's crew of grave robbers and then, on the promise that he can help to produce more food, allowed to live; after all, he is an expert botanist. This symbolic resurrection is immediately followed by a liberating first-time drunken episode in the company of Loola—an 18-year old girl who is blessed with an irresistible dimpled smile and burdened with an extra pair of nipples—who soon becomes the lover of this clownish scientist. Love touches his heart and the affective part of the man blossoms. The scenes with Loola provide incongruous low comedy or Hollywood romance (love among the ruins) in a story inspired by dismay for mankind. The love motif conflicts with the disaster scenario so that, in contrast, Golding appears wise to bar girls from boarding the plane that crashes on his coral island.

The third element of the man—his "glassy essence"—must be drawn from his depths to complete the classic triad of head, heart, and soul. It begins when Poole rescues "a charming little duodecimo Shelley" (91) from a pile of books used to fire the communal bread ovens. Here is the serious philosophical element in Poole's progress: glimpses into Shelley's *Epipsychidion* and *Adonais* furnish an inspired argument for the existence of a soul and a transcendent spiritual reality. Thus the admirably atheistic poet rationalized ubiquitous love incarnated in a multiplicity of female forms and immortalized fellow poet John Keats as an incarnation of the very spirit of beauty. As Poole flees the broken city (and the Arch-Vicar's invitation to eunuchhood) he is assured by lines from *Prometheus Unbound* (1: 152–58) which the narrator interprets:

> Love, Joy and Peace—these are the fruits of the spirit that is your essence and the essence of the world. But the fruits of the apeind, the fruits of the monkey's presumption and revolt are hate and unceasing restlessness and a chronic misery tempered only by frenzies more horrible than itself.   (190)

Poole and Loola flee down into the Mojave as they journey to Fresno, there to join the minority community of Hots who are capable of enduring love and monogamy. In an incredible coincidence they camp at the site of William Tallis's grave. His monument reveals all that the lovers know of this man—that he died in profound grief for the world—but Poole cracks a (symbolic) hard-boiled egg over the grave before the lovers travel on to their new life. The infantile rationalist, who might have served out a destructive career *in nominee Babuini*, has been made whole.

In his last years Huxley came to a happier and more balanced view about the relation of science to the larger culture. His *Literature and Science*, published just before his death, is far more useful to writers on either side of that continuing debate than the heated exchanges of Snow and Leavis in the late 1950s and early 60s, and he avoids the overoptimistic prediction or projection of a "unity of knowledge" found in Edward O. Wilson's *Consilience* (1998). Though Huxley was mentor and guide for many of the ideas and devices that went into Golding's allegory, *Lord of the Flies* offers no real hope for redemption.[6] Golding kills off the only saint available (as history obliges him to do) and demonstrates the inadequacy of a decent leader (Ralph) who is at once too innocent and ignorant of the human heart to save the day from darkness. In later years Golding struggled toward a view in which science and the humanities might be linked in useful partnership, and he tried to believe, as Huxley surely did, that the visible world and its laws were the facade of a spiritual realm. He realized something of this effort in the moral thermodynamics of *Darkness Visible* (1974) and again, somewhat obscurely, in the posthumous novel *The Double Tongue* (1995). His Nobel speech asserts that the bridge between the visible and invisible worlds, one he failed to find in the earlier *Free Fall*, does in fact exist. Thus both novelists recovered to some degree from the trauma of disillusionment with scientific humanism suffered during the war, and both aspired to hope that humanity would somehow evolve beyond the old tragic flaws that assured the rebirth of the devil in every generation.

NOTES

1. Long before Gandhi's death Huxley had come to a "dismal conclusion" on those who attempt to mix politics and religion. See his letter to Kingsley Martin, 30 July 1939:

> So long as the majority of human beings choose to live like *homme moyen sensuel*, in an "unregenerate" state, society at large cannot do anything except stagger along from catastrophe to catastrophe. Religious people who think they can go into politics and transform the world always end by going into politics and being transformed by the world. (E.g. the Jesuits, Père Joseph, the Oxford Group.) Religion can have no politics except the

creation of small-scale societies of chosen individuals outside and on the margin of the essentially unviable large-scale societies, whose nature dooms them to self-frustration and suicide. (*Letters* 443–44)

2. Los Angeles has been destroyed in literature and film by every means imaginable. An enumeration and discussion appears in Davis, notably chapter 6, "The Literary Destruction of Los Angeles," in which he names *Ape and Essence* "the first and greatest of the many 'survivor's tales' situated in Southern California" (345).

3. The genus Papio: large African and Asian primates, including baboons.

4. Huxley quotes some of these lines in his *Literature and Science*, noting that they are still relevant in the ongoing "civil war" between reason and unreason (56–57).

5. Both novelists concluded that the late war demonstrated a psychological state that could legitimately be termed possession. See Huxley's theory in his letter to John Middleton Murry, 19 June 1946 (*Letters* 546–47). The depth of his interest in the subject is evidenced not only in *Ape and Essence* but in his study of a real case of sexual hysteria or possession in a seventeenth-century French nunnery, *The Devils of Loudon* (1952). Golding pursues the matter in *The Inheritors* and again in a contemporary setting in *Darkness Visible*.

6. In a letter to his brother, Sir Julian Huxley, 9 June 1952, Huxley counters the idea that there can be no redemption for fallen man:

> Everything seems to point to the fact that, as one goes down through the subliminal, one passes through a layer (with which psychologists commonly deal) predominantly evil and making for evil—a layer of "Original Sin," if one likes to call it so—into a deeper layer of "Original Virtue," which is one of peace, illumination, and insight, which seems to be on the fringes of Pure Ego or Atman.   (*Letters* 635–36)

Works Cited

Baker, James R., ed. *Critical Essays on William Golding*. Boston: Hall, 1988.

———. "Interview with William Golding." *Twentieth Century Literature* 28 (1982): 130–70.

———. "Why It's No Go: A Study of William Golding's *Lord of the Flies*. *Arizona Quarterly* 19 (1963): 393–405.

———. *William Golding: A Critical Study*. New York: St. Martin's, 1965.

———. "William Golding: Two Decades of Criticism." *Critical Essays* 1–11.

Baker, James R., and William Golding. Correspondence 1962–1993. Harry Ransom Humanities Research Center. University of Texas at Austin.

Biles, Jack I. *Talk: Conversations with William Golding*. New York: Harcourt, 1970.

Carey, John, ed. *William Golding: The Man and His Books*. London: Faber, 1986.

———. "William Golding Talks to John Carey." 1965. *William Golding: The Man and His Books* 171–89.

Davis, Mike. *Ecology of Fear: Los Angeles and the Imagination of Disaster*. New York: Holt, 1998.

Dunaway, David King. *Huxley in Hollywood*. New York: Harper, 1989.

Forster, E. M. Introduction. *Lord of the Flies*. New York: Coward, 1962. ix–xiii.

Golding, William. "Fable." 1962. *The Hot Gates* 85–101.

———. *The Hot Gates*. London: Faber, 1965.

———. "The Ladder and the Tree." *The Hot Gates* 166–75.

———. *Lord of the Flies*. London: Faber, 1954.

———. "A Moving Target." *A Moving Target* 154–70.

———. *A Moving Target*. New York: Farrar, 1982.

———. Nobel Lecture. 1983. Baker, *Critical Essays* 149–57.

———. *Poems*. London: Macmillan, 1934.

———. "Utopias and Antiutopias." 1977. *A Moving Target* 171–84.

Huxley, Aldous. *Ape and Essence*. 1948. Chicago: Dee, 1992.

———. *Letters of Aldous Huxley*. Ed. Grover Smith. London: Chatto, 1969.

———. *Literature and Science*. New York: Harper, 1963.

Monteith, Charles. "Strangers from Within." Carey, *William Golding: The Man and His Books* 57–63.

Raine, Craig. "Belly Without Blemish: Golding's Sources." Carey, *William Golding: The Man and His Books* 101–09.

Szymborska, Wislawa. *View with a Grain of Sand: Selected Poems*. Trans. Stanislaw

Barabczak and Clare Cavanah. New York: Harcourt, 1995.

Time 22 June 1962.

SANFORD E. MAROVITZ

Aldous Huxley and the Nuclear Age:
Ape and Essence *in Context*

On 10 August 1945, four days before Japan surrendered unconditionally and ended World War Two, Aldous Huxley wrote to Victoria Ocampo, editor of a literary journal in Buenos Aires: "Thank God we are to have peace very soon. But I confess that I find a peace with atomic bombs hanging overhead a rather disquieting prospect. National states armed by science with superhuman military power always remind me of Swift's description of Gulliver being carried up to the roof of the King of Brobdingnag's palace by a gigantic monkey."[1]

In 1948, this early Swiftian allusion would indirectly but significantly reappear in *Ape and Essence*, although Huxley had already begun to develop the idea behind it in *Science, Liberty and Peace*, arguing vigorously against the view of Einstein among others that the destructive power of atomic weapons is so great that men will no longer want to wage war. All men are like delinquent fourteen–year–old boys in their quest for gain and power, he says, and they have always found new measures of defense against new weapons, although "there may be no defence against atomic missiles."[2] However intensely "the nationalistic boy–gangster is frightened of what atomic power may do to him and his world ... he continues to think in terms of gang rivalry and his own supremacy. 'If,' he argues, 'our gang can get its scientists to perfect the rocket and the atom bomb, ... then all that need be done is to

From *Journal of Modern Literature* 17, no. 1, (winter 1992) © 1994 by Temple University.

press a few buttons and bang! the war to end war will be over, and I shall be the boss of the whole planet'" (*SLP*, pp. 37–8). All war departments in technologically advanced nations will operate on this basis, Huxley predicts, designing and building more formidable weapons, experimenting and testing secretly until the buttons are inevitably pushed.

Clearly the awesome power of nuclear arms was at the front of Huxley's mind when he wrote these words, and therefore it was probably to be expected that his concern would find its way into his next work of fiction, which appeared the following year. In *Ape and Essence*, he provides an alternate version of the future, a not–so–brave and ravaged old world, the consequence of a nuclear holocaust. To some extent, this work echoes *Brave New World*, published sixteen years earlier. It includes a preoccupation with sex, a look into the future, witty snatches of dialogue, a perverted form of traditional religious practices, considerable didacticism in expository form, and the presence of an alien figure from outside the dystopian setting. But by virtue of its theme—derived from the then–recent nuclear explosions over Japan—the circumstances of *Ape and Essence* are considerably darker and more caustic than those of *Brave New World*, and its message should have been far more compelling. Ironically, however, whereas the stylistically cheerier *Brave New World* ends grimly with the suicide of John the Savage, the effect of the sardonic grotesquerie in *Ape and Essence* is ameliorated by a conclusion that seems to hold promise for a fleeing couple in love and possibly, by extension, for later generations of post–atomic humanity.

Nevertheless, this slight opening for individual hope, following the scenes of carnal barbarism and social perversion that Huxley vividly paints in quick succession, is much less convincing as a prediction of our future than as a relatively happy ending for the book. Reading *Ape and Essence* in the context of Huxley's other contemporary comments on war, nationalism, totalitarianism, and particularly nuclear armament—no one of which can be discussed meaningfully in his thought without reference to the others—leaves one uncertain over the strength of the author's commitment to addressing seriously the moral questions that the work provokes. His real intention in writing this dramatic piece of fiction is clouded, and it is difficult indeed to determine whether his personal investment in it was chiefly that of the moral philosopher or of the imaginative author. In a broader sense, these ambiguities open to question the extent that Huxley's concern over the possibility of nuclear war affected his thought and writing during the post–war years. That his commitment to peace and disarmament was absolute, one may be sure, but that his principal aim in writing *Ape and Essence* was to convert that commitment into a dire warning to the public—

as it seems to be—is not as clear. Instead, in that novel and especially after it, Huxley showed little inclination to surrender other more intense personal interests to the overriding issue of the Bomb. Unlikely as this may appear, the evidence speaks for itself.

Ape and Essence was received poorly by many readers, even devotees of Huxley's earlier work. Donald Watt generalizes accurately on the critical response when he points out that reviewers "frequently ... recoiled from the horrid forecast of the book, the 'ape,' in many cases without acknowledging its generating idealism, the 'essence,'"[3] that is, as represented by the escaping Loola and Poole, the saving remnant, nourished by the divine light of sustaining love (echoing Shelley's "Epipsychidion" and "Adonais"). Anthony Bower acknowledges the importance of Huxley's implicit message in *Ape and Essence* but regrets the lack of a more serious resolution to the problem than "a blend of Eastern mysticism and Western technology." "Splitting the atom could as well be a cause for optimism as for pessimism: the greater the knowledge of science, the greater the chance of [its] ... leading to the establishment of a sane world order."[4]

But Huxley had already rejected this eventuality as plausible when he wrote a year earlier in *Science, Liberty and Peace* that he believes man in a position of power is more tempted to use it for self–aggrandizement than to conform with political agreements meant to restrain him. Consequently, he asserts that atomic energy is and will be for the foreseeable future "politically and humanly speaking, in the highest degree undesirable" (*SLP*, p. 62). Moreover, in *Ape and Essence* itself, the narrator specifically states that the birth of badly deformed babies "could as well be the product of atomic industry as of atomic war."[5] Emphasizing the importance of environmental conservation to overcome world hunger, Huxley wrote to Fairfield Osborn (author of *Our Plundered Planet* [1948]) earlier in the year, "while mankind could do very well without atomic energy, it cannot dispense with bread" (*Letters*, p. 578; 16 January 1948). Clearly, Huxley was aware of nuclear power as a potential source of peacetime energy soon after the Bombs were dropped, but he did not trust it—and that was long before Three–Mile Island and Chernobyl. The novel opens in Hollywood on the day of Mahatma Gandhi's assassination, and Gandhi's humanitarianism thus implicitly contrasts with the egotism and materialism of life in the film capital. Gandhi was killed, the narrator states, because he was caught up in "the sub–human mass–madness of nationalism" (p. 8), a form of regimented insanity that can be cured only from the periphery, not the center. If one works with the system, he becomes caught up in it, used by it, and later dropped; or he begins to apply its policies in attempting to fulfill his own aims. Gandhi's assassination was a prophetic symbol, a warning to anyone who might advocate a policy other than war to achieve peace (p. 9).

The narrator and a filmscript writer discuss a new film being made of the life of Saint Catherine of Siena; in it, the effect of her church politics are minimized in favor of a love theme because otherwise it would be "[t]oo depressing ... [for t]he public" (p. 12). Because these lines anticipate ironically Huxley's own concession to a similar argument a year later, when *Ape and Essence* was being adapted for stage production, they are more significant than their immediate context in the novel might suggest in helping to determine his original aim. When the producer requested in 1949 that Huxley add "human interest" to the staged version being prepared in France and tone down "the atomic–bomb impression that the play gives" [*Letters*, p. 599], Huxley concurred with minimal reluctance, suggesting that perhaps nuclear holocaust had not originally been his principal concern after all.

The form of *Ape and Essence* is that of a filmscript with narrator. Shortly after the script opens, the idea of the play is stated—in a passage from Shakespeare's *Measure for Measure* (II.ii.117–22):

> But man, proud man,
> Drest in a little brief authority—
> Most ignorant of what he is most assur'd,
> His glassy essence—like an angry ape,
> Plays such fantastic tricks before high heaven
> As make the angels weep. (pp. 34–5)

The play is set in California in February 2108, a little over a century after World War III nearly destroyed the earth. Baboons in human roles, with scientists chained, immolate themselves with atomic missiles that finish off what gas clouds from biological warfare missed, and a Belial–worshipping culture emerges from the ruins. Like the failed civilization that it replaces, this culture is ruled by fear, which, ultimately, the narrator says, "casts out even a man's humanity" (p. 51).

Central in the action of the script is Dr. Alfred Poole, an exploring scientist from New Zealand stranded in California when hordes of barbarians attack; his companions leave him behind in fleeing to their boat. He is captured, and as the barbarians commence to bury him alive for their amusement, the Narrator observes, specifying the role of the media in the moral schizophrenia of contemporary Western society:

Cruelty and compassion come with the chromosomes;
All men are merciful and all are murderers.
Doting on dogs, they build their Dachaus;
Fire whole cities and fondle the orphans;

...

Whom shall we persecute, for whom feel pity?
It is all a matter of the moment's mores,
Of words on wood pulp, of radios roaring ... (p. 75).

Huxley later called this attitude a "schizophrenic breach in our moral sensibility"[6]; we sympathize and suffer over harm to individuals—even animals—but have minimal or no feelings for large–scale destruction of life when it is "distant,... abstract and generalized" (*Human*, p. 84). After being rescued, Poole eventually persuades Loola, a dim–witted but voluptuous young woman, to escape with him to the north, where they can live as human beings rather than as slaves and beasts, but first he observes the policies and practices of the post–nuclear culture in California.

"[E]ven without the atomic bomb," he learns from one of the rulers, "men would have destroyed themselves by destroying the world they lived in" through over–industrialization, overpopulation, disregard for conservation and the environment, and through "Progress and Nationalism" (pp. 123–25). In attempting to conquer nature, their Belial nature conquered them. Huxley had anticipated this idea in *Point Counter Point* twenty years earlier; in that novel, Mark Rampion says, "Christianity made us barbarians of the soul, and now science is making us barbarians of the intellect."[7] Philip Quarles (to some extent Huxley's persona) notes of Rampion that his children "have a passion for machinery.... It's as though the young were absolutely determined to bring the world to an end—mechanize it first into madness, then into sheer murder" (*Point*, p. 437).

These perverted practices are implemented by the Belial culture of *Ape and Essence*: "By purely natural means, using human beings and their science as His instruments, [Belial] created an entirely new race of men, with deformity in their blood, with squalor all around them and ahead, in the future, no prospects but of more squalor, worse deformity and, finally, complete extinction" (pp. 132–33). Allied with nations, churches, and political parties, Poole is told, Belial "used their prejudices. He exploited their ideologies. By the time they'd developed the atomic bomb, he had people back in the state of mind they were in before 900 B.C." (p. 184).

Near the conclusion of the novel, however, Poole is certain that ultimately Belial will lose because he "can never resist the temptation of carrying evil to the limit. And whenever evil is carried to the limit, it always destroys itself. After which the Order of Things comes to the surface again," thus making it possible for individuals to live meaningfully by working in concord with it (pp. 197–98). According to John Atkins, "The point of [*Ape and Essence*] is that we know that we are committing suicide and do nothing to stop it.... Man's only hope [in Huxley's view] is that Belial, or the evil in us, always goes to the limit and defeats itself. And then the Order of Things comes to the surface again—but," Atkins asks, "how much destruction will have taken place in the meantime?"[8]

Huxley's idea of an alternating cycle in time may be traced to his earliest poetry, for example, "The Wheel" and "Mole," both first published in 1916. In "The Wheel," alternation is represented in terms of burning energy and stasis rather than chaos and order, as in *Ape and Essence*:

> Weary of its own turning,
> …
> The Wheel must strain, through agony
> On agony contracting, returning
> Into the core of steel.
> …
> But the yearning atoms, as they grind
> Closer and closer, more and more
> Fiercely together, beget
> A flaming fire upward leaping,
> Billowing out in a burning,
> Passionate, fierce desire to find
> The infinite calm....
> …
> And as it burns and anguishes it quickens,
> Begetting once again the Wheel that yearns—
> Sick with its speed—for the terrible stillness
> Of the adamant core and the steel–hard chain.
> And so once more
> Shall the wheel revolve, till its anguish cease
> In the iron anguish of fixity....[9]

The imagery with which Huxley depicts this alternation is a stunning anticipation of billowing atomic flame generated by the atoms of the wheel as they grind closer and more fiercely together; moreover, it makes instantaneous the transformation between the two extreme conditions of existence, the mythic phoenix already dying at the peak of its fiery life. Sybille Bedford, Huxley's chief biographer, sees this poem, among the others in *The Burning Wheel* (his first collection of poetry, 1916), as "the verse of a young man who—after private tragedy—had to begin life in 1914, and is charged with a sense of the moral and physical suicide of the world."[10] This "charged ... sense" doubtlessly remained with Huxley throughout his life. By the time he drafted *Ape and Essence*, however, his perception of individual limitations in the face of incipient global suicide had diminished his capacity to foster universal moral action through his writing.

The other of these two early poems, "Mole," represents the "old mole–soul" tunneling alone and blindly from ages of oblivion into a brief period of light, then "through the sunset's inmost core," and finally, as Necessity dictates, into further ages of oblivion. Huxley's sense of isolation and foreboding as a young man is apparent. "Mole" was first published in a small literary journal called *The Palatine Review*, which Huxley began with a few schoolmates at Balliol early in 1916 as the war was killing off their friends. A short anonymous preface identifying its purpose seems both to foreshadow the oblivion theme of Huxley's poem and to bridge the gap between the world of chaos and that of the poet. Although later, in *Point Counter Point*, Illidge tells Spandrell, shortly before they kill Webley the reactionary, "You can't compare poetry and politics" (*Point*, p. 467), that first number of *The Palatine Review* shows that one can. "The present catastrophe, some have dreamed," says the editor, referring to the war, "is the last storm of adolescence beyond which humanity will advance with a graver and more secure soul. Yet it is with equal possibility the bloody sunset of our civilisation."[11]

It was not until the late 1920s, however, notably in *Point Counter Point* (1928), that Huxley began taking serious issue in print with the practice of resorting to large–scale violence and war as a means of achieving one's aims. In *Brave New World*, he devised an easy way to avert violence in a controlled but not rigorously policed society through the use of soma, a combined hallucinogen and sedative. It is at once comic and serious in the novel, and Huxley would seek its equivalent for many years thereafter in life to help ordinary people cope effectively with tension over ordinary problems. The occasional inhabitants of the brave new world who cannot be made happy through the use of soma are sent to isolated communities to live more satisfying, more fulfilling lives without endangering the rest of society. In this respect, they are comparable with the Hots in *Ape and Essence*, those post–holocaust Californians who either cannot or refuse to conform to the rigid sexual prohibitions of the other Belial worshipers. Both societies are totalitarian, although a grotesque irony pervades the latter work in that it is allegedly a democracy that is being described; the inhabitants are persistently reminded that they have chosen to serve the state. Of course, if they choose otherwise, they become social heretics, traitors, and they are treated accordingly.

Between *Brave New World* in 1932 and *Ape and Essence* in 1948 occurred the rise and fall of Hitler and the development and dropping of the Atom Bombs. In a Foreword to a new edition (but not a revision) of *Brave New World* in 1946, Huxley refers to both of these atrocities, attributing the first to the "nationalistic radicals [who] had their way,"[12] a point that the Arch–Vicar would develop in *Ape and Essence*. Also in this Foreword he first discusses atomic power in a book, acknowledging its omission in *Brave New World* as "[o]ne vast and obvious failure of foresight [that] is immediately apparent" (p. ix). Late the preceding year, he had written to Anita Loos in response to her questions on making a film from *Brave New World*: "Something about the atom bomb will of course have to be brought in. But the point of the original story must be kept—namely, that the really revolutionary changes will come about from advances in biology and psychology, not from advances in physics" (*Letters*, p. 534; 13 October 1945). In the new Foreword, he explains this and his original lapse by indicating that he was focusing in that novel on the effects of the life sciences rather than the physical sciences because although the latter can have prodigious effect on the way life is lived and even destroy it altogether, genetic engineering, psychological conditioning, and other life sciences can "modify the natural forms and expressions of life itself." "The release of atomic energy makes a great revolution in human history," he states, "but not (unless we blow ourselves to bits and so put an end to history) the final and most searching revolution" (Foreword, p. x). He concludes that unless we reverse our priorities so that we use applied science, "not as the end to which human beings are to be made the means, but as the means to producing a race of free individuals, we have only two alternatives to choose from: either a number of national, militarized totalitarianisms, having as their root the terror of the atomic bomb and as their consequence the destruction of civilization;... or else one supra–national totalitarianism ... [evoked by] technological progress in general and the atomic revolution in particular, and developing ... into the welfare–tyranny of Utopia" (Foreword, p. xiv). To Victoria Ocampo early that same year, he wrote emphasizing this confusion of priorities as he would develop the idea in his forthcoming *Science, Liberty and Peace*; he tells her— in a stylistically clumsy manner uncharacteristic of Huxley—that this book will remind people of simple matters which scientists often "like to forget because it is such enormous fun enquiring into the processes of nature and designing bigger and better gadgets that they do not wish to realize that human beings are being sacrificed to applied science" (*Letters*, p. 541; 28 March 1946).

From the 1930s on, Huxley was increasingly concerned with the relation of hunger to totalitarianism, observing that under–nourishment and over–population inevitably lead nations to the loss of freedom. In his Santa Barbara lectures of 1959 he elaborated upon this point by drawing from Bertrand Russell, whose perceptions of short–range military and political prospects at the time seemed to him "extremely realistic and sensible." Russell had posited three alternatives: human extinction through nuclear warfare, reversion to barbarism through the breakdown of the industrial system, and the creation of "a single world state" through either the victory of one side in a nuclear war or the persistent threat of force (*Human*, pp. 98–100). Huxley dramatized the first two of these alternatives in *Ape and Essence*, in which monstrous births are progressively more pronounced and numerous because of gamma radiation; therefore, the Belial–worshipping dystopia, without the industrial capability, energy, or agriculture to improve or even sustain itself, is doomed to extinction.

Given his concern and fears over nuclear armament as he expressed them in the late 1940s, one might think that Huxley would have emphasized the matter more than he actually did in the years that followed, but, strange to say, he seemed to regard nuclear arms as little more than another facet of the war–making mania among nations. It is true that he called for a ban on nuclear tests in 1959 or perhaps earlier (*Human*, p. 89), and he was endlessly amazed at the American government's suicidal development of more complex and powerful armament systems—all at the cost of applying science to the improvement of physical and social conditions for distressed humanity. In 1952, for example, he described to his brother, Julian, a trip he had recently made to a naval research center about two hundred miles from his home in Los Angeles, an enormous station, rich in scientific paraphernalia of all kinds—and in the midst of a desert wilderness. He wrote: "The whole [is] directed exclusively to the production of bigger and better rockets. It was the most frightening exhibition of scientific and highly organized insanity I have ever seen. One vaguely thought that the human race was determined to destroy itself. After visiting the China Lake Research station, one feels quite certain of it. And the whole world is fairly crawling with physicians in barbed wire compounds working three shifts a day *ad majorem Diaboli gloriam*" (*Letters*, p. 645; 20 May 1952). In the summer of 1962, a little over a year before his death, he wrote to Dr. Humphry Osmond, the psychiatrist who had overseen his mescaline experiments, that a few days earlier he had visited the North American Aviation plant, at which he saw how "fabulously well–organized" is the current armament "insanity." He went there to see "the Apollo moon–shot capsule and the latest plane–to–ground missiles, which can turn at right angles, skim along the ground, shoot perpendicularly up into the air to avoid interception and finally be guided, warhead and all, to whatever orphanage or old people's home may have been selected as the target" (*Letters*, p. 936; 19 August 1962). Reference to the orphanage here echoes a similar usage in *Ape and Essence*, which suggests that although he clearly retained an interest in the folly of the arms race, whatever vital personal investment he had made in combating it was by now more in the memory than in the forefront of his mind.

As an illustration, one may note that although Huxley traveled extensively, he apparently had little interest in seeing first–hand the horrifying effects of the two Atom Bombs in Japan. When he had the chance to return to that country, he wrote to his son, Matthew, from India in November that they would go there "perhaps for a few days" (*Letters*, p. 926; 7 November 1961). In fact, he went only to Tokyo for what evidently amounted to little more than a stopover (Huxley to Humphry Osmond, *Letters*, p. 926; 2 January 1962). The following spring, he lectured to the scientists at Los Alamos, a site which should have held a double significance for him. First, it was roughly the setting of the Malpais savage reservation in *Brave New World*, and second, of course, it was the center of Atom Bomb research in the early 1940s. According to Ronald W. Clark, advances on nuclear arms were still being developed there when Huxley visited.[13] Ironically, in his lecture that day he spoke not about nuclear armament but on "Visionary Experiences." He did go to the laboratories and make notes on the radiation experiments in progress, but he apparently wrote nothing on research for atomic weapons.[14]

Perhaps Huxley had come to terms somehow with the prevailing fear and horror of the Bomb. In a limited way, the interest was there, but the persistent presence of nuclear weapons in contemporary life did not grip his imagination as at first it seemed to have done in the immediate aftermath of Hiroshima and Nagasaki, especially while drafting *Ape and Essence*. Yet, even then, one cannot be entirely sure of his intentions in that novel, didactic and pointed as his message appears to be. His letters of the period create an aura of doubt. For example, early in 1947, as the idea of his novel was germinating, Huxley wrote to Anita Loos that he had in mind a futuristic work "about, among other things, a post–atomic–war society in which the chief effect of the gamma radiations had been to produce a race of men and women who don't make love all the year round, but have a brief mating season. The effect of this on politics, religion, ethics etc [sic] would be something very interesting and amusing to work out" (*Letters*, p. 569; 26 March 1947).

This letter suggests that aberrant sexuality rather than nuclear holocaust was his starting point, an implication that gains strength when he speaks of composing the fiction as something not only "interesting" but "amusing" to work out. After completing the novel by February of the following year, he explained to his correspondent at Harper's, who published it, the source of his title from *Measure for Measure* and speculated over the possible use of illustrations (*Letters*, p. 581; 24 February 1948). Early in 1949, he told Victoria Ocampo that he had already completed a dramatization of *Ape and Essence* which he thought "might be very effective on the stage" (*Letters*, p. 589; 9 January 1949), although he said nothing about what kind of effect he wished to achieve. Later the same year, he wrote in French to Georges Neveux (his wife Maria's brother–in–law, who had translated and adapted for the French stage both *The Diary of Anne Frank* and Huxley's own *The Gioconda Smile*) in response to the producer's request for changes in *Ape and Essence* before staging it in France. The producer, Huxley said,

> wants me at all costs to add scenes "with human interest"—that is, scenes in which Poole and Loola's romance would be treated with much greater unction and other scenes in which the incentives for their elopement would become more "idealistic." In a word, De Leon [the producer] wants me to underscore the "positive" side of the play, to proclaim more clearly its spiritual message etc.... I hesitate to take his advice, for I am finding that a bigger dose of "human interest" could destroy the plausibility of the phantasy as a whole—that in trying too hard to reassure the public, one risks spoiling the play. On the other hand maybe he is right in wishing to mitigate a little what you call the atomic–bomb impression that the play gives. But I believe that this mitigation can be produced by means of judicious cuts and the introduction of the spectacle and music. Tell me very frankly what you think.... Not knowing very well what I've written, I am not attached to it and I can envisage no matter what surgical intervention with complete sang froid [*Letters*, pp. 598–99; 2 June 1949].[15]

insufficiently engaged in existence beyond "their intensely private lives," and like everyone else, he shared this common human predicament.

Huxley's telling observation explains not only why his repeated warnings about the bleak future of civilization went largely unheeded, but it also illuminates, perhaps unexpectedly, at least one reason that the character portraits in his early fiction are so remarkably effective. The idiosyncrasies of his characters usually predominated over whatever serious messages they conveyed through lengthy conversations, monologues, and diaries or journals.[16] When this priority was reversed and theme predominated over eccentricity of character, the fiction flattened out and became too overtly didactic.

This point suggests one source of both the strengths and weaknesses of *Ape and Essence* as fiction. At once comical and horrifying, that novel too effectively undermines through humor Huxley's anti–nuclear warning for it to be accepted with the urgency it demands. Poole and Loola are so amusingly sympathetic that they draw too much attention to themselves and their plight, and the frightfulness of the underlying theme loses its efficacy.[17] Unlike *Brave New World*, which ends tragically as the reader is forced to realize the danger of subordinating individualism to social stability, *Ape and Essence* presents a post–atomic horror show but gratifies the reader with a relatively happy ending in which the naive lead couple is saved. Interesting and amusing, as Huxley originally intended it to be, *Ape and Essence* is not compelling, and in this respect it adumbrates the limited impact of his calls for peace.

NOTES

1. Aldous Huxley, *Letters of Aldous Huxley*, ed. Grover Smith (Chatto & Windus, 1969), p. 532. Hereafter cited parenthetically as *Letters*.

2. Aldous Huxley, *Science, Liberty and Peace* (Chatto & Windus, 1947), p. 36. Hereafter cited parenthetically as *SLP*.

3. Donald Watt, ed., "Introduction," *Aldous Huxley: The Critical Heritage* (Routledge & Kegan Paul, 1975), p. 26.

4. Anthony Bower, review of *Ape and Essence*, in Watt, pp. 369–70.

5. Aldous Huxley, *Ape and Essence* (Harper & Brothers, 1948), p. 101. Further references are to this edition.

6. Aldous Huxley, *The Human Situation: Lectures at Santa Barbara, 1959*, ed. Piero Ferrucci (Harper & Row, 1977), p. 85. Hereafter cited parenthetically as *Human*.

7. Aldous Huxley, *Point Counter Point* (Chatto & Windus, 1928), p. 144. Hereafter cited parenthetically as *Point*.

8. John Atkins, *Aldous Huxley: A Literary Study*, rev. ed. (Orion, 1967), p. xxviii.

9. Aldous Huxley, "The Wheel," *Oxford Poetry: 1916* (B.H. Blackwell, 1916), pp. 32–3. This poem, retitled "The Burning Wheel" and slightly modified in punctuation, opens Huxley's first collection of poetry, under the same title; it was also published by Blackwell in 1916; "Mole," too, appears in this collection, pp. 12–4.

10. Sybille Bedford, *Aldous Huxley: A Biography*, 2 vols. (Chatto & Windus, and William Collins Sons, 1973–74), I, p. 67.

11. Anon. [T. W. Earp, ed. (and Aldous Leonard Huxley?)], "Objects," [Preface to] *Palatine Review*, I (January–February 1916), [p. 3].

12. Aldous Huxley, Foreword [to] *Brave New World* (1946; Harper & Row, 1969), p. xi. Hereafter cited parenthetically as "Foreword."

13. Ronald W. Clark, *The Huxleys* (McGraw–Hill, 1968), p. 357.

14. Laura Archera Huxley, *This Timeless Moment: A Personal View of Aldous Huxley* (Farrar, Straus & Giroux, 1968), p. 200.

15. This is Grover Smith's translation. The play was never produced.

16. For development of this idea in relation to Huxley's caricatures and animal imagery, see Sanford E. Marovitz, "Aldous Huxley's Intellectual Zoo," *Philological Quarterly*, LXVIII (1969), pp. 495–507.

17. See Jerome Meckier, *Aldous Huxley: Satire and Structure* (Chatto & Windus, 1969), pp. 194–95.

KERWIN LEE KLEIN

Westward, Utopia: Robert V. Hine, Aldous Huxley, and the Future of California History

> I met a traveller from an antique land,
> Who said—"Two vast and trunkless legs of stone
> Stand in the desert. Near them, on the sand,
> Half sunk a shattered visage lies, whose frown,
> And wrinkled lip, and sneer of cold command,
> Tell that its sculptor well those passions read
> Which yet survive, stamped on those lifeless things,
> The hand that mocked them, and the heart that fed;
> And on the pedestal, these words appear:
> My name is Ozymandias, King of Kings,
> Look on my works, ye Mighty, and despair!
> Nothing beside remains. Round the decay
> Of that colossal Wreck, boundless and bare
> The lone and level sands stretch far away."
> —Percy Bysshe Shelley, "Ozymandias"

In the early 1940s Aldous Huxley was living with his wife Maria seventy miles outside of Los Angeles in the Mojave Desert, amidst the ruins of a failed socialist utopian colony known as Llano del Rio. Huxley, the English author of *Brave New World* (1932), one of the most famous distopian novels

From *Pacific Historical Review* 70, no. 3 © 2001 by the Pacific Coast Branch, American Historical Association.

of the age, had come to California in 1937 to work as a screen-writer. After a stay in Hollywood, he and his wife purchased property in Llano and moved there for the peace, the air, and the mystical quiet. Their front porch looked out toward the abandoned silo of Llano del Rio. Huxley enjoyed his time in the ghost colony but wasted few tears on its memory.[1]

In a 1956 essay, "Ozymandias, the Desert Utopia that Failed," Huxley consigned Llano to the dustbin of history. Shelley's "hands that mocked" had belonged to a "thousand idealists," and the "heart that fed" had beat within a Marxist lawyer named Job Harriman. In 1910 Harriman came close to being elected the first Socialist mayor of Los Angeles. In 1914 he led several dozen families out into the Mojave Desert, and by 1917 some 900 people resided in the community. They built houses, a motel, and a dairy. They planted orchards and alfalfa fields. Llano had its own schools, library, theaters, and mandolin club. Unfortunately, though, the colony seemed not to have its own supply of water, and a succession of crises—which Huxley attributed to incompetence, corruption, and a shortage of toughminded realism—drove most of the colonists to new locations in Louisiana and the Mojave Llano to arid ruin. Of California's Ozymandias in 1942 Huxley believed that only an abandoned silo and a ruined cow byre remained. From the security of his private property, the English writer gazed at the wreckage of tomorrow. "Except in a purely negative way," concluded Huxley, "the history of Llano is sadly uninstructive."[2]

The ruins of the past had gifted Romantics like Percy Bysshe Shelley with edifying visions. The contemplation of bits of history might serve, as in the case of Ozymandias, as a warning against hubris and of the impermanence of human endeavor. Alternatively, the fragments of history might remind viewers of the incredible depth of the past and its awesome pressure upon the fleeting present. Or the sheer monumentality of yesterday might inspire commitments to future greatness. For Huxley, the debris of Llano worked differently. With something like wonder, he noted the innocence with which a Llano colonist in 1917 had chronicled the colony's apparent success: "Its future is clear." For Huxley, the statement showed how radically different from the present were the worlds revealed by history, for a "clear future," in his judgment, was "a thing of the past." Few glasses were cloudier than the future, whether of Llano, Los Angeles, or the world. The Pacific West might well be the land of "tomorrow and tomorrow and tomorrow," but the Englishman found the ruins of the future singularly lacking in monumental romance.[3]

California has long served as a mystic writing pad for forecasts both delightful and dismal, and any history of utopian thought in the twentieth-century United States must reckon with those bygone futures. The very idea of a history of the future acquired a peculiar popular force in the years following World War II, and California's emergence as an economic and cultural center revitalized the old millenarian notions of the Pacific as the end of a westering History (with a capital H). Socialist utopia; suburban paradise; the thousand years of Christ's reign on earth; apocalypse by fire, earthquake, atom, or insurrection; the depths of entropy; the dustbin of history; a technological millennium; the destination of the death instinct—all of these different visions imprinted California's twentieth century. Each end of history set a different tomorrow beside the Pacific and made the future part of an imaginable material space. In the decade following World War II, historians and commentators like Aldous Huxley imagined the place as an archive of the future. The future lay buried in California's past, but with careful excavation, one could write its history. Would that history be an inspirational or a cautionary tale? The most thoughtful students of futures past offered radically different answers. In California, utopia could either culminate or negate history.

In 1953 a young historian, Robert V. Hine, observed that, during the late nineteenth and early twentieth centuries, California had hosted more utopian colonies than any other state or region in the nation. *California's Utopian Colonies* painted the Pacific edge in tones much sunnier than those used by such critics as Huxley. Hine's sympathy for socialist utopias shone through his prose, and that shimmer was the more remarkable for appearing as it did in the red scares of the early 1950s when California's rulers demanded that faculty and staff at the state's universities sign loyalty oaths. Yet Hine's study, which began as an undergraduate honor's thesis ("I was a closet socialist even then," Hine later recalled) and grew into a dissertation at Yale, found a place in California letters. The dissertation was first published by the Huntington Library in San Marino where Hine had done much of his research, and Hine, the foremost student of utopian movements in California, found a career at the new University of California at Riverside.[4]

Why had California invited futurist communities?

According to Hine, the combination of mild climate and rich farmland helped to make communal life attractive, but the very idea of California as the natural home of social experiment provided the necessary cultural capital. The recurring presence of large numbers of new immigrants and in-migrants provided a demographic base for the building of new communities. Labor tried to do the rest. Many of the more famous places, like Llano del Rio, worked hard to achieve self-sufficiency and demonstrate to a selfish world the benefits of communal life. Others invested more heavily in religious or authoritarian visions, but even the occult inspirations of Katherine Tingley's Theosophical Colony at Point Loma appeared in *California's Utopian Colonies* more as a noble experiment than a marker of cultic weirdness. And Hine, a professional historian, attended closely to the empirical detail that Huxley's essay would miss. In the case of Llano, much of the pressure had come from outside as the forces of reaction, led by the conservative *Los Angeles Times*, harassed Llano in print and in court. The Mojave experiment was a victim of history and not of its own internal logic. Ominously, Llano's fate was widely shared. Of the utopian colonies in California surveyed by Hine, virtually all had failed. Hine did not despair of the secular millennium, however, and he touched gently upon the question of the world-historical significance of California's communal experiments. Such projects had been launched with an eye on destiny, and no account could responsibly skirt the topic, but discussions of the meaning of utopian ventures were risky.

Utopian futures were not common coin in 1953. Certainly the professional historiography of the period did not encourage topical adventures. In Peter Novick's account, during these years the American Historical Association presided over the "disappearance of dissident currents in historiography, and [a] retreat into quietude." Intellectual historian Cushing Strout urged his contemporaries to share in "a common respect for moderate means and non-utopian hopes." At Yale, one of Hine's advisers, George W. Pierson, had tried to warn him off his research project, describing California's utopian colonies as so many "superficial diamonds scattered on the intellectual map of reality." But aside from the common usage of "utopian" as a synonym for "simple-minded," the politics of utopia were also suspect.[5]

The word "utopia" hinted at leftist notions, but radicals themselves treated the word and its enthusiasts with disdain. Karl Marx had worked hard to distinguish historical materialism from utopian socialism; Leninists had made utopians into counter-revolutionary demons, and California's most prominent leftist, Carey McWilliams, had employed "utopian" as a near-synonym for fascist in his *Southern California Country* (1946). Throughout his book, the journalist substituted words like "crackpot," "demagogic," "extremist," "sensational," and "Messianic" for "utopian." Few radicals in postwar California would say nice things about utopianism, let alone claim the name.[6]

On the right, things looked even worse. No capital-C Conservative would appeal to the future, let alone invoke utopianism. The technocrats who founded futurology, still a novelty in 1953, would never claim to be utopians. "Utopian" was seen as a synonym for Stalinism, and California, whatever its heritage of social experiment, was no refuge. The University of California dismissed more than a dozen faculty who refused to sign its loyalty oath, UCLA historian and *Pacific Historical Review* editor John W. Caughey among them. After the Huntington published Hine's dissertation, Jack Tenney's Committee on Un-American Activities wrote the author and demanded a list of utopians. Hine refused. Fortunately, the committee forgot about him. Others did not. Many years later, Michelle Nickerson discovered Hine's name in the files of Los Angeles County Supervisor John Anson Ford. Hine's index card was marked with red construction paper. Still, despite the apparent surveillance, no one actually kicked in Hine's door in the middle of the night. Right, left, center—utopianism was politically suspect, but it was so marginal that neither conservatives nor radicals really took it seriously.[7]

California's Utopian Colonies made few explicit political gestures. Hine did not mention Carey McWilliams nor did he allude to McCarthyism. But the historian did not pretend indifference to the modern scene. He noted Arnold Toynbee's assault on utopian idealism in *A Study of History*. Utopias, the Englishman argued, were never as progressive as they appeared; instead, they attempted to arrest the declension of a society whose "members have lost the expectation of future progress." Utopias were utopian in the literal sense of the word: eutopia, no-place. They negated history through apocalyptic leaps into a timeless past or an eternal future, and "in its tragic climax, futurism expresses itself as Satanism."[8]

Hine suspected that Toynbee drew too much from literary utopias and too little from communal experience. It was true that the classical literary utopias, such as Plato's Republic, struck modern readers as depressingly regimented. But "utopia," like any other concept, changed with time and circumstance. California's utopian colonies showed no evidence of stagnation, and Hine turned Toynbee's idea of history as an ascending spiral of progress to different political ends: "The psychological temper of the utopian constantly beckons to an unseen but real goal: from one more experiment in community life may yet emerge—like a phoenix, momentarily dusted with the disappointments of the past—a resplendent, reformed mankind gathered in the ideal society." For Hine, California's utopian experiments may have been millennial in their intent, but neither their successes nor their failures pointed toward eutopia. Hine did not mention Toynbee's allusions to Satan.[9]

The differences between Robert Hine's phoenix and Aldous Huxley's Ozymandias amounted to more than a simple contrast of sunshine and shadow. Huxley's writings of the 1940s and 1950s created a terrifying philosophical history in which Llano, Lucifer, and the apocalypse swirled round and about. If we are to glimpse the breadth of the chasm separating Hine's and Huxley's histories, we need to risk that whirlwind. Much commentary has described Huxley's California writings as dramatically less stormy than the social satires of his English youth, and his turns toward mysticism, parapsychology, and psychedelia—possibilities emerging during his Llano residence—produced texts quite different from *Brave New World*. But Huxley's California history was something less than pacific. *Ends and Means* (1938), the first of the many books Huxley wrote after his arrival in America, had declared that, "at the present moment of time, the 'historical' is almost unmitigatedly evil. To accept the 'historical' and to work for it is to co-operate with the powers of darkness against the light." Huxley, who, like Hine, struggled with blindness for much of his life, kept his face toward the light.[10]

Southern California gave Huxley the materials for anti-history, and in 1948 the high desert of Llano del Rio grounded his bleak endist satire, *Ape and Essence*. In some ways, the book typified an emerging genre of distopian science fiction that imagined the declension of civil society after nuclear holocaust, but the fame of its author guaranteed the work a degree of critical attention that no pulp paperback could hope to attain.[11] The story's premise is a world ravaged by atomic and biochemical war. New Zealand, spared by its remote location, has mounted a scientific expedition to California. There the explorers find a primitive Satanic theocracy in which human sexuality has degenerated into a seasonal rut, romantic love is illegal, and genetic mutation is managed through ritualized infanticide. The Englishman lovingly detailed a memorable series of end-of-the-world images: The public library mined for "fuel" to run the communal bread ovens ("In goes *The Phenomenology of Spirit*, out comes the cornbread"); the harvesting of cemeteries for clothing and valuables; a grim array of biological disasters; a sadistic class of overlords to abuse the dehumanized masses; legends of a protected haven in the North; and the inevitable Ozymandian Los Angeles.

Huxley's screenplay mixed a conventional boy-meets-girl drama with Satanic metaphysics. The romance was straight Hollywood: One of the New Zealand scientists is captured by the Satanists, but they spare his life because they can use his botanical skills. He and one of the young women fall in love and consummate their relationship inside the "moldering pile" of the Los Angeles museum. But sexual devolution (mating allowed only once per year) and social proscription (monogamists are buried alive) obstruct their pursuit of happiness. In the end, of course, boy gets girl, and the two flee Satanic Los

Angeles for Fresno and the North where a last group of rebels is rumored to enjoy erotic freedom. But Huxley twisted the ending. The lovers surmount the San Gabriel Mountains and descend into the high desert where they stare out across the threatening plain. Will they make it? We don't know. We leave them alone at the foot of a single, enormous Joshua tree staring at the gravestone of "William Tallis," the supposed author of *Ape and Essence*.

A polemic against history accompanied this love story. All of Huxley's books were didactic, and *Ape and Essence* was no exception. Characteristically, and crudely, he used a lengthy harangue by the "Arch-Vicar" of the Satanists to make a philosophical point. History, the Arch-Vicar explains to the terrified scientist, is a Satanic invention. The entire dismal history of westering technology, environmental disaster, and world war originated in the mind of Lucifer. "Progress" and "nationalism," the two key demonic inspirations, had deluded humans into believing that the future was clear, predictable, and destined to be better than the past. Events had shown otherwise. Now the future had arrived, and in the wasted remnants of California, survivors of the final battle scrape a polluted living from the dirt. Nor will ritual redeem the faithful. The masses propitiate Satan not in hope of eternal life or millennial ecstasy, but simply to drag out their miserable declension for as long as He will allow. "I tell you, my dear sir," says the Arch-Vicar, "an undevout historian is mad. The longer you study modern history, the more evidence you find of Belial's Guiding Hand."[12]

Huxley imagined "history" as the "public" sphere of work, politics, progress, and institutions like church and state that never rested from their instrumentalist labors. In his rather old-fashioned view, the private sphere of home and hearth offered refuge from historicity. For the average individual in a free society, the majority of moments could pass in ahistorical bliss. Indeed, all organic processes—sleeping, sex, sickness, death—lay "outside the pale of history." Moreover, immediate or mystical experiences of God, Nature, or Spirit also fell outside of the historical flux, and such moments could be intentionally cultivated. Sex, death, and God constituted the first line of defense against history.[13] The final scene of *Ape and Essence* thus returns us to our starting point in "Ozymandias, the Desert Utopia that Failed." William Tallis's grave is not a bad omen, for it marks the edge of the historical frontier across which the lovers may escape into the many little deaths of a romantic and posthistoric future.

That image of the great Joshua tree shading Tallis's burial seems so carefully visualized that it demands a closer look. Did Huxley imagine the grave his own? His essay on Job Harriman's utopian colony appeared eight years after *Ape and Essence*. Allergies had forced the frail Huxley out of his own beloved Llano refuge, but his account of Mojave socialism fell within the narrative landscape he had once surveyed. If the essay criticized a specific utopian enterprise, it also played off a general suspicion of history, aired Huxley's nostalgia for his lost desert years, and hinted at darker concerns.

"Ozymandias, the Desert Utopia that Failed" wove brief citations from primary documents into its history of the buried future while invoking Huxley's memories and, we may speculate, anticipations of his own approaching end. Two or three miles southeast of the Llano ruins, within easy walking distance of the old Huxley place, lay the socialist cemetery where a single enormous Joshua tree "stands like sentinel on guard over the dead." Huxley ended with a mystical allusion of the kind common in his later writing:

> And suddenly the symbol is essentially the same as what it symbolizes; the monstrous yucca in the desert is at once a botanical specimen and the essential Suchness. What we shall all know, according to the *Bardo Thodol*, at the moment of Death may also be known by casual flashes, transfiguringly, while we inhabit this particular pattern of patterns.

California's Ozymandias served not as a historical monument but as a site for antihistorical inspiration, where the proximity of evil to redemptive flashes of eternity highlighted the boundary between history and its salvific alternatives. In the ruins of Llano lay the opportunity to demonstrate the transcendence of an eternal present over the ephemeral past. O History, where is thy sting? Walt Whitman would have liked this moment, an antique land, the circle circled, and history's metaphors run full course: An Englishman using Asian spirituality to transfigure a historical tomorrow on the edge of the American West.[14]

Aldous Huxley's experiments in meditation, hallucinogens, and such mystical revelations as *The Doors of Perception* (1954) carried him further in his journey toward an antihistorical utopia. But Arnold Toynbee had warned that utopian ventures were less an escape from history than a sign of historical decay. A society that had lost its faith in progress would fling up a reactionary ideal to arrest the decline and hold off the inevitable end. Huxley's own work better matched that description than did the abandoned socialist colony at Llano del Rio. Consider the Fresno haven in *Ape and Essence*, with its handful of survivors circled round bourgeois private life while awaiting their doom. Or think of Huxley's Llano ranch, miles above urban history, a Cold War country estate where master and mistress communed with nature in eternal stasis. Huxley's last novel, *Island* (1962), the only work in which he created a livable utopia, followed history's well-worn path. There, Huxley set his asylum from history west of California's shores, upon an imaginary Asian island, round which the lone and level ocean stretched far and away.[15]

"Westward the course of utopia," Robert V. Hine had entitled the opening chapter of *California's Utopian Colonies*. But if California had been overrun by history's imperial march, what then remained? Sex? Death? God? For Hine, the most authentic bohemian experiments showed historicism at its best, as individuals attempted to transcend their alienation through shared commitments to a communal future. For Huxley, the most authentic avant-garde moments came in the attempt of individuals to transcend history by realizing the present. These antithetical visions framed America's millennial dreams: On one side, a synthesis of history's multifarious times. On the other, the Eternal Now.

Huxley's later writings were one of the intellectual sources of the countercultural revolutions of the 1960s, but the social experimentation of those years gave new life to *California's Utopian Colonies* as well. Spurred by the growing interest in communalism, Yale University Press issued a paperback edition of Hine's monograph in 1966. In 1973 Norton, the trade house, picked up the title. And in 1984 the University of California Press issued a revised edition. Almost a half-century after its first publication, *California's Utopian Colonies* remained in print, still the primary scholarly treatment of its topic. In the early 1970s, Hine traveled California gathering material for the new edition of his classic monograph. Hitchhikers, he would later write, were often the best guides to the new millennial West: "Oh, sure, man, right down this road a piece is Table Mountain, and the turnoff with the red symbol on the left, you know, will take you to Heavenly City."

NOTES

1. For the literature on Aldous Huxley, see Eben E. Bass, *Aldous Huxley, an Annotated Bibliography of Criticism* (New York, 1981). David King Dunaway, *Huxley in Hollywood* (New York, 1989), is the best source on this period in Huxley's life.

2. Aldous Huxley, "Ozymandias, the Desert Utopia that Failed," in *Tomorrow and Tomorrow and Tomorrow and Other Essays* (New York, 1956), 84–85, 99, 100; Dunaway, *Huxley in Hollywood*, 161–168, 180–185, 189–191. Compare Mike Davis, *City of Quartz: Excavating the Future in Los Angeles*,

(New York, 1990), 7–8. For the reception of *Tomorrow and Tomorrow and Tomorrow*, see A. C. Ames, *Chicago Sunday Tribune*, Oct. 14, 1956, p. 2; T. F. Curley, *Commonweal*, 65 (Oct. 19, 1956), 77; n. a., *Kirkus*, 24 (July 1, 1956), 465; Cecily Mackworth, *Manchester Guardian*, Nov. 30, 1956, p. 14; V. S. Pritchett, *New Statesman and Nation*, 54 (Oct. 6, 1956), 428; Denver Lindley, *New York Herald Tribune Book Review*, Nov. 11, 1956, p. 6; J. W. Krutch, *New York Times*, Oct. 14, 1956, p. 12; Robert Bierstedt, *Saturday Review*, 39 (Oct. 6, 1956), 26; and A. J. Ayer, *Spectator*, Nov. 9, 1956, p. 649.

3. Huxley, "Ozymandias, the Desert Utopia that Failed," 85.

4. Robert V. Hine, *California's Utopian Colonies* (1953; Berkeley, 1983); Hine, letter to the author, Dec. 29, 1996. Hine contributed a new preface to the 1983 edition of the book that surveys the literature on Llano and other California utopian colonies. See also Hine, "A California Utopia: 1885–1890," *Huntington Library Quarterly*, 11 (Aug. 1948), 387–405; Hine, "Cult and Occult in California," *Pacific Spectator*, 8 (1954), 196–203; Hine, *Community on the Frontier: Separate But Not Alone* (Norman, Okla., 1980); Hine, *California Utopianism: Contemplations of Eden* (San Francisco, 1984); and Hine, *Second Sight* (Berkeley, 1992).

5. Peter Novick, *That Noble Dream: The "Objectivity Question" and the Historical Profession* (Cambridge, Eng., 1988), 325; Cushing Strout quoted in *ibid.*, 324.

6. Carey McWilliams, *Southern California Country* (1946), reprinted as *Southern California: An Island on the Land* (Santa Barbara, Calif., 1973); Kerwin Lee Klein, *Apocalypse Noir: Carey McWilliams and Posthistoric California* (Berkeley, Series No. 7, 1997), Morrison Library Inaugural Address. Although McWilliams invoked Karl Mannheim's influential *Ideology and Utopia: An Introduction to the Sociology of Knowledge* (1929; New York, 1936), trans. Louis Wirth and Edward Shils, Hine's usage falls much closer to Mannheim's use of "utopian" as an oppositional form.

7. Hine, letter to the author, Dec. 29, 1996; Michelle Nickerson, letter to the author, Oct. 27, 2000.

8. Hine, *California's Utopian Colonies*, 166. Hine quoted from D. C. Somervell's abridgment of volumes 1–6: Arnold J. Toynbee, *A Study of History* (London, 1957), 183, 431. The literature on utopianism is too vast to survey here, but the best introductions remain Ernst Bloch, *Das Prinzip Hoffnung* (3 vols., Frankfurt, Germany, 1959); Frederik L. Polak, *The Image of the Future* (2 vols., 1955; New York, 1961), trans. Elise Boulding; and Frank E. Manuel and Fritzie P. Manuel, *Utopian Thought in the Western World* (Cambridge, Mass., 1979). A growing region of more recent utopian studies concentrates upon gender and sexuality. See Marleen S. Barr, ed., *Future*

Females (Bowling Green, Ohio, 1981); Barr and Nicholas D. Smith, eds., *Women and Utopia* (Lanham, Md., 1983); Ruby Rohrlich and Elaine Baruch, eds., *Women in Search of Utopia* (New York, 1984); Frances Bartkowski, *Feminist Utopias* (Lincoln, Nebr., 1989).

9. Hine, *California's Utopian Colonies*, 178.

10. Aldous Huxley, *Ends and Means* (New York, 1937), 69; Dunaway, *Huxley in Hollywood*, 33–54. On Huxley and history, see Robert S. Baker, *The Dark Historic Page: Social Satire and Historicism in the Novels of Aldous Huxley, 1921–1939* (Madison, Wisc., 1982).

11. Aldous Huxley, *Ape and Essence* (New York, 1948); Dunaway, *Huxley in Hollywood*, 218–237. See the reviews of the book by C. J. Rolo, *Atlantic Monthly*, 182 (Sept. 1948), 102; J. C. Garrett, *Booklist*, 45 (Oct. 15, 1948), 66; Theodore Kalem, *Christian Science Monitor*, Aug. 19, 1948, p. 11; Anne Fremantle, *Commonweal*, 48 (Oct. 8, 1948), 622; n. a., *Kirkus*, 16 (June 15, 1948), 289; Anthony Bower, *Nation*, 167 (Aug. 21, 1948), 210; n. a., *New Republic*, 119 (Aug. 23, 1948), 21; Alfred Kazin, *New York Herald Tribune Weekly Book Review*, Aug. 22, 1948, p. 3; A. S. Morris, *New York Times*, Aug. 22, 1948, p. 5; J. H. Jackson, *San Francisco Chronicle*, Aug. 19, 1948, p. 10; John Woodburn, *Saturday Review of Literature*, 31 (Aug. 21, 1948), 8; n. a., *Time*, 52 (Aug. 23, 1948), 76. See the two different manuscript versions of *Ape and Essence: A Play* in the Aldous Huxley Collection 2009, Box 2, in Special Collections, University Research Library, University of California, Los Angeles. Neither treatment included the "Hollywood" frame. Both featured more extended treatments of the love story. Neither was ever produced.

12. Huxley, *Ape and Essence*, 125–126. See the retrospective assessments of *Ape and Essence* in John Clute, "When the Wheel Stops," *New Statesman and Society*, 6 (Dec. 17, 1993), 61–62; and Mike Davis, *Ecology of Fear: Los Angeles and the Imagination of Disaster* (New York, 1998), 345–346.

13. Huxley, "Variations on a Philosopher," in Huxley, *Tomorrow and Tomorrow and Tomorrow*, 64. Salvation, in Huxley's increasingly mystical view, was possible in the "here and now" through the redemption of time by eternity, and here he could draw upon Christian mysticism: "'Time,' says Meister Eckhart, 'is what keeps the light from reaching us.'" See *ibid.*, 139. See also Baker, *The Dark Historic Page*, 7–8, and Dunaway, *Huxley in Hollywood*, 243–244.

14. Huxley, "Ozymandias, the Desert Utopia that Failed," 101–102.

15. Aldous Huxley, *The Doors of Perception* (New York, 1954); Huxley, *Island* (New York, 1962); Dunaway, *Huxley in Hollywood*, 294–303, 360–366.

DAVID BRADSHAW

The Best of Companions: J. W. N. Sullivan, Aldous Huxley, and the New Physics

On 18 December 1921 Virginia Woolf noted in her diary that the scientific journalist J. W. N. Sullivan was 'too much of the indiarubber faced, mobile lipped, unshaven, uncombed, black, uncompromising, suspicious, powerful man of genius in Hampstead type for my taste'[1] and the following month she reiterated her aversion to the 'too black and hairy and singular' Sullivan in a letter to E. M. Forster.[2] Other inter-war writers, however, responded more favourably to Sullivan. In chapter 28 of W. J. Turner's *The Duchess of Popocatapetl*, for instance, a novel based on the Australian critic's memories of London in the 1920s, the reader is introduced to '[t]hat gay, romantic, brilliant, and lovable Irishman, J. W. N. Sullivan, whose hyperbolical rhapsodies and conjurations on Beethoven, Newton, and Einstein' had so endeared him to the book's twin protagonist, Henry Airbubble. More straightforwardly reverential, the narrator hails Sullivan as 'a man of powerful mind, capable of sharp penetration, rapid co-ordination, and lucid exposition altogether removed from the ordinary ... one of the most lovable, brilliant, and uncomplaining of men, who lived and died with an heroic fortitude that equalled his gusto and love of life.'[3] Turner had first become acquainted with Sullivan in the early 1920s when, as literary editor of the *Daily Herald* between 1920 and 1923, he had employed Sullivan as one of his science correspondents. From then on the two men met regularly for

From *The Review of English Studies* 47, no. 186 (1996) © 1996 by Oxford University Press.

evenings of spirited *bonhomie* in the company of Mark Gertler, Ralph Hodgson, S. S. Koteliansky, John Middleton Murry, James Stephens, and others.[4] Sullivan was also a close friend of Aldous Huxley between the wars, especially in the early 1920s, and a major influence on the development of his thought. To date, however, their relationship, and Sullivan's wider role as an exponent of the new physics of relativity and quantum theory within both the modernist avant-garde and the more traditional recesses of English literary culture, have remained uninvestigated.

Huxley's veneration for Sullivan is evident in the following letter which he sent to his father from Florence on 25 January 1924:

> We have staying with us now a most interesting man, J. W. N. Sullivan (whom I think you have met, by the way, in connection with articles about the Einstein theory for *Cornhill*). He has a very clear, hard and acute intelligence and a very considerable knowledge, not merely on his own subjects—mathematics, physics and astronomy—but on literature and particularly music. A stimulating companion. He was brought up at Maynooth under the Jesuits; they intended him to be a controversial apologist and seeing the bent of his mind trained him on Thomas Aquinas ... But after he had been with them for a year or two they turned him out—though at that time he was still a firm believer—telling him that they could see that with his mind he would inevitably become a sceptic. Which he did—three years later! Fairly acute psychological insight on the part of the reverend fathers—for whose intelligence, indeed, he retains the highest respect.[5]

In the words of Sullivan's son, this biographical sketch 'is all moonshine!'[6] In fact, as Charles Singer revealed in 1938, John William Navin Sullivan (1886–1937) 'had only remote Irish connections' and had been born and brought up in Poplar in the East End of London, 'the only son and eldest of three children of an official of a well known Protestant Mission.'[7]

Why Sullivan should have deceived Huxley in such an extravagant manner is unclear, but the most likely explanation would seem to be that he was sensitive about his unremarkable background and believed that the Maynooth canard would imbue him with some of the social and intellectual glamour which Huxley and other members of his set seemed to possess in abundance. As Sullivan's daughter puts it:

A man whose father could not read or write until he was 18 and who had himself left school aged 14, but had entered social circles which included Bertrand Russell, Lady Ottoline Morrell and Aldous Huxley could not be unaware of the values of the class system ... When he met my mother's family, in their view he was to be 'discouraged at all costs' on the grounds that he was socially unsuitable, or as one of her brothers put it 'impossible.'

In another letter, Mrs Ridley mentions that Sullivan's second wife, Vere Bartrick-Baker,

> was told [the Maynooth] story and ... shortly after JWN's death she wrote to the Principal ... asking for information about the time he was supposed to have been studying there and the Principal responded with some tact that delighted as he would have been to be able to claim JWNS as a former student, there was alas ... The story was completely untrue. Vere was, naturally, very upset and angry.[8]

Sullivan himself offered a less fanciful but hardly less hazy account of his early years in a short autobiographical preface he wrote for the American edition of *But for the Grace of God*, his semi-autobiographical novel of 1932. Sullivan's self-portrait, which in the event was not used by his American publishers, is held by the Harry Ransom Humanities Research Center, University of Texas at Austin (hereafter the HRHRC). It reads as follows:

> As a boy I lived in a sort of perpetual day-dream. My great preoccupations were mathematics and music. I was taught music from a very early age—six or seven, I believe. Mathematics I discovered for myself. I was very shy with strangers and lived a very solitary life. On leaving school I joined a large electrical concern in the technical department. After a time my mathematical bent attracted the attention of the head of the concern, and he very generously paid for me to continue my education at London University. On finishing my course there I went to America. I found life there, in many ways, very agreeable. I liked the people I met—their ease and frankness. But after a time there life seemed to me to lack mental excitement. I came to England for a 'refresher' and then could not bring myself to return to America. Then came the war. It completely

disorganized my life, and at the end of it I took up writing
professionally ...[9]

While it contains no mention of Maynooth, Sullivan's sketch
nevertheless comprises an idiosyncratic blend of lacunae and hyperbole. As
far as this article is concerned, however, the crucial point is not that Sullivan
had a proclivity to gild the truth, but that Huxley was inclined to believe him
and deemed his bogus schooling under the 'reverend fathers' to be entirely
in keeping with Sullivan's quirky and exceptional mind.[10] Having been
mischievously unreceptive to Sullivan's claims for the new physics in the
early 1920s, by the time of Sullivan's visit to Florence in the early months of
1924 Huxley had come to regard his friend as nothing less than a savant.
From one perspective, Huxley's intellectual development can be understood
in terms of his dependence on a sequence of guru figures who provided him
with both inspiration and a framework for his ideas. Preceding D. H.
Lawrence and Gerald Heard, Sullivan fulfilled the role of Huxley's first such
guru when he inducted his friend into the exhilarating *Zeitgeist* of the new
physics during their time together in Italy. Above all, during his stay at
Huxley's house Sullivan impressed on his host the '*entente cordiale*' which, as
a result of the Einsteinian revolution, now existed between physical science
and metaphysical speculation. By examining Huxley's relationship with
Sullivan in detail, it is possible not only to appreciate why Huxley registered
the Einsteinian shift of 'paradigm'[11] so vividly in his *Little Mexican* collection
and *Those Barren Leaves*, but also to understand why mysticism became the
dominant theme of his third novel and why Huxley wrote about scientists
and mathematicians so often and so enthusiastically in the mid-1920s in such
works as *Along the Road*.

Sullivan spent the early part of the First World War working as an
ambulance driver in Serbia before taking up a post under Middleton Murry
at the War Office in June 1917. 'My new job in the Intelligence has been
working me, on an average, from 10 till 10, Saturdays included,' Sullivan
wrote to Grant Richards the following month. '10–7 are the hours, but I
usually have to take some work home.'[12] Within a year Sullivan had become
completely exhausted and Huxley first met him in June 1918 when Sullivan
spent a period of time at Lady Ottoline Morrell's Garsington Manor
recuperating from some kind of nervous breakdown. Murry had written to
Lady Ottoline informing her that his colleague was 'suffering from brain-fag'
and had asked if Sullivan might be allowed to convalesce at her Oxfordshire
home:

It is very necessary that he should take the sick-leave he has in the country. On the other hand he has a wife—a very nice little person—and he can't afford to go.

Would you do Katherine and me, and art, and Sullivan the good turn of letting him live for three weeks in the cottage?... He is, as I have told you, a very good man indeed and a dear friend of mine ...[13]

On 30 June 1918, having returned to his work with Murry, Sullivan wrote to Lady Ottoline:

This is the first occasion since my return to London that I have sufficient leisure to write even a short letter. I see now that the quite special pleasure with which I look back on Garsington is because it gave me an opportunity to live as a live human. Life in London is merely a busy death ... I want to thank you and Mr Morrell for an abiding experience.[14]

In her memoirs Lady Ottoline recalled that after meeting him at Garsington Sullivan 'became a great friend of Aldous.'[15] The following year Murry appointed Sullivan and Huxley assistant and second assistant editor respectively of the *Athenaeum* magazine. Many years later Huxley informed Murry's biographer that Sullivan had been his 'closest associate' on the *Athenaeum*,[16] and it is clear that from now on a warm relationship began to develop between the two men.[17] By October 1919 Huxley was telling Lady Ottoline that he had been 'seeing a lot of funny old Sullivan of late—and liking him very much—he's a most interesting and remarkable creature. We discuss Life with great gusto.'[18]

In a short tribute to Sullivan which appeared after his death on 12 August 1937, *The Times* noted that when Einstein's general theory of relativity 'made a big stir shortly after the War [Sullivan] was one of the few people in England able to penetrate behind the symbols,'[19] and it seems certain that one of the topics which he and Huxley would have discussed with 'great[est] gusto' was the new physics. The general theory of relativity had been developed by Einstein between 1905 and 1915, but it was not until November 1919, when a special joint session of the Royal Society and the Royal Astronomical Society heard 'that the results of the analysis of photographs taken of stars in the vicinity of the sun during a solar eclipse [29 May] had been completed and it strongly supported predictions of Albert Einstein's general theory of relativity,'[20] that both Einstein and relativity received widespread scientific and popular acclaim. The joint meeting took place on 6 November and the following day a report of it appeared in *The Times* under the thunderous headlines:

REVOLUTION IN SCIENCE.

NEW THEORY OF THE UNIVERSE.

NEWTONIAN IDEAS OVERTHROWN.

The Times quoted the President of the Royal Society, Sir Joseph J. Thomson, who told those present at the joint session that they had been privileged to hear 'one of the most momentous, if not the most momentous, pronouncements of human thought.' Thomson was firmly of the view that, as a result of the eclipse observations, 'the Einstein theory must now be reckoned with, and that our conceptions of the fabric of the universe must be fundamentally altered.'[21] Thomson's words were taken up by the newspaper in a leader which proclaimed that 'it is confidently believed by the greatest experts that enough has been done to overthrow the certainty of ages and to require a new philosophy of the universe, a philosophy that will sweep away nearly all that has hitherto been accepted as the axiomatic basis of physical thought.'[22] The next day *The Times* reported that Sir Joseph Larmor, author of *Aether and Matter* (1900), Lucasian Professor of Mathematics at Cambridge and the University's MP, had been 'besieged by inquiries as to whether Newton had been cast down and Cambridge "done in"'[23] and the paper carried something concerning Einstein or his celebrated theory (including, on 28 November, an article by Einstein himself) more or less daily for the rest of the year. But the relativity sensation was not confined to the national press. For the next few years an unremitting banquet of books, pamphlets, papers, and other publications, in which every conceivable aspect of Einstein's theory was explained, discussed, challenged, or lampooned, fed the appetite of an astonished reading public. Phenomenally speaking, Charlie Chaplin was the German-Swiss physicist's only serious rival in the early 1920s.[24]

Following the eclipse revelations, Huxley would have been as aware of the relativity furore as everyone else, but as an editor of the *Athenaeum* and a close 'associate' of Sullivan, he would have been more primed than most for the stirring disclosures of November 1919. In April of that year Katherine Mansfield reported to Virginia Woolf that Murry had discussed 'the theory of relativity with Sullivan'[25] and we can almost take it for granted that Sullivan and Huxley would have addressed the same hot topic on more than one occasion during 1919. Moreover, between 9 May and 6 June 1919 Sullivan had provided the *Athenaeum*'s readers with a series of articles which 'mark an important step in the dissemination of relativity.'[26] Apart from an article on Darwin which appeared in the *Daily Herald*[27] and a review of Havelock's Ellis's *The Philosophy of Conflict* which was published in the *Nation*,[28] Sullivan wrote exclusively for the *Athenaeum* between November 1919 and February 1921 and a great deal of his output dwelt on aspects of relativity.[29] Given the intimacy of their personal and professional relationships, it seems safe to assume that Huxley and Murry would have read most if not all of Sullivan's contributions to the *Athenaeum*. But persuading his literary colleagues that in the wake of relativity, science was in the ascendant and literature in danger of becoming an intellectual sideshow, appears to have proved a much more difficult task than Sullivan might have hoped or expected.

Standing in for Huxley as the *Athenaeum*'s 'Autolycus' on 21 May 1920, Sullivan offered his readers this glimpse of an unnamed yet easily recognizable 'friend':

> 'See life steadily and see it whole' … The last time I heard Matthew Arnold's phrase was from a young and esteemed contemporary with whom I was lunching. He was deploring the 'short-windedness' of modern poets; he thought the time had come for poets to essay 'comprehension.' He mentioned 'the Universe,' and then he quoted Matthew Arnold's phrase. He is a very pleasant and exceptionally intelligent young man. He frankly cannot understand religious people and he finds the scientific mind unsympathetic; he took a good degree at Oxford and is learned in eighteenth-century French literature. Our conversation was interrupted by two men coming to sit at our table and discussing their own affairs rather loudly. They appeared to be cinema actors, and the extraordinary oddity of some of their sentiments caused my friend and myself to exchange whimsical smiles. He made a little gesture of comic despair as we went out: 'Such is life in the great West,' he murmured.[30]

Huxley's antipathy to 'the scientific mind' was part and parcel of his desire as a young man to slough an intellectual inheritance which he found oppressive. Even so, in what may have been in part a retort to Sullivan's remark, Huxley commented in the following month's *London Mercury* that although Chaucer seems 'as much at home among the stars as he is among the birds and beasts and flowers of earth,' 'There are some literary men of to-day who are not merely not ashamed to confess their total ignorance of all facts of a "scientific" order, but even make a boast of it. Chaucer would have regarded such persons with pity and contempt.'[31] While Sullivan no doubt welcomed these sentiments he seems not to have been reassured by them. For the 13 June 1919 issue of the *Athenaeum* (that is, the week following the publication of the last of his quintet of articles heralding the general theory of relativity), Sullivan wrote an article entitled 'Science and Literature' in which he pondered 'the serious possibility that literature has lived its day, that the literary man may come to be regarded with something of the impatience with which one watches the activities of the theologian.' Sullivan went on to note that he could see 'no signs that contemporary writers realise how inadequate their work is to the modern consciousness.'[32]

The publication of *Crome Yellow* in November 1921, in which the relativity uproar is the first target of Huxley's broadscale iconoclasm, must have confirmed Sullivan's worst suspicions about the 'inadequa[cy]' of his literary companions. Although the only explicit reference to relativity occurs in chapter 10 of Huxley's first novel—'Tell me, Mr. Barbecue-Smith,' Priscilla Wimbush intones, '—you know all about science … [t]his Einstein theory. It seems to upset the whole starry universe. It makes me so worried about my horoscopes'—*Crome Yellow*'s opening chapter is a clear satire on the Einstein craze.[33] Sitting in a dusty train compartment *en route* from London to Crome, Denis Stone bemoans the journey's 'two hours cut clean out of his life' (p. 2). In 1920 steam locomotion and the relativity commotion had become inseparably coupled together in the mind of the reading public after Einstein had enlisted the assistance of 'our old friend the railway carriage' in his own book on relativity.[34] By the following year, when Huxley was writing *Crome Yellow*, the train had become relativity's most favoured explanatory vehicle. A comment by Sullivan on encountering two trains in H. Wildon Carr's book on relativity highlights their pervasiveness at this time. 'We knew that something complicated was coming,' Sullivan remarks, 'because we are always meeting these trains in expositions of Relativity.'[35] By involving Denis Stone in speculations which juxtapose the buzz-words 'time' and 'train' and by making him construe space old-fashionedly as a kind of etherial permanent way, Huxley's more alert readers would have recognized *Crome Yellow*'s opening scene as a witty spoof on the advent of relativity.

From another angle, when the eclipse observations confirmed that starlight was indeed bent in its passage through the sun's gravitational field, as Einstein had predicted, Euclidean geometry was spectacularly overthrown. In the 'warped' universe of space-time, it was recognized, parallel lines *would* meet before reaching infinity, and much was made of this phenomenon in the interpretive literature.[36] Consequently, Denis Stone's observation later on in the novel that '[p]arallel straight lines ... meet only at infinity' (p. 30), combined with the sub-Georgian obsolescence of his poetry, accentuates the reader's impression of Crome being not the sanctuary of learning and culture which its architecture and history would merit, but an outlandish and uncivilized backwater.[37] In *Point Counter Point* Huxley uses exactly the same technique to emphasize the arrant pigheadedness of Everard Webley. During an exchange with Edward Tantamount, Webley shrugs his shoulders: '"Dotty old lunatic!" he said to himself, and aloud, "Parallel straight lines never meet, Lord Edward"'.[38]

Having at last disembarked at Camlet station, Denis Stone sets off for Crome on his bicycle. Almost immediately he is

> overcome by the beauty of those deeply embayed combes, scooped in the flanks of the ridge beneath him. Curves, curves: he repeated the word slowly, trying as he did so to find some term in which to give expression to his appreciation. Curves—no, that was inadequate ... What was the word to describe the curves of those little valleys?... *Galbe*. That was a good word; but it was French ... Curves, curves ... (pp. 4–5)

As experienced by Denis Stone, the English countryside is little more than a sublunary province of the vast, 'bent' universe of relativity. By seating his protagonist in a train, having him fret about the relentless march of clock time, and making him muse obsessively on nature's curvilinear form, Huxley may well have disheartened Sullivan, but he could not have chosen a neater ploy to signal *Crome Yellow*'s up-to-the-minute satire. Perhaps it is an indication of how close Sullivan and Huxley were in the early 1920s that, notwithstanding *Crome Yellow*'s irreverent treatment of relativity, the two men remained warm friends. It was also during this period that Huxley gradually began to take on board the philosophical significance of the new physics, if not their technical complexity.[39]

Huxley was not the only literary figure to benefit from Sullivan's expertise. We know, for instance, that Huxley, Conrad Aiken, Sullivan, and T. S. Eliot lunched together at least once in the early 1920s[40] and Michael Whitworth has argued that Sullivan played a key role in the formation of Eliot's understanding of scientific concepts and that these played a more substantial role in Eliot's work than has been acknowledged hitherto.[41] On 13 June 1922 Sullivan published a short critical article on Eliot in *The Times* following 'a most interesting conversation with him about his poetry,'[42] and that August Sullivan gave Ezra Pound 'a lucid explanation of something he says is Einstein' in Paris and told Pound he was writing a book on the scientist.[43] While it is unfortunate that no further details have come to light concerning Sullivan's exchanges with Eliot and Pound, unpublished letters from Sullivan to Middleton Murry in the HRHRC may well suggest the kind of line Sullivan was taking with other literary peers at this time.

On 22 April 1922 Sullivan told Murry that an article he had written on Beethoven for *John O'London's Weekly* and a *TLS* review of Hermann Weyl's *Space-Time-Matter*[44] conveyed 'very thinly, the intellectual aspect of [his] "attitude" to life.' The *John O'London's* piece is a review of H. E. Krehbiel's English language edition of A. W. Thayer's monumental life of Beethoven (New York, 1921). Towards the end of his review Sullivan writes:

> The unearthly serenity that we find in [Beethoven's] late music is the crown of a struggle that faced everything, avoided nothing, and which overcame. We see just what he meant when he reproached Goethe for being moved to tears by music. He jumped up and spoke scornfully. 'Artists are fiery; they do not weep,' said Beethoven. It was the fire, and not the tears, which enabled Beethoven to be triumphant. It is the history of this process which would be the real Life of Beethoven.[45]

Sullivan would eventually publish his own 'history' of Beethoven's spiritual development in 1927, but he had already embarked on a study of the composer in 1922, as he mentions in a long and important postscript to his letter of 22 April:

> The Nation has arrived and I have read your review of Ulysses. I have not yet read the book myself—I have read passages when it was lying about. I am prepared to think the book is a great one— in a way—but I think you are altogether too generous when you say that 'every thought a super-subtle modern can think' is

somewhere in Ulysses.[46] You also said something equivalent about Proust. You know this is a mere *façon de parler*. The chief reason why present literature is so little important is precisely because the most important thoughts, carrying the most tremendous implications, are *not* represented in literature. There have been two streams of thought; one has now broadened out into a mighty river and all the intellectual life of the future will be carried on it; the other, the 'super-subtle modern' business, is nothing whatever but a back water *now*. You have not realized this because you have not yet seen that *the sceptre has changed hands*. Old Bernard Shaw, in his Preface to *Back to Methuselah*, unspeakably crude and narrow as he is, is essentially more up-to-date than any of you. This is enormously important, my dear old man. The way to a life of unprecedented vigour and range has now been glimpsed. The fact that it is based on science gives it its strength. Science is its basis, but it is co-extensive with the whole of what men can think and feel. And you have had glimpses of something of the kind—but I suppose they have all been separate sparks as yet. The thing has come to me in a much more complete way (I am only at the beginning, of course, of course) because it is much easier to get to it via mathematics and music than any other way. My present business is to make this clear and I am, naturally, writing a book about it (called—remembering an old suggestion of yours—Beethoven, although that individual has not yet appeared in it) and if I come to Paris I'll bring some of the manuscript. We are, I assure you, living at the birth of a Renaissance—an unprecedented Renaissance. I could mention a dozen new books to you, having most repulsive and technical titles, where the first steps are being formulated. But I find no reflection of this in literature, although I find a vague expectancy, a sense of something impending, in one or two sensitive literary men.[47]

Murry must have responded to Sullivan's letter with a defence of his point of view. On 8 May 1922 Sullivan replied:

I've just read your letter. It is a very nice and reasonable letter, although it is full of statements and assumptions that make me want to argue for hours. But I will first of all deliver my knockout blow, and then speak quiet and healing words to your woe-begone and humbled spirit. Let me comfort you with your own words. 'Another great division is into those which stress the reality of the ego, and those which stress the reality of the external world.' You go on to say that if Relativity can change one of those attitudes for another you would be persuaded that it is going to bring a Renaissance. Well, that is just what Relativity Theory has done. My notorious modesty prevents me from quoting myself, so I will quote Eddington. 'Mind exalts the permanent and ignores the transitory; and it appears from the mathematical study of relations that the only way in which mind can achieve her object is by picking out one particular quality as the permanent substance of the perceptual world, partitioning a perceptual time and space for it to be permanent in, and, as a necessary consequence of this Hobson's choice, the laws of gravitation and mechanics and geometry have to be obeyed. Is it too much to say that mind's search for permanence has created the world of physics?'

And what is the 'content' of this something that the mind has singled out as matter? Here Eddington says: 'All through the physical world runs that unknown content, which must surely be the stuff of our own consciousness.'[48] Well, aren't you knocked out? …

The general question of the relations of science to literature involves the study of the influence of science in forming the *Zeitgeist* characteristic of any age. My 'middle' I mentioned to you is about that, so I'll wait till that appears before going on with that part of our discussion. You appear to be thinking of the *direct* relations of science and literature. They, I agree, are almost non-existent, because literary men have to get their science indirectly. But, in this indirect way, the influence of science is enormous …

Yes, I want the Weyl review back. I took great pains with it, and it is far the best I have done. It even enabled Oliver Lodge and some Oxford professor to see what the theory might be about, for they wrote very nice letters to the Times newspaper about it.[49]

As if backing up his letter, Sullivan published a signed article in the *Daily Herald* almost immediately after writing to Murry in which he acclaimed relativity as 'probably the greatest intellectual achievement the world has ever seen. [Einstein],' he wrote, 'has completely revolutionised the thought of his time, and it may take centuries before his achievement is fully understood in all its bearings.'[50] 'Mystery, but more wonderful and full of promise than ever, has been restored to the universe,' Sullivan had written four days previously when concluding another article on the Einsteinian revolution.[51]

Sullivan's letter of 8 May prompted Murry to respond with an article on 'Literature and Science' which was published in *The Times* on 26 May. A dispute as to whether 'the sceptre' had really 'changed hands,' anticipating the more well-known and belligerent 'two cultures' controversy of 1959, was now in full swing. 'A friend of mine wrote to me the other day that "the sceptre has passed from literature to science." He is, of course, a man of science himself,' wrote Murry, before going on to observe that it 'seemed rather strange that he should use such a very literary phrase to express his triumph.' While conceding that his friend was 'a brilliant man,' Murry could not accept that Sullivan's metaphor was well chosen, for the reason that 'the kingdom of literature has certainly not been incorporated into the kingdom of science, nor is it likely to be. You might as well try to marry "Boyle's Law" to a bookcase.' Murry concluded:

> I suspect that what my friend has in his head is that the Einstein theory is a discovery of supreme philosophical importance; that for the first time the metaphysical doctrine of philosophical idealism has been backed by scientific proof; and that this will have a determining influence upon the future evolution of literature. The last of these propositions is most doubtful.[52]

The 'middle' Sullivan referred to in his letter to Murry of 8 May was eventually published on 24 June 1922. Completed as a direct response to Murry's 'Literature and Science' piece, Sullivan pointedly entitled his article 'Science and Literature.' While recognizing that 'the kingdom of literature [had not been] incorporated into the kingdom of science,' Sullivan argued that 'science does influence literature, in the same way that religion and philosophy have influenced literature, because it throws light on the nature of man and of his destiny ... Science cannot be, and is not, ignored, except by mere entertainers.' In similar words, perhaps, to those he had already addressed to Eliot and Huxley and which Pound would hear in two months' time, Sullivan concluded his article with the following remarks:

Science is to be judged, finally, by the light it throws on man and his destiny. And this is one of the criteria for literature—a very important one, although not the only one. And it may well be that the scientific man quoted by Murry, was right when he said that the sceptre has passed from literature to science, if he meant that, at present, science has something more important to say about these things than literature has. Certainly the Einstein theory will influence, not only science, but also philosophy ... If the literary mind is to be a mind through which no big and vitalizing conceptions, however pertinent to man's destiny, are to be allowed to pass unless they have occurred to other literary minds, then literature must be rescued from the literary expert ... When you have tabulated the qualities which go to make up a big literary or scientific man you will find they are not purely literary or purely scientific. You will find they each have some resemblance to the ideal philosopher, the man interested in everything, and powerful enough to turn everything into grist for his mill.[53]

Sullivan's conviction that relativity strengthened the hand of metaphysical idealism was shared by a broad constituency of intellectuals in the 1920s. Eddington concluded *Space Time and Gravitation* with the observation that

where science has progressed the farthest, the mind has but regained from nature that which the mind has put into nature.

We have found a strange foot-print on the shores of the unknown. We have devised profound theories, one after another, to account for its origin. At last, we have succeeded in reconstructing the creature that made the foot-print. And Lo! it is our own. (pp. 200–1)[54]

Eddington developed this point at length in *The Nature of the Physical World*, in which he embraced the 'frank realisation that physical science is concerned with a world of shadows,' and that the 'idea of a universal Mind or Logos would be ... a fairly plausible inference from the present state of scientific theory; at least it is in harmony with it.'[55] The expository trend epitomized by Eddington's work reached its apogee in Sir James Jeans's highly successful *Mysterious Universe* (1930).[56] But if, by the end of the decade, Jeans was the most popular proselytizer of the mentality of the new physics, in the early 1920s Sullivan had held centre stage. In *The Reign of Relativity* (1921) Viscount Haldane observed that '[m]en of science are now advancing with sure steps into a domain which for long they did not think of entering ... In this borderland they are bound to meet the metaphysician,'[57] and in *Daedalus or Science and the Future* (1924), his nephew, J. B. S. Haldane, predicted that Kantian idealism would provide 'the basal working hypothesis, first of physics, and then of every-day life ... for some centuries,'[58] but it was undoubtedly their contemporary, J. W. N. Sullivan, who provided the reading public with its most regular, accessible, and rousing accounts of the new physics and the philosophical mind-set they seemed to entail.

In view of their 'most interesting conversation' and his 'Medallion' of the poet, it seems almost certain that Sullivan had Eliot in mind when he spoke of finding 'a sense of something impending in one or two literary men.'[59] In the light of Sullivan's 'Medallion' of Huxley, it seems most unlikely that his erstwhile co-editor was the other. In his evaluation of Huxley's work Sullivan reiterates criticisms of his friend's attitude to life which he had almost certainly expressed both in person and in their correspondence. As well as his assessments of the writings of Eliot and Huxley, Sullivan wrote short appraisals of Wyndham Lewis (6 June), E. M. Forster (17 June), and Katherine Mansfield (27 July) for *The Times*. 'At first sight,' wrote Sullivan, 'Mr. Aldous Huxley seems to be distinguished from our other young writers chiefly by his lack of earnestness.' He continued:

A large number of delightfully ridiculous people are scattered over this planet, all quaintly earnest about something or another. With a smiling and somewhat languid urbanity—for he is never bitter, never cruel—Mr. Huxley acts as a Showman to this World's Fair ... He does not, we suppose, disbelieve in the existence of great teachers, but he knows that he is not one. And he turns a very wary eye on anyone who professes to tell him more about life than that it is quite meaningless. More superficial, less sincere, and less intelligent, he shares the attitude of Anatole France, as that writer is usually presented to us. But the other Anatole, the Anatole of burning indignation, of passionate sympathy, the valiant champion of unpopular causes—there is no trace of this in Mr. Huxley.[60]

It seems very much as if *Crome Yellow* rankled with Sullivan in the same way that *Brave New World* was to irritate another of Huxley's scientific friends, H. G. Wells.

Early in 1923, Sullivan reached a wider audience with the publication of *Aspects of Science*.[61] Sullivan probably chose his title as yet another rejoinder to Murry, who had issued his *Aspects of Literature* in 1920. According to Singer, Sullivan's selection of essays from his *Athenaeum, Nation and Athenaeum* (of which he was now science editor), and *TLS* journalism proved 'an unqualified success.' Extracts from *Aspects* were published in *John O'London's Weekly*, which claimed that '[w]hen Einstein visited this country [in the summer of 1921] he declared that Mr. Sullivan was the only man to put intelligent questions to him about his theory of Relativity,'[62] and there is hardly a single piece in Sullivan's volume in which the Einsteinian liberation of science from the thrall of nineteenth-century materialism is not trumpeted with fervour. In all his writings on Einstein in the 1920s Sullivan's abiding theme is the '*entente cordiale*' which now existed between physics and metaphysics. In his essay of this title he wrote:

> Those who are interested in current 'serious' literature, and more particularly that branch of it which deals in a speculative way with those vague but impressive problems which have always haunted men, the existence of God, the 'meaning of the Universe' and so on, cannot have failed to notice the unaccustomed prestige now enjoyed by science ... Compared to the crude materialists of [T. H.] Huxley's day, it is evident that the modern man of science has greatly improved his social standing; he now frequently talks to the best people, on equal terms, on such subjects as the Good and the Beautiful.

Sullivan goes on to emphasize that, following the Einsteinian revolution, science, philosophy, and religion have moved closer together and brought into being a new branch of literature, 'works which seem to result from a close collaboration between, say, a professor of physics, an archdeacon and a Bond Street crystal-gazer.'[63]

By September 1923 Huxley was recommending Sullivan to H. L. Mencken as a man who 'writes well on scientific (physics and astronomy) themes,'[64] and in revising an essay for inclusion in his *On the Margin* volume, Huxley showed that he had at last come round to Sullivan's point of view and that he was now ready to acknowledge the significance of the new physics in his writings. In 'The Subject-Matter of Poetry' (1920), Huxley had simply stated that only Laforgue had 'succeeded in making real poetry out of science ... he is science's only lyrist.'[65] However, when he refashioned his article in

1923, Huxley not only dropped the title's definite article but wrote more expansively about the new physics:

> It is very rarely that we find a poet who combines the power and the desire to express himself with that passionate apprehension of ideas and the passionate curiosity about remote strange facts which characterize the man of science and the philosopher. If he possessed the requisite sense of language and the impelling desire to express himself in terms of beauty, Einstein could write the most intoxicating lyrics about relativity and the pleasures of pure mathematics. And if, say, Mr. Yeats understood the Einstein theory—which, in company with most other living poets, he presumably does not, any more than the rest of us—if he apprehended it exultingly as something bold and profound, something vitally important and marvellously true, he too could give us, out of the Celtic twilight, his lyrics of relativity.

Huxley goes on to argue that there would be 'real novelty in the new poetry' if only it would absorb 'any of the new ideas and astonishing facts with which the new science has endowed the modern world.' He concluded his article with the following words:

> The twentieth century still awaits its Lucretius, awaits its own philosophical Dante, its new Goethe, its Donne, even its up-to-date Laforgue. Will they appear? Or are we to go on producing a poetry in which there is no more than the dimmest reflection of that busy and incessant intellectual life which is the characteristic and distinguishing mark of this age?[66]

A sort of 'up-to-date Laforgue' is the role which Huxley was soon to assume as the author of *Those Barren Leaves*. But even in *Antic Hay*, published in November 1923, there are signs that Huxley was attempting to produce the kind of hybrid literature which Sullivan had forecast in his 'Entente Cordiale' piece. Although towards the end of chapter 1, when he learns that understanding 'perfectly and without effort the quantum theory'[67] forms part of the lavish fantasy life of Gumbril Junior, the reader might assume that Huxley's second novel is to continue *Crome Yellow*'s flippant treatment of the new physics, the absurd Lypiatt does at least speak with the genuine passion and insight of Sullivan, and echoes Huxley's own idealist position, when he asks:

What are science and art, what are religion and philosophy but so
many expressions in human terms of some reality more than
human? Newton and Boehme and Michelangelo—what are they
doing but expressing, in different ways, different aspects of the
same thing?... One reality ... there is only one reality ... We are
all trying to talk about it ... The physicists have formulated their
laws, which are after all no more than stammering provisional
theories about a part of it. The physiologists are penetrating into
the secrets of life, psychologists into the mind. And we artists are
trying to say what is revealed to us about the moral nature, the
personality of that reality, which is the universe. (p. 64)

None the less, it was only after Sullivan joined Huxley in Florence in January
1924 that he was able to instil into his host a more profound understanding
of the new physics and the metaphysics they seemed to authenticate. Indeed,
it may be argued that mysticism only became the focus of *Those Barren Leaves*
because Sullivan, with his infectious and visionary grasp of Einstein's work,
was a guest at Huxley's home until late April 1924, during which period the
'*entente cordiale*' was at the forefront of Sullivan's mind and Huxley's third
novel was commenced.

NOTES

1. *The Diary of Virginia Woolf*, ed. A. O. Bell and A. McNeillie (London,
1978), ii. 150.

2. *The Question of Things Happening: The Letters of Virginia Woolf,
1912–1922*, ed. N. Nicolson and J. Trautmann (London, 1976), 499 (21 Jan.
1922).

3. W. J. Turnèr, *The Duchess of Popocatapetl* (London, 1939), 241–8. A
later chapter, ch. 38, takes the form of a dialogue between Sullivan and
Airbubble.

4. 'Sometimes the rendezvous was a restaurant. At one time [Dorothy]
Brett was allowed to preside at her Pond Street house, because, as she said,
she was too deaf to intervene' (*Mark Gertler: Selected Letters*, ed. N.
Carrington (London, 1965), 185).

5. *Letters of Aldous Huxley*, ed. G. Smith (London, 1969), 227 (hereafter,
Letters). Although Sullivan may well have discussed the possibility of 'articles
about the Einstein theory' with Leonard Huxley (editor of the *Cornhill* from
1917 until his death in 1933), none were published. Sullivan's sole

contribution to the magazine seems to have been a playlet entitled "The New Temptation of St. Anthony,' *Cornhill*, NS 41 (Sept. 1916), 309–13.

6. Letter from Mr Navin Sullivan to the author, 1 Dec. 1989. I am grateful to Mr Sullivan for allowing me to quote from his father's unpublished writings.

7. Singer's 'Memoir' prefaced Sullivan's posthumous *Isaac Newton 1642–1727* (London, 1938), pp. ix–xx. Hitherto, it has provided the only published account of Sullivan's life. According to Sullivan's daughter, Mrs B. Navina Ridley, however, Singer's profile was based mainly on an interview with Sullivan's sister and requires amending in places. In particular, Mrs Ridley feels that Sullivan's childhood was less genteel than Singer made out. 'Certainly I recognize the childhood depicted in *But for the Grace of God* [Sullivan's novel of 1932], obviously autobiographical in parts, as far more "like" what I knew of the grandparents and my aunts and the kind of home they had. (There was *no* music).'
Mrs Ridley observes that her grandmother 'was not, I think, a teacher' and that her grandfather, John William Sullivan, 'was a second generation Irish immigrant. He was a seaman [who] seems quite suddenly to have been promoted to a white-collar job as an official of an "Inland Mission".' Letter from Mrs B. Navina Ridley to the author, 17 Jan. 1990. I am grateful to Mrs Ridley for allowing me to quote from her letters.

8. Letter from Mrs B. Navina Ridley to the author, 13 Feb. 1990.

9. MS A.A. Knopf Misc, n.d. [1931].

10. The other possibility, of course, is that Huxley was hoaxing his father. However, this would have been uncharacteristic of their relationship, and there is no evidence of any similar occurrence in the *Letters* or elsewhere.

11. Stanley Goldberg (*Understanding Relativity: Origin and Impact of a Scientific Revolution* (Oxford, 1984), 322) paraphrases T. S. Kuhn's argument in his seminal study of *The Structure of Scientific Revolutions* (1962; 2nd edn. 1970) that 'science does not proceed in a linear, continuous, progressive development but is punctuated by discontinuous, precipitous, revolutionary breaks' or paradigm shifts.

12. HRHRC, 29 July 1917.

13. Murry to Lady Ottoline Morrell, HRHRC, n.d. [late May 1918]. I am grateful to the Society of Authors as the literary representatives of the Estate of John Middleton Murry for permission to quote from this letter. On 14 June Murry told Katherine Mansfield that he had received 'a note from Sullivan at Garsington this morning. He seems comfortable enough and writes of everybody being "extraordinarily kind," so that's all right. I can't help feeling a bit jealous of his holiday though, because I think I'm suffering

from exactly the same "brain fag" as he, and have to do his work into the bargain' (*The Letters of John Middleton Murry to Katherine Mansfield*, ed. C. A. Hankin (London, 1983), 175). Sullivan had married Sylvia Mannooch the previous year, not Vere Bartrick-Baker as stated in *The Collected Letters of Katherine Mansfield*, ed. V. O'Sullivan and M. Scott (Oxford, 1987), ii. 291.

14. HRHRC.

15. R. Gathorne-Hardy (ed.), *Ottoline at Garsington: Memoirs of Lady Ottoline Morrell 1915–1918* (London, 1974), 260.

16. Huxley to F. A. Lea, Henry W. and Albert A. Berg Collection, The New York Public Library, Astor, Lenox and Tilden Foundations, 17 July 1957. 'I could tell you much of [Sullivan],' Huxley continued, 'but very little of Murry.' For more information on Huxley, Sullivan, Murry, and the *Athenaeum*, see Lea's *The Life of John Middleton Murry* (London, 1959), 65–82.

17. On 6 Feb. 1955 Huxley told his publisher that he had written 'to Mrs Sullivan 2 or 3 days ago in response to a letter (not a cable) of hers, asking for permission to reprint my letters to J. W. N. Sullivan, if and when she writes a book about him. I said yes—conditionally ...' Grover Smith comments in a footnote: 'The letters to Sullivan remained unpublished in Huxley's lifetime, when his conditional permission was effective, and their present whereabouts is unknown' (*Letters*, 731). Huxley's letters to Sullivan have still not surfaced. They are not in the possession of either of Sullivan's children and it is likely that they were destroyed at some point in the late 1950s, probably by Sullivan's widow.

18. HRHRC, 3 Oct. 1919.

19. 'Mr. J. W. N. Sullivan: A Gifted Interpreter of Science,' *The Times* (13 Aug. 1937), 14. In order to attribute to Sullivan articles and reviews in *The Times* and *TLS* which were by custom published anonymously, extensive reference has been made in this article to the marked copies of *The Times* and the *TLS* held by News International plc at its London premises. However, owing to a gap in this archive, it has not been possible to identify Sullivan's obituarist.

20. Goldberg, *Understanding Relativity*, 307–8.

21. *The Times* (7 Nov. 1919), 12.

22. 'The Fabric of the Universe,' *The Times* (7 Nov. 1919), 13.

23. 'The Revolution in Science,' *The Times* (8 Nov. 1919), 12.

24. For more information about the advent of relativity, see R. Clark, *Einstein: The Life and Times* (London, 1973), 227–58 and *Nature*, 106 (17 Feb. 1921), a special issue of the journal which is solely devoted to the theory and which includes a 'Bibliography of Relativity,' 811–13. A. J. Friedman and C.

C. Donley, *Einstein as Myth and Muse* (Cambridge, 1985) and L. Calcraft, 'Einstein and Relativity Theory in Modern Literature,' in M. Goldsmith, A. Mackay, and J. Woudhuysen (edd.), *Einstein: The First Hundred Years* (Oxford, 1980), 163–79, provide useful overviews of the new physics' impact on literature.

25. *Collected Letters of Katherine Mansfield*, ii. 314.

26. Michael Whitworth, 'Physics and the Literary Community, 1905–1939,' D.Phil thesis, Oxford University (1995), 44. See also pp. 301–7 and 320–61. The *Athenaeum* articles in question are: 'A Crucial Phenomenon,' no. 4645 (9 May 1919), 303; 'On Relative Motion,' no. 4646 (16 May 1919), 337; 'The Notion of Simultaneity,' no. 4647 (23 May 1919), 369; 'The Union of Space and Time,' no. 4648 (30 May 1919), 402; and 'The Equivalence Principle,' no. 4649 (6 June 1919), 433.

27. 'Great Names: Charles Darwin (1809–1882),' *Daily Herald* (20 Oct. 1920), 7.

28. 'A New-Fashioned Humanist,' *Nation*, 26 (8 Nov. 1919), 184, 186.

29. See e.g. 'Science and Culture,' *Athenaeum*, no. 4672 (14 Nov. 1919), 1190, and 'The Entente Cordiale,' *Athenaeum*, no 4693 (9 Apr. 1920), 482; both articles repr. in Sullivan's *Aspects of Science* (London, 1923), 36–40 and 77–81 respectively (hereafter, *Aspects*). Whitworth's thesis contains a full checklist of Sullivan's contributions to periodicals between 1915 and 1937.

30. 'Marginalia by Autolycus,' *Athenaeum*, no. 4699 (21 May 1920), 672. This pseudonymous piece and Sullivan's other pseudonymous and anonymous contributions to the *Athenaeum* have been identified through reference to the file of marked copies of the magazine now housed in the Centre for Interactive Systems Research, Department of Information Science, City University, London. In addition to Huxley being Arnold's great-nephew, there are at least three clues which indicate he is the 'friend' in question. (1) In 'Subject-Matter of Poetry,' *On the Margin: Notes and Essays* (London, 1923), 26–38, Huxley was to argue that 'most of the world's best poetry has been content with a curiously narrow range of subject-matter ... poets do not concern themselves with fresh conquests.' (2) The *Athenaeum*'s reviewing of French literature was generally shared between Huxley and Murry. (3) In a letter to H. L. Mencken of Dec. 1922 Huxley asks 'How goes life in the Great West?' (quoted in D. Bradshaw (ed.), *The Hidden Huxley: Contempt and Compassion for the Masses 1920–36* (London, 1994), 19).

31. 'Chaucer,' *London Mercury*, 2 (June 1920), 179–89. Repr. in *On the Margin*, 203–29.

32. *Athenaeum*, no. 4650 (13 June 1919), 464.

33. *Crome Yellow* (London, 1921), 95 (subsequent quotations in the text).

34. Albert Einstein, *Relativity: The Special and General Theory: A Popular Exposition*, trans. R. W. Lawson (London, 1920), 16.

35. 'An Abstruse Theory,' rev. of Carr's *The General Principle of Relativity*, *Athenaeum*, no. 4723 (5 Nov. 1920), 621–2.

36. See e.g. the 'Prefatorial Dialogue' in E. E. Slosson's *Easy Lessons in Einstein: A Discussion of the More Intelligible Features of the Theory of Relativity* (London, 1920), p. vi.

37. For a more detailed examination of this aspect of *Crome Yellow*, and Huxley's broader sense of the decadence of the 'old traditional ruling class,' see Bradshaw (ed.), *The Hidden Huxley*, 8–15.

38. *Point Counter Point* (London, 1928), 80 (further page-refs. in the text).

39. I should like to record my gratitude to Mr H. R. Weinberg for sharing with me his interesting observations on Huxley and the new physics.

40. C. Aiken, *Ushant: An Essay* (New York and Boston, 1952), 277.

41. See Michael Whitworth's very interesting '*Pièces d'identité*: T. S. Eliot, J. W. N. Sullivan and Poetic Impersonality,' *English Literature in Transition 1880–1920*, 31/2 (1996), 149–70.

42. Sullivan to Lady Ottoline Morrell, HRHRC, 30 June 1922. Sullivan's anonymous article is entitled 'Medallions III: Mr. T. S. Eliot: The Exact Critic,' *The Times* (13 June 1922), 14. Four months later, we now know, Sullivan wrote the *TLS*'s unsigned notice of the first number of the *Criterion*, during the course of which he makes complimentary remarks about *The Waste Land* (26 Oct. 1922), 690; see Samanyu Satpathy, 'Eliot and J. W. N. Sullivan,' *N & Q* 240 [NS 42] (June 1995), 216. Although Satpathy rightly goes on to describe Sullivan as 'one of the unsung figures behind the modernist revolution in the arts,' he suggests less convincingly that Eliot 'may have received lessons on Thomism from Sullivan who, as Huxley told his father "was brought up at Maynooth under the Jesuits".'

43. T. Materer, *The Selected Letters of Ezra Pound to John Quinn 1915–1924* (Durham, NC and London, 1991), 216. Letter dated 10 Aug. 1922.

44. 'The Complete Einstein,' *TLS*, no. 1056 (13 Apr. 1922), 237.

45. 'Beethoven the Man,' *John O'London's Weekly*, 6 (11 Feb. 1922), 610–11.

46. J. M. Murry, 'Mr. Joyce's "Ulysses",' *Nation and Athenaeum*, 31 (22 Apr. 1922), 124–5. Murry wrote of *Ulysses*: 'Every thought that a super-subtle

modern can think seems to be hidden somewhere in its inspissated obscurities.'

47. HRHRC, 22 Apr. 1922.

48. Sullivan is quoting from A. S. Eddington's *Space Time and Gravitation: An Outline of the General Relativity Theory* (Cambridge, 1920), 198 and 200 respectively. In the second quotation, 'own' is Sullivan's embellishment. Sullivan had reviewed Eddington's book in the *Athenaeum*, no. 4707 (16 July 1920), 85–6.

49. HRHRC, 8 May 1922. Sir Oliver Lodge was the most prominent exponent of the ether theory in the 1920s and one of relativity's most vociferous opponents. Written on the day 'The Complete Einstein' had been published, Lodge's letter commended Sullivan's 'remarkably able and well-informed' review of Weyl's book: 'Mathematics and Physics,' *The Times* (15 Apr. 1922), 13. The only other letter published under the caption 'Mathematics and Physics,' in which *The Times*'s readers were urged to heed Lodge's praise, was written by one Max Judge from an address in Pall Mall, London (21 Apr. 1922), 8.

50. 'Albert Einstein (1879),' *Daily Herald* (24 May 1922), 7.

51. 'The Return of Mystery,' *Nation and Athenaeum*, 31 (20 May 1922), 252–3. Repr. in *Aspects*, 151–8.

52. J. M. Murry, 'Literature and Science,' *The Times* (26 May 1922), 16. Repr. in *Pencillings: Little Essays on Literature* (London, 1923), 53–61.

53. 'Science and Literature,' *Nation and Athenaeum*, 31 (24 June 1922), 452, 454.

54. There may well be an allusion to this passage in ch. 24 of *Crome Yellow*. After Denis Stone stumbles upon Jenny Mullion's large red notebook of caricatures, it is said that 'periodically he would make some painful discovery about the external world and the horrible reality of its consciousness and its intelligence. The red notebook was one of these discoveries, a footprint in the sand. It put beyond a doubt the fact that the outer world really existed' (p. 259).

55. A. S. Eddington, *The Nature of the Physical World* (Cambridge, 1928), pp. xvii, 338.

56. 'Mind no longer appears as an accidental intruder into the realm of matter,' Jeans asserted, 'we are beginning to suspect that we ought rather to hail it as the creator and governor of the realm of matter' (*The Mysterious Universe* (Cambridge, 1930), 148).

57. R. B. Haldane, *The Reign of Relativity* (London, 1921), 33–4.

58. J. B. S. Haldane, *Daedalus or Science and the Future: A Paper Read to the Heretics, Cambridge on February 4th, 1923* (London, 1924), 13–15. Sullivan

reviewed *Daedalus* during his stay with Huxley in Florence: 'Scientific Prophecies,' *TLS*, no. 1151 (7 Feb. 1924), 74.

59. T. S. Eliot mentions Einstein in passing and argues that Joyce's 'parallel use of the Odyssey' has 'the importance of a scientific discovery' in his 'Ulysses, Order, and Myth,' *Dial*, 75 (Nov. 1923), [480]–3.

60. 'Medallions: I. Mr. Aldous Huxley: A Juggler of Ideas,' *The Times* (22 May 1922), 16.

61. The British Library's copy is stamped '28 Feb 1923' [192].

62. Anon, 'J. W. N. Sullivan,' *John O'London's Weekly*, 9 (7 Apr. 1923), 19.

63. 'The Entente Cordiale,' *Athenaeum*, no. 4693 (9 Apr. 1920), 482. Repr. in *Aspects*, 77–81.

64. *Letters*, 220. Of course, Huxley did not derive his understanding of relativity exclusively from Sullivan. For instance, he spent part of Christmas Day 1922 in reading, 'with more profit than I generally derive from such literature,' the *Encyclopaedia Britannica*'s article on the subject ('Music in the Encyclopaedia,' *Weekly Westminster Gazette*, 1/46 (30 Dec. 1922), 14). The article in question is J. H. Je[ans], 'Relativity,' *The Encyclopaedia Britannica: The New Volumes, Constituting with the Twenty-Nine Volumes of the Eleventh Edition, the Twelfth Edition* (London, 1922), xxxii. 261–7.

65. 'The Subject-Matter of Poetry,' *Chapbook*, 2 (Mar. 1920), 11–16.

66. 'Subject-Matter of Poetry,' *On the Margin*, 26–38. Huxley returned to this topic in '"And Wanton Optics Roll the Melting Eye"' in *Music at Night* (London, 1931), 32–42.

67. *Antic Hay* (London, 1923), 15 (further page-refs. in the text).

RONALD HOPE

Aldous Huxley's Philosophy

I was sixteen when Aldous Huxley's *Ends and Means* was published, and a year older when it came my way in the public library. By that time I had romped through *Crome Yellow*, *Antic Hay* and *Brave New World*. Today, the young do not seem so well served by the winners of the Booker Prize, but no doubt that is the plaint of all the generations. However, those of us who grew up in the Huxley era had much to look forward to and best of all, in my opinion, was *The Perennial Philosophy*, the book of Huxley's prime. And it is, perhaps, worth taking another look at it as we celebrate the 2000th anniversary of the birth of Christ.

Text and Pretexts had been an annotated anthology of verse. *The Perennial Philosophy* was an annotated anthology of mysticism, with chapter headings like 'Charity,' 'God in the World' and 'Time and Eternity.'

This perennial philosophy – the phrase is borrowed from Leibniz—is the highest factor common to all religions, a 'minimum working hypothesis,' and Huxley's character Sebastian had already reflected upon it in *Time Must Have a Stop*. The primary assumption is that there is a Godhead behind the universe, behind all appearance. This unity both pervades the universe and is above and beyond it. 'Behold but the One in all things,' says the mystic Kabir; 'it is the second that leads you astray.'

From *Contemporary Review* 278, no. 1621 © 2001 by Contemporary Review Co. Ltd.

Most of us, claimed Huxley, have some consciousness of this unity, a consciousness implicit in our use of words. One is the embodiment of Good; two is the embodiment of Evil. Thus the Greek prefix '*dys*,' as in dyspepsia, and the Latin 'dis' as in dishonourable; and the German '*Zweifel*,' which means doubt. Bunyan, he pointed out, had his Mr Facing-both-ways and American slang its 'two-timers.' He might have added the double-crossers.

Granted the underlying unity in all things, Huxley argued that it was possible for human beings to love, know and become identified with the Godhead, to become one with God, and to achieve this identity with God is the purpose and end of human life. It is, of course, a message that has been conveyed by many other thinkers.

This end, however, cannot be realised unless a certain path is followed. We can have direct knowledge of God only by union, and this union cannot be achieved while we remain selfish and egoistic. 'The more there is of I, me, mine,' wrote Sebastian, 'the less there is of the Ground'. And the only way of dying to self, of annihilating the Ego, is the way of humility and compassion, the way of disinterestedness. It is because people have been unwilling to follow this path to salvation that human history has been what it has. People don't see why they shouldn't 'express their personalities' and 'have a good time.' 'They get their good times,' says Huxley; 'but also and inevitably they get wars and syphilis and revolution and alcoholism, tyranny and, in default of an adequate religious hypothesis, the choice between some lunatic idolatry, like nationalism, and a sense of complete futility and despair.' Everybody realises that this is a sad state of affairs but 'throughout recorded history most men and women have preferred the risks, the positive certainty of such disasters to the laborious whole-time job of trying to get to know the divine Ground of all being. In the long run we get exactly what we ask for.'

Huxley did not, of course, suggest that there was any proof, in the mathematical sense, of the existence of God. We cannot divide matter by nothing and call it infinity, as one of Huxley's fictional characters tried to do. But there is, according to Huxley, abundant evidence that certain people, by no means extraordinary except in this mystical respect, have directly experienced and realised the spiritual Absolute, have become united in God.

Then what of we 'ordinary, nice, unregenerate' people, what can we do about it? The answer is that our will is free and it is up to us. We can either identify ourselves exclusively with our self-ness and its own interests to the exclusion of God, in which case we shall be either passively damned or actively fiendish; or we can identify ourselves exclusively with the divine within us and without, in which case we shall be saints. As is the case with the current British Prime Minister, there is also a 'third way,' the way of life for the majority of us. Those who follow the third way are neither saint nor fiend. At one moment, or in one set of circumstances, they are selfish; at another moment, or in another set of circumstances, they are humble, contrite and compassionate. These are too godly to be wholly lost, but too self-centred to achieve enlightenment and total deliverance.

Human craving, Huxley suggests, can be satisfied only by following the saintly path. To some extent our path will vary according to our temperament. Broadly speaking, we are all Pickwicks, Hotspurs or Hamlets, or some complicated combination of more than one of these. On the earthly plane, the Pickwick in us is characterised by gluttony, the love of comfort and the love of social approval. Pickwick can find God only through devotion, a deliberate disciplining of his merely animal gregariousness and merely human kindliness into devotion to the personal God, and universal goodwill and compassion towards all sentient beings.

The path of works is for Hotspur. He must rid himself of the usual and fatal accompaniments of the love of action—love of power and the desire to hurt—and work without regard to the fruits of his work, in a state of complete non-attachment.

'For Hamlet, there is the way of knowledge, through the modification of consciousness, until it ceases to be ego-centred and becomes centred in and united with the Divine Ground.' For all of us—Pickwick, Hotspur and Hamlet – it boils down to the denial of Self, and thence the achievement of a knowledge of God.

Of course, none of this is easy. Above all, we must be charitable—charitable in the original sense of the word and not as it is used in the debased verbal currency of our day. Charity includes within itself disinterestedness, tranquillity and humility. 'Where there is disinterestedness, there is neither greed for personal advantage nor fear for personal loss or punishment; where there is tranquillity, there is neither craving nor aversion ...; and where there is humility there is no censoriousness and no glorification of the ego...'

'There isn't any secret formula or method,' scribbled the dying Bruno in *Time Must Have a Stop*, echoing as he did so the words of St François de Saes. 'You learn to love by loving—by paying attention and doing what one thereby discovers has to be de done.' But to put this doctrine into effect requires constant awareness and discipline. To give but one example, the kind of talk in which most of us indulge is morally evil and spiritually dangerous, for most of what we say is inspired by greed, sensuality, self-love, malice, uncharitableness or pure imbecility. All these idle words stand between us and God.

The path to salvation today is as difficult as it has always been. On every side we are urged to be as extraverted and as uninhibitedly greedy as possible since it is only the restless and distracted who spend money on the things that advertisers want to sell. We are encouraged to 'love' and 'adore' different kinds of clothes, cars, food and drink. We must chasten these desires and passions.

That is not to say that we must deliberately seek out physical austerities, because this may have the wrong effect. This can nourish that pride in ourselves which it should be our aim to destroy. What we must endeavour to achieve is a 'holy indifference' towards the things in time, not merely towards the physical satisfactions, but also towards the mental satisfactions—the success, for example, of a cause to which we have devoted our best energies. If it succeeds, well and good; but if it suffers defeat, that also is well and good, if only in ways which to a time-bound mind are here and now entirely incomprehensible.

What, it may be asked, is the reward for all this effort? It is not, necessarily, a 'better world,' though this would follow if there were better people in it. To the exponents of the perennial philosophy, the question of a 'better' world, of whether progress is inevitable or even real, is not a matter of primary importance. For them the important thing is that individual men and women should come to the unitive knowledge of God; and what interests them in the social environment is not its progressiveness or non-progressiveness, whatever these terms may mean, but the degree to which it helps or hinders individuals in their advance towards the final end.

This obviously has an important political corollary as well as a personal implication. Power always corrupts. 'All great men are bad.' The political corollary is that we should live, not in great nation states, but in units sufficiently small to be capable of shared spiritual existence and of moral and rational conduct. Such social rearrangement as decentralisation, small-scale property-owning and small-scale production would do much to prevent ambitious individuals and organisations from being led into temptation.

In seeking this deliverance out of time and into eternity we cannot lose sight of the fact that we are living in time. The life of a mystic is not a life of inaction; nor does it lead to suicide for in committing suicide we do not escape the boundaries of time. But the mystic's work, as Huxley pointed out in *Grey Eminence*, must always be marginal; it is always started on the smallest scale and, even when it expands, it is never organised on a large scale, for there lies the way of corruption.

Deliverance, when and if it comes, is out of the limitations imposed upon us by time and into eternity. By definition, we cannot say what eternity is like in terms of things in time. The most that writers on the subject have been able to do in describing their experiences to those without faith is to use such phrases as 'seeing the light' or, as Huxley does, 'participating in the eternal Now of the Divine Ground.' The mystic can do no other than speak in a mysterious way.

More can be said, perhaps, about hell than heaven because we already know hell pretty well. If you do not choose to be saved, if you do not choose to become immortal, you survive. That is you persist in one of the forms of time. And persisting in time *is* hell, because the elements of hell are the elements of self, covetousness, envy, pride and wrath. If you have fallen from grace and God, life can be nothing in itself but an extremity of want, continually desiring, and an extremity of desire, continually wanting: you have become the economic man!

In *Time Must Have a Stop* Huxley made some attempt to describe this state of survival in time after death when Eustace Barnack died, but the attempt did not come off. In *The Perennial Philosophy* he takes a leaf out of his brother Julian Huxley's great work on *Evolution* and suggests that the other animals, indeed all creation, have already made their choice. They have chosen, not the ultimately best, but the immediately most profitable form, and are thus debarred from realising the supreme good. As Villiers de l'Isle-Adam wrote, only man in all the universe, has not yet come to an end.

That Huxley's thought had been moving in the direction of the perennial philosophy for some time was obvious to anyone familiar with his work. Some of the reviewers when the book appeared seemed to find evidence for a sudden conversion round about 1934, but his disgust for earthly things is displayed over and over again in his early novels. In *Antic Hay*, Lypiatt is disgusted with 'hoggish materialism'; and Gumbril Junior remarks after his first love affair, 'Is that all?' Coleman's relish, in *Antic Hay*, in 'the hundreds of thousands of couples' who 'are at this moment engaged in mutually caressing one another in a manner too hideous to be thought of' seems little different from Huxley's relish in *The Perennial Philosophy* for a metaphor which describes personal love – a by no means ignoble thing – as 'slime.' At the age of fifty it was perhaps easier for Huxley to seek the perennial philosophy. In his youth he had been attracted to as well as disgusted by the earthly pleasures.

'The earthly paradise,' he exclaims in *Texts and Pretexts*, 'the earthly paradise! With what longing, between the bars of my temperament, do I peer at its bright landscape, how voluptuously sniff at its perfumes of hay and raspberries, of honey-suckle and roast duck, of sun-warmed flesh and nectarines and the sea! But the bars are solid; the earthly paradise is always on the further side. Self-hindered, I cannot enter and make myself at home.'

By the time he wrote *The Perennial Philosophy* that brightness of the landscape had dimmed and the vision of a new paradise had eclipsed it. The conflict between the life of the senses and the life of the spirit was over; and so largely was the novel-writing. 'I have a premonition,' said Gumbril on one occasion, 'that one of these days I may become a saint. An unsuccessful flickering sort of saint, like a candle beginning to go out.'

After writing *The Perennial Philosophy* Huxley thought of himself, perhaps, as a flickering sort of saint; but those who do not share his curious temperamental difficulties may remain unconverted. After all, he left unsolved the perennial problem of why pain and suffering are so unevenly distributed; and is it true that all people may become mystics if they want to? Perhaps, like the animal world (and as Huxley intimated), many of us are already fixed in our ways. Many of the ordinary, nice, unregenerate people may not be willing to exchange the pleasures they know for the unknown pleasure of becoming united in God. It may be useless to suggest to these that they are really unhappy for they may not know it. With Huxley's contemporary, Richard Aldington, they may cry instead:

> ... *we who do not drug ourselves with lies*
> *Know, with how deep a pathos, that we have*
> *Only the warmth and beauty of this life*
> *Before the blankness of unending gloom.*

Aldington also used the image of the candle, but to him its flame represented life, and it burned most clearly and flickered least when fed by earthly love. He was unrepentantly for Twoness, the good and the bad that we have to live with.

DAVID LEON HIGDON AND PHILL LEHRMAN

Huxley's 'Deep Jam' and the Adaptation of Alice in Wonderland

In his Los Angeles *Times* 'Drama and Film' column of 19 November 1945, Philip K. Scheuer reported that Walt Disney had taken definite steps towards realizing his 23-year-old dream of filming *Alice's Adventures in Wonderland*. He had signed Aldous Huxley, 'distinguished novelist and an authority on Carroll,' to 'work out the details' for *Alice and the Mysterious Mr. Carroll* which would combine animation with live action and star Disney's discovery, Luana Patten, who was 'being groomed for the role.'[1] Very little is known of Huxley's involvement with this project or his general work in film, largely because of the loss of 4,000 of his annotated books and other papers in a disastrous fire in 1961 and the assumed disappearance of other documents;[2] however, discovery in the Walt Disney Studio Archives of important story meeting notes, Huxley's 'treatment' of the story (reproduced in the appendix, below), and Huxley's script for part of the film now provides the necessary information for exploring why Huxley's script was ultimately rejected, why Huxley was attracted to the project in the first place, and how an established novelist fared in the world of Hollywood studios.

From *The Review of English Studies* 43, no. 169 (1992) © 1992 by Oxford University Press.

II

Alice in Wonderland has tempted a number of film directors, yet it has never received a fully satisfactory adaptation. As early as 1903, the Englishmen Cecil M. Hepworth and Percy Stow had filmed the work, and the American directors, J. Searle Dawley and Norman Z. McLeod, had adapted it in 1910 and 1933. Walt Disney's Laugh-O-Gram Studio in Kansas City, Missouri, very freely borrowed Alice for a series of fifty-seven 'Alice in Cartoonland' short subjects between 1922 and 1926, short subjects ranging from 'Alice among the Cannibals' and 'Alice Chops the Suey' to 'Alice's Circus Daze.'[3] Surveying them, Richard Schickel concluded that 'about the only thing the pictures had going for them was their inexpensiveness to the distributors and the gimmick, quite crudely done, of mixing a live actor in the same frames with cartoon characters.'[4] The idea of filming Carroll's book, though, stayed with Disney. In 1933 he was contemplating a version starring Mary Pickford,[5] and between 10 December 1938 and 8 April 1941 he met with various members of the Disney staff a total of eleven times to discuss the project.

At a meeting on 14 January 1939 Disney analysed for his staff the problems with previous Alice films and concurrently dismissed the English audience and Carroll fans, saying it was more crucial to maintain a 'Carroll spirit' than to remain faithful to the text:

> I'll tell you what has been wrong with every one of these productions of Carroll. They have depended on his dialogue to be funny. But if you can use some of Carroll's phrases that are funny, use them. If they aren't funny, throw them out. There is a spirit behind Carroll's story, there. It's fantasy, imagination, screwball logic.... but it must be funny. I mean funny to an American audience. To hell with the English audiences or the people who love Carroll.... I'd like to make it more or less a 1940 or 1945 version—right up to date. I wouldn't put in any modern slang that wouldn't fit, but the stuff can be modernized. I want to put my money into something that will go in Podunk, Iowa, and they will go in and laugh at it because they have experienced it. They wouldn't laugh at a lot of English sayings that they've never heard or that don't mean anything to them. Yet we can keep it very much Carroll—keep his spirit. (*SM* 1–2)[6]

Dorothy Blank quickly added that the character of Alice was absolutely crucial, because

> She is the only real person in it. The other[s] are dream creatures. If the audience doesn't believe that any of those things would amuse her, that they are unbelievable to her—that was one of the biggest things wrong with the Paramount picture (1932). It was just a pretty girl walking through. Nothing seemed to affect her. (*SM* 2)

By the 13 November 1939 meeting, Disney and his staff were worrying about matters of plotting, when Stuart Buchanan suggested they secure advice from someone 'who is an *Alice in Wonderland* fiend.' Disney responded: 'I'm scared of that. If we could get a straight line on the thing, then it might not hurt to have someone come in and try to switch it around so it sounds a little more like *Alice in Wonderland* so we'll please those *Alice in Wonderland* authorities' (*SM* 1). No such authority had been added by the time of the 8 April 1941 meeting when Disney reverted to his interest in combining live action with cartoon animation as a means of solving the plotting difficulties:

> I've been wondering if we could do this thing with a live action girl.... Here's the value in the live girl over trying to animate it—we can animate a girl, make her run around and things—but carrying this story is different. There's a lot of story here with the girl, and trying to carry the story with a cartoon girl puts us in a hell of a spot. We might, in the whole picture, have, say, a dozen complicated trick shots, but the rest of them would be closeups and working around it. (*SM* 1)

At this point, however, demands for wartime educational and propagandistic films and the depletion of staff by the Selective Service draft forced Disney to delay all further work on *Alice in Wonderland*, *Peter Pan*, and *Wind in the Willows*.[7]

III

Immediately following the conclusion of the Second World War, Disney Studios began work on three animated features: *Cinderella*, *Peter Pan*, and

Alice in Wonderland (only the first succeeded at the box office). At this point, Aldous Huxley joined the project. The Huxleys had just begun to settle into their new home at Wrightwood when the offer came. A Disney Archive memo from Jack Lavin to Hal Adelquist records the terms of the agreement:

> Our agreement with Aldous Huxley specifies our paying him $7500 to write a treatment on [*sic*] 'Alice in Wonderland.' His services commenced as of October 18, 1945. Huxley agrees to deliver the treatment to us no later than January 15, 1946. We are to pay him $2500 on the execution of the agreement and $5,000 upon delivery of the treatment by Huxley to us.
>
> We have an option on Huxley's services to do a screenplay, to be exercised not later than 14 days after the delivery of the treatment to us. In the event of our exercising the option we are to pay him $15,000 payable $5,000 upon exercise of the option and $10,000 upon delivery of the screenplay, including all additions, changes and revisions. (5 Nov. 1945 Memorandum)

Five days earlier, Huxley had confided his plans to Anita Loos, who had been instrumental in securing him work on the earlier MGM *Pride and Prejudice* script.[8] He wrote:

> I am about to sign up with Disney for the script of an *Alice in Wonderland*, which is to be a cartoon version of Tenniel's drawings and Carroll's story, embedded in a flesh-and-blood episode of the life of the Rev. Charles Dodgson. I think something rather nice might be made out of this—the unutterably odd, repressed and ridiculous Oxford lecturer on logic and mathematics, seeking refuge in the company of little girls and in his own phantasy.[9]

Work apparently moved quickly, because Huxley delivered his synopsis on 23 November 1945. The following day, he wrote to Victoria Ocampo about his interest in the Carroll side of the treatment, recording his family ties to Oxford in the 1860s:

> It would be nice to be able to reconstruct the university of the period, ... with its long-drawn struggles between tory High Churchmen and liberal Modernists, under Jowett and Pattison. But, alas, there is no time in an hour of film—and even if there were time, how few of the millions who see the film would take

the smallest interest in the reconstruction of this odd fragment of
the forgotten past! So I have to be content with bringing out as
many of the oddities of Dodgson as possible, and with preventing
producer and director from putting in too many anachronisms
and impossibilities for the sake of the story.[10]

Even if we did not know of Huxley's work on various film projects
both before and after the *Alice* project, we would know of his interest in film
and the genres of this form through his use of a filmscript in *Ape and Essence*
(1948), which may possibly record his own disillusionment with his work
with Disney.[11] Before the *Alice* project, Huxley had earned $15,000 in 1938
for a script on the life of Madame Curie, even though his script was never
used, and he later worked on scripts with Jan Murfin for *Pride and Prejudice*
(Metro-Goldwyn-Mayer, 1940) and with Robert Stevenson and John
Housman on *Jane Eyre* (Twentieth-Century Fox, 1944).[12]

Considering the interest in dissolving the distinctions between genres
in the 1920s and 1930s, it is easy to see why Huxley would have been
interested in a project combining live action and animation. In many ways,
such a project would have promised full exploitation of the agenda for the
'musicalization of fiction' enunciated by Philip Quarles in *Point Counter Point*
(1929) when he called for the juxtaposition of apparently disparate
fragments, 'the change of moods, the abrupt transitions.'[13] Huxley's
immediate task, though, was to create a live-action frame tale which would
not only provide the transitions into Wonderland but also successfully tame
the episodic nature of Carroll's book.

In the fourteen-page synopsis he prepared, Huxley addressed these
two necessities by immediately establishing Dodgson/Carroll and Alice as
characters so at the mercy of comic blocking figures that they have a keen
need to escape from reality. Dodgson/Carroll's potential nemesis is
Langham, an Oxford vice-chancellor, High Church and ultra-Tory in
attitude, who has the power to block Dodgson's hopes of becoming a
librarian free from the onerous chores of lecturing. Langham disapproves of
Dodgson's interest in the theatre and in photography, for he 'does not think
that gentlemen in holy orders should fool with chemicals and dark rooms'
(*SY* 2). Miss Beale, a far more formidable figure, endangers Alice's hopes of
achieving some happiness in childhood and also threatens a compromising
unmasking of Dodgson/Carroll. She disapproves not only of photographs
and plays, but even more so of any failure to observe each and every
propriety.

In the synopsis, Dodgson visits Ellen Terry at the theatre, where she quickly discerns that he is Lewis Carroll, because he had once told her stories about the Cheshire Cat. Miss Beale, in the mean time, has locked Alice in the garden house as punishment. Alice begins to imagine objects in the garden house as beings in Wonderland, turning a rope, for example, into Wonderland's Caterpillar. After talking with a horse whose stable backs on to the garden house, Alice escapes, experiences an exciting but frightening series of misadventures in the Oxford streets, and finally arrives at the theatre where Ellen Terry entrusts her to the hands of Dodgson. As Ellen and Dodgson tell Alice stories, the live action dissolves into animation of Wonderland scenes but returns to live action when Miss Beale arrives. Huxley, worrying about 'a certain weakening of the dramatic effect,' argued that 'at this point we should touch the lowest point of Dodgson's and Alice's fortunes, and the passage from this low point to the happy ending should be abrupt and almost miraculous' (*SY* 12). He proposed the arrival of Queen Victoria, a true *deus ex machina*, the presentation of Dodgson/Carroll to her, and the immediate lionization of Dodgson by his opponents whom Alice now envisions 'as cartoon animals clustering round a Dodgson, who remains the only human figure in the whole collection' (*SY* 13). In the brief epilogue, the audience is intended to see Carroll and Alice triumphant: he in his library, she at the hay-party with a new, young governess.

Huxley's emphasis on Dodgson/Carroll and Ellen Terry may have been rooted in 'autobiographical nostalgia,' in that his own idealized mother, Julia Arnold, apparently was a favourite of Dodgson, who photographed her as a 'Bulgarian peasant' and again in 'Turkish fashion,' posed in his study while gazing 'through' a looking-glass.[14] There is also extant a message to 'Judy' in an 1884 letter from Dodgson to Ethel Arnold:

> You will be kind enough to tell Judy (with my love, which I send *most* reluctantly) that I may forgive, but cannot forget, her utterly heartless behaviour in my rooms yesterday. You were not present, and I will not pain your sensitive nature by describing it. But I will be even with her some day. Some sultry afternoon, when she is here, half fainting with thirst, I will produce a bottle of delicious cool lemonade. This I will uncork, and pour it foaming into a large tumbler, and then, after putting the tumbler well within her reach, *she shall have the satisfaction of seeing me drink it myself*—not a drop of it shall reach *her* lips![15]

Huxley's script, dated 5 December 1945, translates the synopsis into dialogue and directions. Miss Beale, for instance, types herself immediately when she responds to Grove's suggestion that 'there are other points of view' with the icy rejoinder, 'Not in *my* family. My dear father, the late Canon Beale of Canterbury, would *never* have admitted that there were other points of view' (*SC* 2). With these words she would have joined a long line of Disney villainesses, stretching from the Wicked Queen in *Snow White* (1938) to Cruella de Ville of *A Hundred and One Dalmatians* (1961). The comic potential inherent in the situations of the synopsis takes shape as visual effects, comic juxtapositions, and word play, including a throwaway scene involving the tongue-twister 'She sells sea shells on the salt sea shore' (*SC* 8–9). Mainly, though, Huxley concentrated his attention on making Alice a 'real little girl' and on highlighting the affinities between her and Dodgson. Alice is overly curious about the people in his photographs, prepared to be shocked on learning that Ellen Terry performed breeches roles, and completely unable to maintain poses for the forty-five seconds required by the camera, so much so that Dodgson tells her the next sitting will be 'under chloroform' (*SC* 15).

Most importantly, the 5 December script completely changes the entry into Wonderland. It now occurs in his studio, not in the theatre, and it occurs when he places the proofs of his book in Alice's hands. The scene, though, was struck through at some point in pencil, and Alice eventually enters Wonderland in dissolves as Dodgson begins to tell the story—effects not too distant from those in *The Wizard of Oz* (1939). The transition has now been effected, and Carroll's book takes over with its 'Drink Me' bottle, 'Eat Me' cake, living flowers in the garden, and the frenetic White Rabbit. It becomes clear that all these exist in the imagination of Alice, because we then merge back into live action with Dodgson checking his stoves, before another dissolve into Wonderland with the hookah-smoking Caterpillar. At this point the now obviously incomplete script ends. Huxley was not exaggerating, though, when he sent the script to Disney along with a note reading: 'I think the story is becoming more closely knit, smooth & dramatic than it was, & it should soon be ready to be worked out more fully.'[16]

IV

Fortunately, a complete transcript of the 7 December 1945 story meeting has survived. Huxley met with Disney and his staff, Cap Palmer, Dick Huemer, Bill Cottrell, Ham Luske, D. Koch, and Joe Grant, who had been working in one way or another on the project since 1938. The transcript gives us considerable insight into the transformation of a 'Hollywood' script into a motion picture and how the work of an individual scriptwriter becomes the production of a group. Huxley was relatively quiet during the session, speaking only forty-nine times and only briefly each time. Mr Huxley, as 'Cap,' 'Dick,' 'Bill,' 'Ham,' and 'Joe' called him, may have had the last words concerning the end of his treatment, but the eventual Disney *Alice* was certainly 'Walt's' creation.

Some speculation centred, of course, on casting. Disney had, during the past decade, considered Mary Pickford and Ginger Rogers. Huxley suggested Fanny Brice for the Ellen Terry role; Joe Grant saw Harold Lloyd as a perfect Dodgson/Carroll, and before the meeting concluded Disney suggested Cary Grant as Dodgson/Carroll (*SM* 2, 18). Generally, though, more important matters were discussed. Those at the meeting were particularly concerned with relationships established between the characters and the absolute necessity of a happy ending. A third of the way through the meeting, Disney clearly saw a way to achieve the happy ending. He told the group:

> There is this chance to have a scene in the end where they all go on a picnic—there is Dodgson, Grove, Alice, Terry, Mrs. Terry, and the new governess. And the new governess is not so bad to look at, and it is quite a change for Grove, so Grove becomes a sort of comic figure in a way. Or, there is another play. There could be a suggestion that Mrs. Terry and Grove become rather friendly. But we could do the same thing through the new Governess who is an entirely different character. That could be a very happy setting and you would leave with a very happy thought. (*SM* 8)

He returned to this conclusion several more times, once noting:

> And we are driving toward another underlying point which is that often times the best sense is non-sense. I'd like to finish the whole thing by coming out with some bit of nonsense that makes very good sense—and the implication would be—'There, that's what we've been trying to tell you.' (*SM* 22)

At the end of the meeting, he summarized the directions the discussion on the ending had taken thus:

maybe in the last scene we see Mr. Carroll with all these little characters around him and all of a sudden he turns into the little character we want him to be. We can just make a tag ending. Suddenly the whole thing changes. We make an overlap right on into this fantasy and don't go into any other scenes. Everybody's happy. Grove is all right and when the queen comes you can bring Miss Terry and her mother in. Everybody can be happy while this is happening. It's a natural place to bring everybody together. (*SM* 24)

He had heeded Huxley's earlier advice to do as little as possible with Queen Victoria, not only because they were 'on very dangerous historical ground because actually she was an old woman without any sense of humour at all' but also because it was best 'to keep her this remote and comic figure' (*SM* 10).

Not surprisingly, Disney was also concerned with Dodgson/Carroll's sexuality, insisting that his relationship with Ellen Terry should be played up because 'we don't want him to look like a "queer"' (*SM* 1), and much attention was paid to the various possibilities of love attractions for him in the script. Disney continued to worry about this matter throughout the discussion, saying at one point, 'I don't want to see us build up any sex story here.... We don't bring sex into it at all,' to which Cap Palmer added, 'Just a healthy interest in a grown woman' (*SM* 15–16).

Things were far more complicated when discussion focused on the other characters, and Disney proposed his 'suggested romance' (*SM* 1) between Dodgson/Carroll and Ellen Terry; Ham Luske said 'that could be cute' (*SM* 2), and further found a way of acquainting the Terrys with Alice by having them pass her on Dodgson's stairs. Disney also strongly wanted to established the theme of non-sense as early as the personal relationships were delineated. He wanted to have Carroll give lessons in nonsense to Alice, lessons which would turn Miss Beale even more adamantly against Dodgson/Carroll as the film sharply opposes Beale's and Carroll's ideas on bringing up children. Disney put it thus:

But to strengthen the whole thing, Beale is trying to bring this child up in a certain way. When she comes back from Dodgson's, the child has come back with a certain amount of Nonsense and a certain philosophy along those lines. If he has said, for example, 'Going through life with nothing but Sense is like trying to run a race with one foot.' Well, now, that's a heck of a philosophy to

give a child—in other words, it clashes with what Beale is trying
to do. (*SM* 3)

Although there was complete agreement about Miss Beale's character,
there were differences of opinion as to how her villainy should be expressed.
Suggestions were offered as diverse as jealousy of Ellen Terry, merciless
domination of Grove (at various times Alice's guardian, uncle, and father),
inhumane punishment of Alice, and her attempt to use her knowledge of
Carroll's identity to solidify her position. Huxley, though, suggested her
ultimate humiliation: having to ask Dodgson/Carroll to endorse her pension
petition (*SM* 9). Ham Luske let his imagination range freely, suggesting a
scene culminating in Dodgson, Beale, and Alice kneeling before Queen
Victoria; it would, he said, offer 'cute scenes of Alice trying to get into the
Palace' (*SM* 11). All in all, Miss Beale was a rich field on which the story
editors exercised their imaginations. Disney concluded, 'I'd like to work it so
that there's only one heavy in the picture and that's Beale and we can lay
everything on her. Have no other heavy, you see?' (*SM* 17). The discussion
suggests that Miss Beale, rather than Dodgson/Carroll or Alice, was the key
figure in every way for the film's plotting and that eventually she was turned
into a direct descendant of Charles Dickens's Gradgrind in *Hard Times*: 'The
thing that makes the whole story pay off is that there is a conflict between
Beale and her theory on how Children should be handled—there should be
no nonsense at all—everything has to drive toward something practical' (*SM*
22).

V

Maria Huxley remembered that 'this [was] the first movie he liked doing,'[17]
but Huxley never saw his work used. Reportedly, Disney rejected Huxley's
synopsis as being 'too literary.'[18] The Disney *Alice in Wonderland* was not
released for another six years, on 28 July 1951, and Huxley's name was not
among the thirteen story editors listed in the screen credits. The film
contained no live action, for the almost thirty-year goal of Disney had been
discarded in 1946.[19] A full-length live-action film had been shot in-house for
the animators to consult, as they had observed the live deer during the
production of *Bambi*, but it took five years and a reported $5 million before
the animated version was completed.[20]

The episodic nature of the material hampered the pacing and
continuity of the film. It has its memorable moments—the Cheshire Cat, the

living flowers, the march of the cards—but audiences and critics did not like it. The *New Yorker* critic, for instance, wrote: 'In Mr. Disney's *Alice* there is a blind incapacity to understand that a literary masterwork cannot be improved by the introduction of shiny little tunes, and touches more suited to a flea circus than to a major imaginative effort.'[21] The film's directing animator, Ward Kimball, analysed the problems much more specifically, holding that the film

> degenerated into a loud-mouthed vaudeville show. There's no denying that there are many charming bits in our *Alice*, but it lacks warmth and an overall story glue. *Alice* suffered from too many cooks—directors. Here was a case of five directors each trying to top the other guy and make his sequences the biggest and craziest in the show. This had a self-cancelling effect on the final product.[22]

Even Disney himself came to consider Alice 'as a prim and prissy little person, lacking in humor and entirely too passive for her role in the story.'[23] Disney's daughter has written that 'Father had been dubious about *Alice*' and 'millions of people didn't care what happened to Alice' as they had cared about Cinderella.[24]

Whatever the reasons for the failure of *Alice in Wonderland*, it is highly doubtful whether or not Huxley's hand could have prevented it, but it was undoubtedly a disaster in Walt Disney's mind. It was the only one of the major animations he allowed to be shown on the 'World of Disney,' but the film was not reissued. Even its 16-millimetre form was later withdrawn from distribution.

Carroll's work was filmed as *Alice au pays des merveilles* by Lou Bunin, Marc Maurette, and Dallas Bower in 1949; Jonathan Miller directed a 1966 English television version; and William Sterling filmed it in 1972.

APPENDIX

ALDOUS HUXLEY'S ALICE IN WONDERLAND SYNOPSIS

Montage shots as before.

When we get to Oxford, Langham is reading to Grove a letter he has just received from the Lord Chamberlain's office, saying that the Queen is interested in the authorship of 'Alice,' understands Carroll is an Oxford don and desires Langham, as Vice-Chancellor, to make enquiries in the University. (This ties up with the last sequence of the MONTAGE and fits in with the final discovery, at the time of the Queen's visit.) Langham regards this request almost as an insult to the dignity of his office, and is much annoyed at being asked to take an interest in children's books. He says he proposes to take no action about the Lord Chamberlain's letter.

Meeting with Dodgson, whom they find absorbed in a playbill announcing coming performances at the local theatre. Grove rather likes Dodgson—though he regards him as a harmless lunatic. For Langham, however, no lunatic is harmless if his lunacy threatens to bring discredit on the High Church, conservative party in the university. Talk about the theatre. Dodgson explains that he is especially interested in these performances on account of Ellen Terry, whom he knew as a child, when she made her first stage appearance. Langham expresses disapproval of theatre-going for clergymen. Grove changes the subject by talking of Alice and the picture Dodgson is to make of her—to be sent to her parents in India. More disapproval by Langham, who does not think that gentlemen in holy orders should fool with chemicals and dark rooms.

They take leave of Dodgson. Langham expresses his disapproval as in the existing version; says he will do his best to see that Dodgson does not get the librarianship for which he has applied. Grove defends him, but is reduced to silence by the imperious Langham.

Scene between Grove and Miss Beale, retaining Miss Beale's request for help in securing her pension.

Scene between Miss Beale and Alice, with the addition that, before letting Alice get down from her chair, Miss Beale reads her one of Dr. Watts' edifying rhymes for children, or some other similar production, characteristic of the period.

Lecture scene, the same as at present, except that the undergraduates audibly snigger when Dodgson's stammer gets too bad. (This gives point to the intensity of Dodgson's desire to get the librarianship, which means the end of lecturing and its humiliations.)

On the stairs we bring out the characteristics of the two undergraduates we shall see later, waiting for Miss Terry. One is a member of the 'fast set'—handsome, athletic, devil-may-care; the other a hero-worshipping follower, of slight physique and timid character. On the stairs, as he leaves the lecture, the 'fast set' youth divests himself of his cap and gown, the light overcoat he is wearing and his trousers—revealing the fact that he is dressed for horseback riding in bottle green tail-coat, breeches and high boots. (This is based on an episode in 'Tom Brown at Oxford' and may be regarded as authentically of the period.) It is the youth in riding clothes who tells Alice that he hopes she will enjoy her logic lesson.

Scenes between Dodgson and Alice as before, except that we should at some point introduce a conversation in which Alice expresses a wish that she might escape from the grind of lessons and Dodgson says, in humorous terms, that his wish is just the same—to be able to give up lecturing and devote himself to writing. [pencilled '?' in left margin] We should also, I think, make Alice mention her father and mother and express her longing for their return. This must not be sentimental; but it is necessary to underline that the child is temporarily an orphan and at the mercy of a governess and an old man, who do not understand or truly love her.

Scene of the return home and release of the mouse. This is the same as before, except that, when Miss Beale first appears, Alice starts to tell her about the little girls who dress up as boys and act in plays—and may she do that one day? This naturally incenses Miss Beale yet further against Dodgson.

Grove's interview with Dodgson after the mouse episode is more friendly, more in sorrow than in anger, than in the present version. He speaks to Dodgson as a sincere well-wisher, giving the younger man advice for his own good, telling him how careful he must be if he wants to secure so important a post as the librarianship.

Scene with the doll as at present.

Time lapse and scene between Alice and Miss Beale in the Schoolroom, as at present. Dodgson's note is brought in. Alice first looks at the photo and shows it to Miss Beale, who disapproves. Then she reads the note, which announces that the afternoon performance of 'Romeo and Juliet' is for May 3rd and that he will make final arrangements for picking her up when he comes to tea, as she has asked him to do, on May 2nd. Miss Beale is doubly outraged—first by the fact that an invitation should have been issued without her permission, second because Dodgson proposes to take Alice to the theatre. Alice is forced to write an answer, cancelling her invitation and saying that she cannot go to the theatre on account of her religious principles.

Scene of Alice hiding the letter to Dodgson, as at present.

Time lapse, scene in Dodgson's room on May 2nd. Dodgson is alone, working on one of his mathematical problems. He murmurs the calculations to himself as he writes them down. Then something in the problem, or something in the environment, suggests a nonsense idea, and he starts to write a few lines of the 'Snark' or of one of the nonsense poems in 'Through the Looking Glass.'

Drinks a pot of beer [pencilled '?' in left margin] with the janitor and puts half a crown on a horse. The messenger returns and takes him to Ellen's dressing room.

Scene in the dressing room. Ellen, dressed as Ophelia, is having her hair done by her mother. Ellen says she feels flattered by his visit, for it is rare that he deigns to pay any attention to anyone who is not a child. Mrs. Terry humorously calls him the most fickle and faithless of men—dropping all his child friends as soon as they show signs of growing up, Dodgson admits that he gets on best with women when they are under seven or over seventy—the Terrys are the exception who prove the rule. The Terrys now draw him out, and he talks to them more freely than he could do to Alice about the librarianship and his desire to escape from the humiliating and painful duty of lecturing and to concentrate on his own writing. He now gives Ellen a copy of 'Alice,' saying that the book is by an old friend of his, Mr. Carroll. 'Alias Mr. Dodgson,' says Ellen, as she turns the pages. He protests. She answers that the evidence against him is overwhelming. Has he forgotten that he used to tell her stories about a creature called the Cheshire cat? In the end, he admits that he is the author, but begs that the secret may not be divulged. At the university he is known as a logician and mathematician; it would do his reputation no good and spoil his chances for the librarianship if he came to be known as a writer of nonsense. The call boy now knocks at the dressing-room door. Asking permission to bring Alice after the next day's performance, Dodgson goes out.

Scene in the bookshop, as at present.

Scene with Miss Beale, Polly and Susan in the forecourt of Dr. Grove's house. We establish the fact that the children have driven in from their home in the country, some miles from Oxford, and have just left an invitation for Alice to attend the hay party which their parents annually give in June. Dodgson is also invited.

Scene between Alice and Miss Beale regarding the discovery of the unposted letter—as before.

Scene of Dodgson's entry on all fours—as before, except that, at the end, the punishment decreed for Alice includes, as well as solitary confinement, a prohibition to go to the hay party.

[pencilled '?' in left margin] Scene in the garden house. This begins as at present. We cut out the scene of the committee discussing the librarianship and substitute a scene between Miss Beale and Grove. Grove expresses concern about the severity of Alice's punishment, but Miss Beale assures him that this is how it was always done in the best and most pious families. Grove ends by agreeing, as he always does when confronted by a personality stronger than his own.

Miss Beale now raises the subject of the pension. She is getting very anxious, as she only has two more weeks to get her application in—if she fails to send it in time, she will have to wait another two years. Grove admits he has done nothing and says definitely that he can't do anything. The affairs of his kinsman, who is trying to get the job at Barchester, are in a rather delicate situation and Grove cannot afford to waste his influence with the Bishop on anyone else. Charity, he concludes, begins at home. In desperation Miss Beale asks him if he knows of anyone else who could give her a recommendation to the Bishop. Grove answers that the Bishop is an old friend of Dodgson's father [pencilled '?' in left margin] and has known Dodgson from childhood. Too late Miss Beale wishes that she had kept on better terms with Dodgson.

At this point they are interrupted by the sound of screaming and knocking from the garden house. Grove is shaken and suggests letting Alice out. Miss Beale tells him to leave the matter to her and, going to the door of the garden house, tells Alice that if she doesn't stop her noise, she will be kept in confinement all night as well as all day.

Cut to Alice, who now makes a deliberate effort to get rid of her terrors. This she does by pretending she is in Wonderland and that things are not what they seem. The rope hanging from the beam becomes in her imagination the Wonderland caterpillar. A terrifying stuffed tiger's head, lying among the lumber, turns into the Cheshire Cat, and she finds that she can make it appear and vanish at will. Then she reminds herself (talking to herself aloud) that in Wonderland there is always a way out of the tightest corner, always a garden at the bottom of every rabbit hole. For instance, what would you see if you opened that little shuttered window there in the back wall? With much difficulty she unfastens it, opens and finds herself looking into the face of a horse. Alarmed, she hastily closes it; then recollecting that anything can happen, cautiously re-opens for a better look. The garden house backs onto the stables of the house behind, and she is looking into these stables. Reassured, Alice now starts talking to the horse and, in her fancy, hears it talking back. It tells her its name, and when she asks if it would like a piece of her bread, it replies by enquiring rather cagily, if the bread is buttered. Alice explains that it isn't, as she is being punished. The horse agrees to have a taste, and Alice fetches the bread and gives it a fragment, which the horse takes in its mouth, then lets fall on the floor, saying 'I can't swallow the stuff without butter.' Then it suggests that Alice should crawl through the bars. Alice takes its advice, squeezes through and, standing on the manger, closes the shutter after her. Then she jumps down, says good-bye to the horse and goes out into the stable yard, which has a gate leading into the street. She sees a groom approaching and dashes off in a panic through the gate and along the street. She turns into a narrow side street and halts, recovering her breath and straining her ears for sounds of pursuit. All is quiet. Reassured, she goes on, talking to herself about the best way of getting to the theatre. She knows how to get there from Cornmarket Street. She now meets a band of ragged street urchins, who ask her questions, pull her hair, steal the contents of the pocket of her pinafore; suddenly one of them shouts, 'Police!' and they all scatter. Alice turns, sees the towering form of a policeman approaching, remembers Miss Beale's blood-curdling accounts of what happens to children who fall into the clutches of the Law, and takes to her heels down a side street. The street ends in a court-yard, one side of which is occupied by a blacksmith's shop.

'What are you looking for, missie?' the blacksmith asks.

Alice sees that there is another entrance to the smithy and, saying, 'They're after me,' she dashes past the smith and out through the door on the opposite side. Still running, she crosses a crowded street and is nearly run over by a horse-drawn omnibus. As she reaches the sidewalk, an old lady stops Alice and asks her kindly if she has lost her way. Alice starts to answer, when she catches sight of another policeman some way down the street. Breaking away from the old lady, she darts into an alley. Turning a corner, she finds herself confronted with an enormous mastiff, almost as tall as she is. Alice almost turns tail, then remembers the police and decides to brave the dog. 'Nice Fido,' she says. 'Nice little puppy dog.' To her great relief the dog wags its tail, and, when she goes on, it accompanies her. The alley debouches into a narrow cul de sac. In the high brick wall opposite is a door, beside which hangs the playbill announcing today's performance of 'Romeo and Juliet.' 'The theatre!' Alice cries. Running to the door, she asks the janitor for Miss Terry. The man looks at her curiously, asks her name and, when she tells him, sends someone to ask Miss Terry if she knows a little girl called Alice; then he turns to speak to someone else. While he does this, Alice slips past and follows the messenger into the theatre. She sees actors dressed up, property men carrying jewels, swords, golden flagons—it is all part of Wonderland. The messenger goes onto the stage, where most of the actors are assembled, in costume, talking together and eating a sandwich lunch. He gives his message to Mrs. Terry, who shakes her head and says they don't know any little girl called Alice. At this Alice emerges from the dark nook in which she has been hiding, runs to Mrs. Terry and begs not to be sent away. Incoherently she explains that she was to have been brought by Mr. Dodgson, but wasn't allowed to come, was punished, ran away, has all the police in Oxford on her track. Ellen and the other players gather round; everyone is very kind. Mrs. Terry tells the messenger to take a cab and bring Mr. Dodgson back immediately. Listening to the child's story, Mrs. Terry becomes indignant. This is the way she herself was brought up, and she has vowed to do what she can to prevent such horrors being perpetrated on other children. Alice now confides to Ellen her system for overcoming fear by pretending to be in Wonderland. Ellen thinks this is an excellent idea and tells her that this is what the theatre is for—to take people out of Dull-land and Worry-land and carry them into Wonderland. And she adds that there are all kinds of Wonderlands—beautiful, sad Wonderlands like the 'Romeo and Juliet' and funny, nonsense Wonderlands, like the story Mr. Dodgson has written. Alice corrects her: the story was written by Mr. Carroll. And she describes Mr. Carroll's peculiarities. Ellen laughs. 'So you know why you can never see Mr. Carroll?' she asks and, when Alice says no, she whispers something in her ear. 'You mean that Mr. Dodgson ...?' says Alice. 'Sh-sh,' says Ellen. 'It's a great secret. If you told anyone, the queen might say, "Off with his head."' And she goes on to ask Alice if she remembers how the Queen carried on at the croquet party. She starts telling the episode and the other actors join in, taking the various parts. Alice looks on spellbound.

dissolve into animation.

Return to live action at the entry of Dodgson, whom Ellen greets as the White Rabbit but Dodgson is in no mood for joking. He is greatly worried over what has happened and wants to take Alice home immediately. But the Terrys won't hear of it. 'She shan't go back,' says Mrs. Terry, 'until I've had a talk with that old dragon of hers.' Dodgson finally agrees to join in the dramatic story telling.

We go on with the animation.

At the height of one of the Queen's 'off with his head' scenes, an all too familiar voice breaks in, saying 'There she is!' Returning abruptly to live action, we see Miss Beale, supported by Dr. Grove and two policemen. Alice screams in terror, 'don't let them take me!' and throws herself into Ellen's arms. The man who plays Romeo mock-heroically draws his sword and stands in a posture of defence. But Miss Beale, with an unexpected flourish of her umbrella, knocks the sword out of his hand and advances on Alice.

Mrs. Terry comes forward indignantly. 'You ought to be ashamed of yourself' she tells Miss Beale, 'frightening a poor little child out of her wits with your abominable stories of hanging and prisons.' 'You too,' she adds, turning to Grove, and she orders him to send the policemen away. Grove, as usual, bows before the stronger personality, explains apologetically that the policemen helped them to get on Alice's trail, then tips the men and sends them away. Mrs. Terry returns to Miss Beale, and Dodgson is left with Grove, stammeringly trying to explain. Grove, feeling himself in a stronger position, adopts his most pompous manner, telling Dodgson that hitherto he had supported his application for the post of librarian, but that now, after what has happened, he cannot vote for a candidate whose eccentricities and irresponsible behaviour have led to such deplorable results.

At this point we have to decide whether or not there is a time lapse between the theatre episode and the arrival of the Queen.

If there is a time lapse, then we require a very full scene between the Terrys and Miss Beale, in which Miss Beale finally agrees not to punish Alice any further when they get home. In such a scene the Terrys would overcome Miss Beale's hostility to them as actresses by evoking a fellow feeling on the ground that both actresses and governesses are wage slaves, looked down upon by the rich and respectable, and ruthlessly exploited by them.

Having established this, they could then start to talk with equal realism about other matters, such as child psychology in general and Alice in particular. If we don't have a scene of this kind, ending with a promise of good behaviour by Miss Beale, it is difficult to see how Alice could be persuaded to go home. The child would have to be dragged away by main force and in a state of hysterics. Moreover the audience would feel very uncomfortable at the thought of what might happen to Alice, after falling once again into Beale's clutches. On the other hand, if we insert a scene along the lines indicated above, the result will be a certain weakening of the dramatic effect; for at this point we should touch the lowest point of Dodgson's and Alice's fortunes, and the passage from this low point to the happy ending should be abrupt and almost miraculous. For this reason I am inclined to think that the Queen's arrival should take place on the same afternoon as the episode in the theatre. If this is the case we can arrange the story along some such lines as the following.

At some time during the scenes following Grove's and Miss Beale's arrival, Alice lets out the secret of Dodgson's identity with Carroll.

In his talk with Dodgson Grove brings up Dodgson's authorship of a nonsense book as yet another reason why he is unfit for a post of honour and responsibility in the university. Leaving the others in the theatre, he goes off there and then to discuss the matter with Dr. Langham.

We follow Grove to Langham's study, where he starts to talk about Dodgson and the librarianship. But Langham has more pressing problems on his mind. The Queen is arriving unexpectedly within the next half hour and this announcement has been accompanied by a message expressing her majesty's wish to have the author of Alice presented to her. Langham is in a tight corner, as he has ignored the earlier request contained in the Lord Chamberlain's letter (read by him in the first sequence) and he will therefore cut a very poor figure with the Queen, when she turns up.

Grove now announces excitedly that he knows the secret and without divulging Dodgson's name, he leaves Langham in order to fetch the author of 'Alice' for presentation to the Queen.

Cut to the theatre. Grove comes bustling in, tells Dodgson that the Vice-Chancellor wants to see him immediately. Dodgson takes leave of the Terrys with the air of a condemned criminal going to execution. Grove, Dodgson, Alice and Miss Beale all get into a cab and drive off.

Approaching the main gate of Christ Church they find that the Queen has arrived and a crowd is assembling. Grove and his party leave the cab, and push their way through the crowd to where Langham and the other university dignitaries are paying their respects to the Queen. Langham is in the act of telling her Majesty that he does not know who the author of 'Alice' is, when Grove pushes Dodgson forward. (Alice is terrified lest the Queen should order Dodgson's head to be cut off).

Dodgson is presented, as in the present version. The Queen drives off. Dodgson is flattered and lionized by those who previously looked askance at him. Miss Beale is all smiles, apologizes for any little misunderstandings there may have been in the past and, when Dodgson expresses a wish to let by-gones be by-gones, goes on to ask if he will help her with pension business. Dodgson hesitates a moment; then asks if this means that she will not have to teach anymore children in the future. Miss Beale answers that, if she gets her pension, she will be able to resign immediately. Dodgson takes the form and says he will submit it to the Bishop at once with the warmest possible recommendation.

Alice now has a vision of the flatterers as cartoon animals clustering round a Dodgson, who remains the only human figure in the whole collection.

EPILOGUE:

A gothic doorway with the word 'Librarian' painted on the door. A scout knocks and goes in. We see Dodgson sitting at a table, writing. The walls of the room are lined with book shelves, filled with ancient folios and quartos. The scout announces that the carriage is at the college gate. Dodgson picks up his hat and umbrella and goes out. On the way he meets [illegible line] their delight that old Dodo should have given up his dreary lectures. Dodgson climbs into the carriage, and we cut to the carriage entering the gates of a park. In the park is a large meadow, newly mown and covered with hay-cocks. There are some grown-ups and a great many children, who are looking for presents in the hay. A little merry-go-round worked by hand stands in one corner of the meadow; a Punch and Judy show in another. Alice comes running up to Dodgson and introduces him to her new governess a young and charming girl, who seems to be enjoying the hay-party almost as much as Alice herself.

At this moment a stout, effusive, middle-aged lady comes up to Dodgson, apologizes for addressing him without a formal introduction, but says she could not resist telling the distinguished author of 'Alice' how much she loves his wonderful book. Dodgson bows and, without speaking, takes a printed card out of his pocket and hands it to her, then bows again and moves away, leaving the lady looking at the card, on which is printed: 'The Rev. Charles L. Dodgson takes no responsibility for any publication not issued under his own name.' The stout lady looks after him and, through her eyes, we see Dodgson walking away, holding Alice with one hand, Polly with the other, while Susan brings up the rear, carrying his umbrella.

The End

NOTES

1. Los Angeles *Times*, 19 Nov. 1945, Part I, p. 11.

2. See Laura Archera Huxley, *This Timeless Moment: A Personal View of Aldous Huxley* (New York, 1968), who writes: 'His system of reading was extremely helpful, not only for him but for me also. Aldous always read with a pen—he would mark passages which were of special importance, sometimes comment on them with a few words on the page itself, then at the end of the book note the subject and the page.... Unfortunately, I have now very few books marked in this way. The fire destroyed his 4,000 volumes, most of which contained these private reference annotations' (p. 275). For those scholars interested in the intellectual development of Huxley and in tracing the development of the individual works, this was a grave loss.

3. See Leonard Maltin, *The Disney Films* (New York, 1973), 279–80 for a complete listing of the Alice in Cartoonland short subjects.

4. Richard Schickel, *The Disney Version: The Life, Times, Art and Commerce of Walt Disney*, rev. edn. (New York, 1985), 105.

5. Bob Thomas, *Walt Disney: An American Original* (New York, 1976), 220.

6. These and the subsequent quotations from the synopsis, script, and meeting notes are quoted with the permission of the Studio Archives, The Walt Disney Company. The specific documents are: (1) 14 Jan. 1939 Story Meeting (*SM*); (2) 13 Nov. 1939 Story Meeting (*SM*); (3) 8 Apr. 1941 Story Meeting (*SM*); (4) 7 Dec. 1945 Story Meeting (*SM*); (5) 5 Nov. 1945 Jack Lavin Memorandum to Hal Adelquist; (6) 23 Nov. 1945 *Alice in Wonderland* Synopsis, 14 pp. (*SY*); (7) 5 Dec. 1945 *Alice in Wonderland* Script, 31 pp. (*SC*).

7. Thomas, *Walt Disney*, 176–7.

8. In her essay, 'Aldous Huxley in California,' Anita Loos recalled how she secured Huxley the job by recommending him to the producer. The position paid $2,500 a week, and Huxley was adverse to taking the job so long as his 'family and friends [were] starving and being bombed in England.' Loos suggested that he could send them whatever amount from his salary he wanted, and this settled the matter. See *Harper's Magazine*, 228 (May 1964), 55.

9. *Letters of Aldous Huxley*, ed. Grover Smith (New York, 1969), 535.

10. Ibid. 536.

11. The flyleaf inscription on the *Ape and Essence* script possibly echoes Huxley's feelings over the several rejections: 'An original Treatment by William Tallis, Cottonwood Ranch, Murcia, California.... Rejection slip sent

11–26–47. No self addressed envelope. For the Incinerator,' *Ape and Essence* (New York, 1948), 14.

12. His scenario, 'Success,' never found a taker from a studio. For a further survey of and discussion of Huxley's film scripts, see Virginia Martha Clark, 'Aldous Huxley and Film,' unpub. dissertation, University of Maryland, 1983. Clark's dissertation does not discuss the *Alice in Wonderland* episode.
According to George Woodcock, in 1957 Huxley 'was reduced to preparing the outline for an animated cartoon of *Don Quixote* to be played by Mr. Magoo,' *Dawn and the Darkest Hour: A Study of Aldous Huxley* (New York, 1972), 218.

13. *Point Counter Point* (New York, 1928), 301. In the Anita Loos letter, cited in note 9, Huxley discussed the adaptation of *Brave New World* for film. He commented, 'it will probably be necessary, for film purposes, to write the scenes in the future in the form of cut-forwards from a contemporary starting point' (*Letters*, 534). The proposed cutting from present to future, in a quite different world, closely resembles what he was to do in moving from Oxford to Wonderland. This dialogic imagination, of course, stands behind many of the effects for which Huxley is famous.

14. *A Selection from the letters of Lewis Carroll to His Child-Friends*, ed. Evelyn M. Hatch (London, 1933), 186, 94.

15. Letter LXII to Ethel Arnold, ibid. 96.

16. Letter of 23 Nov. 1945, quoted with permission of Laura Archera Huxley.

17. Sybille Bedford, *Aldous Huxley: A Biography* (New York, 1974), 447. Bedford also quotes a Maria Huxley letter in which she notes that Matthew Huxley 'helped him out instantly over a deep jam in the Alice situation' (p. 447). The nature of the assistance and the nature of the jam remain unidentified.

18. Woodcock, *Dawn and the Darkest Hour*, 218.

19. Maltin, *The Disney Films*, 101.

20. Ibid. 102.

21. Quoted ibid. 103.

22. Quoted ibid.

23. Schickel, *The Disney Version*, 295.

24. Diane Disney Miller, as told to Pete Martin, *The Story of Walt Disney* (New York, 1957), 214. Miller saw several reasons for the failure of the film: 'For one thing, *Alice* is a literary classic, but it's heavy with intellectual appeal and light on emotional appeal. Such stories are as tricky as TNT: they can be a success or they can blow a picture sky high' (p. 214).

Chronology

1894	Born on July 26 in Godalming, Surrey, England to Leonard and Julia Huxley. His grandfather, Thomas Henry Huxley, was an important scientist who developed Darwin's theories on evolution, as well as a thinker who first used the term "agnostic." He also has distant maternal relation to famed English poet Matthew Arnold.
1908	Huxley's mother dies of cancer.
1910	Eye illness renders Huxley temporarily blind, foiling plans for medical school, for which he had been preparing. Later, although his vision recovers, Huxley does not gain sufficient sight to fight in World War I.
1916	Earns BA from Balliol College, Oxford University. While there, Huxley makes his first literary friendships, with Lytton Strachey, Bertrand Russell, and D. H. Lawrence. Also publishes first book, a collection of poems entitled *The Burning Wheel*.
1917	Hired as schoolmaster at Eton College in Eton, England.
1919	Becomes staff member of *Athanaeum* and *Westminster Gazette*. Marries Maria Nys.
1920	Huxley's only child, Matthew, is born. In the decade following, the Huxleys travel a great deal, living in London intermittently. They visit Italy, India, and America for more extended visits.

1921	*Crome Yellow* published in London; the following year it is published in New York. It would be reprinted in both countries in the year of Huxley's death.
1923	*Antic Hay* published.
1924	As a result of early novel successes, Huxley is able to leave his editorial jobs to pursue writing full time.
1925	*Those Barren Leaves* published. Huxleys travel around the world for most of the year.
1928	*Point Counter Point* published in the United States.
1931	During a fevered four months, Huxley writes *Brave New World*.
1937	Huxleys move permanently to the United States. By 1938, they are settled in Hollywood, and Huxley begins work as a screenwriter.
1940	Huxley writes the screenplay for the film adaptation of Jane Austen's *Pride and Prejudice*.
1946	Following World War II, Huxley pens a new introduction to *Brave New World*, recanting his stated idea of the novel, that mass social sanity was impossible in the world of his time. Huxley also publishes *The Perennial Philosophy*, Huxley's own collected writings (with others) further defining "social sanity" and musing on means of achieving it.
1954	Publishes *The Doors of Perception*, a nonfictional account of his experiences with hallucinogens and other "mind-expanding" substances, including LSD. The account provided another facet to Huxley's fame, and the book was a counterculture sensation in the years that followed. The rock group, The Doors, claim to have taken the inspiration for their name from this book. In all, Huxley's chemical experimentation lasted through the 1950s and into the 1960s.
1955	Maria Huxley dies.
1956	Publishes *Heaven and Hell*, another book chronicling drug experiences. He also remarries, to Laura Archera.
1958	Publishes *Brave New World Revisited*, essays which addressed problems only thematically present in the novel, as well as in a great deal of Huxley's other work.

1959	American Academy of Arts and Letters awards Huxley the Award of Merit for the Novel.
1962	Publishes *Island*, considered by some to be the utopian antidote to *Brave New World's* dystopia.
1963	Dies November 22, 1963. His ashes were returned to England and laid to rest in his parents' grave.

Contributors

HAROLD BLOOM is Sterling Professor of the Humanities at Yale University and Henry W. and Albert A. Berg Professor of English at the New York University Graduate School. He is the author of over 20 books, including *Shelley's Mythmaking* (1959), *The Visionary Company* (1961), *Blake's Apocalypse* (1963), *Yeats* (1970), *A Map of Misreading* (1975), *Kabbalah and Criticism* (1975), *Agon: Toward a Theory of Revisionism* (1982), *The American Religion* (1992), *The Western Canon* (1994), and *Omens of Millennium: The Gnosis of Angels, Dreams, and Resurrection* (1996). *The Anxiety of Influence* (1973) sets forth Professor Bloom's provocative theory of the literary relationships between the great writers and their predecessors. His most recent books include *Shakespeare: The Invention of the Human*, a 1998 National Book Award finalist, and *How to Read and Why*, which was published in 2000. In 1999, Professor Bloom received the prestigious American Academy of Arts and Letters Gold Medal for Criticism.

MILTON BIRNBAUM is former Professor of English and Dean of the College of Arts and Sciences at American International College. He is author of *Aldous Huxley's Quest for Values*.

JOHN ATTARIAN is a freelance writer and a contributing editor to *Religion & Liberty*. His work has appeared in such publications as *Modern Age*, *Crisis* and *The Freeman*.

SALLY A. PAULSELL, at the time the article was written, was an associate faculty member at Indiana University–Purdue University in Columbus,

Indiana. She contributed an essay on Aldous Huxley to *British Short Fiction Writers 1914-1945*.

JEROME MECKIER is Professor of English at the University of Kentucky, and the author of *Aldous Huxley: Satire and Structure*, *Innocent Abroad: Charles Dickens' American Engagements*, and the editor of *Critical Essays on Aldous Huxley*.

NINA DIAKONOVA is Professor of English at the University of St. Petersburg in Russia. Her articles have appeared in a number of American journals.

JAMES R. BAKER is the editor of Penquin's edition of *Lord of the Flies*, as well as *Critical Essays on William Golding*.

SANFORD E. MAROVITZ is University Professor Emeritus of English at Kent State University. He co-edited *Artful Thunder: Versions of the Romantic Tradition in American Literature* and co-authored *Bibliographical Guide to the Study of Literature of the U.S.A.*

KERWIN LEE KLEIN is associate professor of history at the University of California, Berkeley. He is the author of *Frontiers of Historical Imagination: Narrating the European Conquest of Native America, 1890-1990*.

DAVID BRADSHAW is Hawthornden Fellow and Tutor in English Literature at Worcester College, Oxford. He is the editor of several books on Aldous Huxley, including *Between the Wars Essays and Letters* and a critical edition of *Now More Than Ever*.

RONALD HOPE, a scholar who discovered Huxley at a young age and grew up in Huxley's era, considers *The Perennial Philosophy* to be the book of Huxley's prime.

DAVID LEON HIGDON is Paul Whitfield Horn Professor Emeritus of English at Texas Tech University. He is the author of *Time and British Fiction*, and *Shadows of the Past in Contemporary British Fiction*, and has served as the general editor of *Conradiana*. He is also the editor of *Almayer's Folly* for the Cambridge University Press Joseph Conrad edition.

PHILLIP LEHRMAN holds a BA (1971) and MA (1973) in Music from the University of Southen California. He was Assistant Conductor of the New York Philharmonic in 1973–74, studying with Leonard Bernstein, an Assistant Professor at the University of Wisconsin from 1974–78, and an Associate Professor and Conductor at Texas Tech University from 1979–89.

Bibliography

Aplin, John. "Aldous Huxley's Music Criticism: Some Sources for the Fiction." *English Language Notes* 21 (September 1983): pp. 58-62.

John Atkins, John. *Aldous Huxley*. Columbus: Orion Press, 1968.

Baker, Robert S. "Aldous Huxley: History and Science Between the Wars." *Clio* 25 (Spring 1996): pp. 293-300.

——. *Brave New World: History, Science, and Dystopia*. Boston: Twayne, 1990.

Bedford, Sybille. *Aldous Huxley: A Biography*. New York: Knopf, 1974.

Begnoche, Suzanne R "Aldous Huxley's Soviet Source Material: An Unpublished Letter."*English Language Notes* 34 (March 1997): pp. 51-6.

Birnbaum, Milton. *Aldous Huxley's Quest for Values*. Knoxville: University of Tennessee Press, 11971.

Bowering, Peter. *Aldous Huxley: A Study of the Major Novels*, London: Athlone Press, 1968.

Brander, Laurence. *Aldous Huxley: A Critical Study*, Cranbury: Bucknell University Press, 1970.

Brook, Jocelyn. *Aldous Huxley*, London: Longmans, Green, 1954.

Clark, Ronald W. *The Huxleys*, New York: McGraw, 1968.

Dasgupta, Sanjukta. *The Novels of Huxley and Hemingway: A Study in Two Planes of Reality*, New Delhi: Prestige, 1996.

Deery, Jane. *Aldous Huxley and the Mysticism of Science*, New York: St. Martin's Press, 1996.

Dunaway, David King. *Aldous Huxley Recollected: An Oral History*, Alta Mira Press, 1998.

Firchow, Peter Edgerly. *The Ends of Utopia: A Study of Aldous Huxley's 'Brave New World,'* Cranbury: Bucknell University Press, 1984.

_____. *Aldous Huxley: A Satirist and Novelist*, Minneapolis: University of Minnesota Press, 1972.

Gibson, William L. "Four Samples of Oral Biography." *The Oral History Review* 24, no. 2 (Winter 1997): pp. 101-6.

Greenblatt, Stephen J. *Three Modern Satirists: Waugh, Orwell, and Huxley*, New Haven: Yale University Press, 1965.

Holmes, Charles M. *Aldous Huxley and the Way to Reality*, Bloomington: Indiana University Press, 1970.

Huxley, Julian. *Aldous Huxley: A Memorial Volume*, New York: Harper, 1965.

Huxley, Laura Archera. *This Timeless Moment: A Personal View of Aldous Huxley*, New York: Farrar, Straus, 1968.

Izzo, David Garrett. *Aldous Huxley and W.H. Auden: On Language*, Locust Hill Press, 1998.

Keulks, Gavin. "Aldous Huxley: A Centenary Bibliography (1978-1995)." *Journal of Modern Literature* 20 (Winter 1996): pp. 223-38.

Klein, Kerwin Lee. "Westward utopia: Robert V. Hine, Aldous Huxley, and the future of California history." *Pacific Historical Review* 70, no. 3 (August 2001): pp. 465-76.

Kuehn, Robert E., ed. *Aldous Huxley: A Collection of Critical Essays*, Englewood Cliffs: Prentice-Hall, 1974.

Leal, R. B. "Drieu La Rochelle and Huxley: Cross Channel Perspectives on Decadence." *Journal of European Studies* 15 (December 1985): pp. 247-59.

Mathisen, Werner Christie. "The Underestimation of Politics in Green Utopias: The Description of Politics in Huxley's *Island*, Le Guin's *The Dispossessed*, and Callenbach's *Ecotopia*." *Utopian Studies* 12, no. 1 (2001): pp. 56-78

Meckier, Jerome. "Aldous Huxley, Evelyn Waugh, and Birth Control in Black Mischief." *Journal of Modern Literature* 23, no. 2 (Winter 1999/2000): pp. 277-90.

_____. "Aldous Huxley: Dystopian Essayist of the 1930s." *Utopian Studies* 7, no. 2 (1996): pp. 196-212.

_____, ed. *Critical Essays on Aldous Huxley*, Boston: G. K. Hall, 1996.

_____. *Aldous Huxley: Satire and Structure*, New York: Barnes & Noble, 1969.

Morissey, Thomas J. "Armageddon from Huxley to Hoban." *Extrapolation* 25 (Fall 1984): pp. 197-213.

Nugel, Bernfried. *Now More than Ever: Proceedings of the Aldous Huxley Centenary Symposium, Munster, 1994,* New York: P. Lang, 1996.

Sexton, James. "Brave New World, the Feelies, and Elinor Glyn." *English Language Notes* 35 (September 1997): pp. 35-8.

————. "Aldous Huxley's *Bokanovsky*." *Science-Fiction Studies* 16 (March 1989): pp. 85-9.

Super, R. H. "Aldous Huxley's Art of Allusion—the Arnold Connection." *English Studies* 72 (October 1991): pp. 426-41.

Thody, Peter. *Huxley: A Biographical Introduction,* New York: Scribner, 1973.

Varricchio, Mario. "Power of Images/Images of Power in Brave New World and Nineteen Eighty-Four." *Utopian Studies* 10, no. 1 (1999): p. 98-114.

William, Donald. "Which Urges and Reasonably So The Attraction of Some for Others." *The Yale Review* 86, no. 4 (Oct. 1998): p. 18-31.

Wilson, Keith. "Aldous Huxley and Max Beerbohm's *Hardy*." *Notes and Queries* 31 (December 1984): p. 515.

Woodcock, George. *Dawn and the Darkest Hour: A Study of Aldous Huxley,* New York: Viking, 1972.

Acknowledgments

"Marking and Remembering: Aldous Huxley" by Milton Birnbaum. From *Modern Age* 37, 1 (Fall 1994): 163-166. © 1994 by the Intercollegiate Studies Institute, Inc. Reprinted by permission.

"*Brave New World* and the Flight from God" by John Attarian. From *Modern Age* 38, 1 (Fall 1995): 332-342. © 1995 by the Intercollegiate Studies Institute, Inc. Reprinted by permission.

"Color and Light: Huxley's Pathway to Spiritual Reality" by Sally A. Paulsell. From *Twentieth Century Literature* 41, 1 (Spring 1995): 81-107. © 1995 by *Twentieth Century Literature*. Reprinted by permission.

Meckier, Jerome. "Aldous Huxley's Modern Myth: Leda and the Poetry of Ideas." *English Literary History* 58 (1991), 439-469. © The Johns Hopkins University Press. Reprinted with permission of The Johns Hopkins University Press.

"Aldous Huxley, Satiric Sonneteer: *The Defeat of Youth*" by Jerome Meckier. From *Contemporary Literature* 29, 4 (1988): 583-605. © 1988 by the Board of Regents of the University of Wisconsin System. Reprinted by permission.

"Aldous Huxley in Russia" by Nina Diakonova. From *The Journal of Modern Literature* 21, 1 (Fall 1997). © 1997 by the Foundation for Modern Literature. Reprinted by permission of Indiana University Press.

"Golding and Huxley: The Fables of Demonic Possession" by James R. Baker. From *Twentieth Century Literature* 46, 3 (Fall 2000): 311-327. © 2001 by *Twentieth Century Literature*. Reprinted by permission.

"Aldous Huxley and the Nuclear Age: Ape and Essence in Context" by Sanford E. Marovitz. From *The Journal of Modern Literature* 17, no. 1, (winter 1992): 115-125. © 1994 by Temple University. Reprinted by permission.

"Westward Utopia: Robert V. Hine, Aldous Huxley, and the Future of California History" by Kerwin Lee Klein. From *Pacific Historical Review* vol. 70, no. (August 2001): 465-476. © 1983 by American Historical Association, Pacific Coast Branch. Reprinted by permission.

"The Best of Companions: J. W. N. Sullivan, Aldous Huxley, and the New Physics" by David Branshaw. From *The Review of English Studies* 47, 186 (1996): 188-206. © 1996 by Oxford University Press. Reprinted by permission.

"Aldous Huxley's Philosophy" by Ronald Hope. From *Contemporary Review* 278, no 1621 (February 2001): 102-106. © 2001 by Contemporary Review Co. Ltd. Reprinted by permission.

"Huxley's 'Deep Jam' and the Adaptation of *Alice in Wonderland*" by David Leon Higdon and Phill Lehrman. From *The Review of English Studies* 43, no. 169 (1992): 57-74. © 1992 by Oxford University Press. Reprinted by permission.

Index